Germany's Wild East

Social History, Popular Culture, and Politics in Germany
Kathleen Canning, Series Editor

Recent Titles

Bodies and Ruins: Imagining the Bombing of Germany, 1945 to the Present
David Crew

The Jazz Republic: Music, Race, and American Culture in Weimar Germany
Jonathan Wipplinger

The War in Their Minds: German Soldiers and Their Violent Pasts in West Germany
Svenja Goltermann

Three-Way Street: Jews, Germans, and the Transnational
Jay Howard Geller and Leslie Morris, Editors

Beyond the Bauhaus: Cultural Modernity in Breslau, 1918–33
Deborah Ascher Barnstone

Stop Reading! Look! Modern Vision and the Weimar Photographic Book
Pepper Stetler

The Corrigible and the Incorrigible: Science, Medicine, and the Convict in Twentieth-Century Germany
Greg Eghigian

An Emotional State: The Politics of Emotion in Postwar West German Culture
Anna M. Parkinson

Germany's Wild East: Constructing Poland as Colonial Space
Kristin Kopp

Beyond Berlin: Twelve German Cities Confront the Nazi Past
Gavriel D. Rosenfeld and Paul B. Jaskot, Editors

Consumption and Violence: Radical Protest in Cold-War West Germany
Alexander Sedlmaier

Communism Day-to-Day: State Enterprises in East German Society
Sandrine Kott

Envisioning Socialism: Television and the Cold War in the German Democratic Republic
Heather L. Gumbert

The People's Own Landscape: Nature, Tourism, and Dictatorship in East Germany
Scott Moranda

German Colonialism Revisited: African, Asian, and Oceanic Experiences
Nina Berman, Klaus Mühlhahn, and Patrice Nganang, Editors

Becoming a Nazi Town: Culture and Politics in Göttingen between the World Wars
David Imhoof

For a complete list of titles, please see www.press.umich.edu

Germany's Wild East

Constructing Poland as Colonial Space

Kristin Kopp

The University of Michigan Press
Ann Arbor

For my parents

First paperback edition 2017

Published in the United States of America by
The University of Michigan Press
Manufactured in the United States of America
♾ Printed on acid-free paper

2020 2019 2018 2017 5 4 3 2

A CIP catalog record for this book is available from the British Library.

Library of Congress Cataloging-in-Publication Data

Kopp, Kristin Leigh.
Germany's wild east : constructing Poland as colonial space / Kristin Kopp.
p. cm.—(Social history, popular culture, and politics in Germany)
Includes bibliographical references and index.
ISBN 978-0-472-11844-1 (cloth : alk. paper)—ISBN 978-0-472-02858-0 (e-book)
1. Germany—Relations—Poland. 2. Poland—Relations—Germany. 3. Germany—Territorial expansion—Philosophy. 4. Germany—Intellectual life—19th century. 5. Germany—Intellectual life—20th century. 6. German literature—19th century—History and criticism. 7. German literature—20th century—History and criticism 8. Colonies in literature. 9. Germans—Poland—History. I. Title.
DD120.P7K67 2012
303.48'243043809034—dc23 2012012805

ISBN 978-0-472-03682-0 (pbk. : alk. paper)

Acknowledgments

Many different people and institutions have made the research and writing of this book possible. I am particularly grateful to the Alexander von Humboldt Foundation for its generous financial and institutional support, and also extend great thanks to the Research Board and Research Council of the University of Missouri, the Doreen B. Townsend Center for the Humanities at the University of California, Berkeley, the Social Science Research Council's Berlin Program for Advanced German and European Studies, the Humanities Research Council, and the Kościuszko Foundation, who all provided funding and support at various stages of the project.

I benefited immensely from presenting and discussing my work-in-progress at lectures and workshops hosted by the Bucerius Institute for Research of Contemporary German History and Society in Haifa, the Munk Centre for International Studies in Toronto, the Kolloquium Osteuropäische Geschichte and the Oldenburger Ringvorlesung zur Geschichte in Oldenburg, the Literaturwissenschaftliches Forschungskolloquium at the Slavic Institute in Berlin, the Osteuropa-Kolloquium in Frankfurt (Oder), the Zentrum vergleichender Geschichte Europas in Berlin, and the Institut für Zeitgeschichte in Vienna. My warm thanks to Arnd Bauerkämper, Werner Benecke, Jennifer Jenkins, Magdalena Marszałek, Siegfried Mattl, Amos Morris-Reich, Sylvia Sasse, Zur Shalev, and Philipp Ther for making these exchanges possible. My special thanks to Hans Henning Hahn, who both organized several public presentations in Oldenburg, and also made it possible for me to teach a rewarding summer seminar with his history students at the Carl von Ossietzky University.

For the advice, feedback, and support they provided at various stages of this book's preparation, I am grateful to Leslie Adelson, Eric Ames, Jeff Bowersox, Winson Chu, Sara Hall, Jennifer Jenkins, Jennifer Kapczynski, Marcia Klotz, Sara Lennox, Vejas Liulevicius, Paweł Lutomski, Jerzy Maśnicki, Bradley Naranch, Robert L. Nelson, Annemarie Sammartino, Gregor Thum, Heidemarie Uhl, Tobias Weger, Lora Wildenthal, Gotthart Wunberg, and Andrew

Zimmermann. I am especially grateful to Geoff Eley for his support of my project and for introducing my volume into his series.

Some of the best ideas in this book were developed in dialogue with Klaus Müller-Richter, a truly cherished critic and interlocutor who provided extensive feedback on my written work and ideas-in-progress. My deepest thanks also to Anton Kaes and Hinrich C. Seeba who oversaw the dissertation out of which this book arose. Their enthusiasm and intellectual generosity not only made the original project possible but also exemplified the role to which I now aspire as a scholar and colleague.

I feel extremely fortunate to be a member of the German program at the University of Missouri, where I have great colleagues who work to create an environment conducive to research and the exchange of ideas while also being great friends that I always enjoy hanging out with. For their support and collegiality, and simply for picking up slack during the final phases of this project I thank Roger Cook, Stefani Engelstein, Monika Fischer, Sean Franzel, Sean Ireton, Megan McKinstry, Brad Prager, Olaf Schmidt, Carsten Strathausen, and our irreplaceable administrative associate, Jennifer Arnold.

Many friends and family members have supported me through the difficult phases of this project and celebrated its joyful milestones along the way. Robert Wilson Jr. has been a partner in the best sense of the term; I am grateful for his love and support, and particularly thank him for his rapidly evolving culinary skills and unflagging enthusiasm for life away from the desk on the seat of a bicycle. I also extend my gratitude to Carol Bayley, Carlos Cabana, Heather Duncan, Kayla Duncan, Matthias Erdbeer, Amy Evans, Wolfgang Fichna, Geraldine Janecyk, Daniel Kramer, Denise Leto, Paweł Lutomski, Jill Mackey, Siegfried Mattl, Klaus Müller-Richter, Debra Prager, Annemarie Sammartino, Daniela Schmeiser, Werner Schwarz, Kuba Szalowski, Brigitta Wagner, Robert Wilson III, and all of the members of the BTWH international working group for the memorable meals, shared travels, and late-night conference cocktails that have given me so much pleasure over the past years. My warmest thanks to Susanne Lowenthal who has been my dear friend and mentor since my days as an undergraduate, and to Joanna Niżyńska, who generously shared her time, wisdom, and humor through this lengthy process. My parents, Peter and Judy Kopp, have carried the weight of this book with me throughout its development and provided everything from financial help to intellectual curiosity and emotional support. I've had so much fun sharing this project with them, and dedicate it to them with much love.

Contents

Introduction: Germany's Wild East

In 1893 the cartographer and activist Paul Langhans published the first edition of his *Deutscher Kolonial-Atlas* (German colonial atlas).[1] Germany had just begun acquiring overseas colonies in the previous decade, and Langhans was one of the very first to offer such a cartographic overview of Germany's new empire. The atlas engaged the public's fascination with the colonization project by presenting a wide range of information addressed to a popular audience; in addition to political maps recording Germany's new landholdings, cultural maps depict the spread of German accomplishments and the forthcoming challenges in the new colonies: maps of train lines built by Germans in East Africa and routes forged into the outback of Cameroon by German research expeditions alternate with maps locating ore deposits in German Southwest Africa and the spread of cannibalism in German New Guinea. Such maps followed standard European colonial convention; these overseas territories had all been brought under German control and, in the wealth of knowledge displayed, the maps affirmed German mastery over these spaces and showed Germans that they, like other European colonial powers, were in the business of bringing civilization to the world's primitive periphery.

While, in these respects, Langhans's colonial atlas resembled those of other European powers, it also contained significant anomalies: in addition to the maps of German colonial "protectorates" in Africa and the Pacific, Langhans includes maps of every region into which any sizable number of Germans had ever migrated and settled. Prominent in this section of the atlas are maps of "German Colonization in the East," which feature broad expanses of territory in Eastern and Southeastern Europe. The maps depict various historical pursuits in the East, each of which is labeled as a form of German "colonization." The establishment of medieval trade routes along the northern European coast ("The trade colonies of the German Hansa"), the facilitated settlement and land reclamation projects of the early modern period ("The German colonization of Lithuania in 1736"), and the existence of contemporary German enclaves abroad ("German colonies in Wolhynien") are thus all linked by a colonial denominator. As Germany's closest neighbor to the east, Polish space dominates this section of the atlas, with maps depicting events ranging from the eastward penetration of the Teutonic Knights to the contemporary establishment of German settlements in predominantly Polish regions of Prussia under the aegis of Bismarck's inner colonization campaign.

Such inclusion of adjacent continental space broke with the conventional European image of a "colony," which referred exclusively to overseas landholdings.[2] But Langhans argued for an expanded colonial model, insisting that the German colonial experience—and hence the nature of its colonies—differed from those of its European counterparts, and that an alternative definition was therefore necessary to comprehend the totality of the German colonial endeavor. In the introduction to the *Kolonial-Atlas,* he begins by justifying his alternative model.

> The modern movement championing the German acquisition of overseas protectorates . . . has led to such a lopsided meaning of the word "colony" in everyday language . . . that it seemed risky to name this book, which is a cartographic representation of the entirety of Germanic settlement activities, "Colonial Atlas." We did so nonetheless because we have repeatedly found it necessary to insist that the German Empire's current colonial project did not just suddenly appear, but that it is instead framed and contextualized by centuries of colonial activity . . . . The contents of the following pages are meant to address this inner connection between all German settlements.[3]

To a certain extent, Langhans is only manipulating a semantic instability: the German word *Kolonie,* like its English equivalent *colony,* is a portmanteau term, analogous to the suitcase that opens to expose two separately contained but collectively enclosed halves. When the term is introduced, context and convention determine which of the word's multiple meanings becomes operative. On the one hand, *Kolonie* can refer to almost any form of group settlement, from *Ferienkolonien* (vacation colonies) to *Schrebergartenkolonien* (garden colonies) to *Verbrecherkolonien* (convict colonies). Similarly, many of the settlements created in conjunction with land reclamation projects inside of Germany's own borders are still referred to as "colonies," such as the so-called *Fehnsiedlungen* in East Friesland. When the East Friesians today speak of neighboring "colonies," they engage just one half of the portmanteau term, along with the conventional set of connotative attributes activated by it: resilience, entrepreneurship, mastery over nature, and so forth.

On the other hand, *Kolonie* refers to "a territory, particularly an overseas territory, that has been conquered by an imperial state and economically exploited, and that is held in political dependency and social backwardness."[4] This version of *Kolonie* assumes a certain type of relationship between foreign newcomers and native locals, and therefore, in addition to the connotations of resilience and entrepreneurship attending the first meaning of the term, this *Kolonie* includes elements of foundational violence, racialized models of human order, global imaginations of imperial center and periphery, etc.

Both of these meanings—which we can perhaps refer to as "weak" and "strong"—are contained within the term *Kolonie.* In late nineteenth-century discussions of Eastern European space, we see the manipulation of this portmanteau term in a series of strategic substitutions. For centuries, Germans had referred to their settlement colonies in Poland and further east in the weak sense of the word, but now, Langhans resignifies all instances of this term into its strong sense and thereby asks his readers to bring the history of German settlement in the European East into conceptual alignment with forms of colonization undertaken overseas. By including maps of Polish space in his colonial atlas, Langhans rather forces the reader to think these two forms of colonization together, to seek their "inner connections," to see them as two manifestations of the same principle.

We observe Langhans struggling here with the insecurity of German colonial belatedness. After the unification of Germany in 1871, the country had leaped quickly from nation-state to colonial empire by acquiring "protectorates" in Africa and the Pacific. But this rapid expansion did not alleviate Germany's newcomer status on a centuries-old colonial scene dominated by the likes of England and France. Proponents of German colonization wanted to catch up with these colonial powers and therefore encouraged the acquisition of even more overseas territory; detractors, meanwhile, argued that Germany was not yet ready for such an undertaking and should refrain from further straining its resources and capabilities.

With his *Kolonial-Atlas,* Langhans seeks to strengthen Germany's identity as a colonial power by arguing that it was not actually a newcomer to the colonial project after all. To achieve this objective, he introduces an alternative narrative of German history that reinvents past settlement, migration, and trade events as acts of "colonization." Because this eastward migration had taken place over several centuries, Langhans's inclusion of eastern space greatly extended the geographic expanse and the temporal duration of the conventional German colonial narrative. Langhans does not introduce new historical data (the fact that Germans migrated eastward has never been seriously debated); instead, he reinterprets existing data to change the story it tells.

To present this argument visually, Langhans relies more on suggestive titles for his maps than on any unexpected adaptations of cartographic convention. The atlas contains 30 maps (overlaid with some 300 insets), 5 of which are devoted to Eastern European space—roughly the same number as are dedicated to each of Germany's overseas colonies. Therefore, before one even arrives at the maps themselves, the atlas's allocation of its resources already ascribes a significant degree of importance to Eastern Europe.

The first of the European maps, "The spread of Germandom in Europe," depicts the percentage of Germans found in various regional populations beyond the German state borders. Eastern Europe is overlaid with islands of space in which Germans are shown to make up anywhere between 1 and 70 percent of the local population. At first glance, this map seems to offer an objective depiction of familiar German migration patterns, but the map's title alters the conventional meaning attributed to this migration: it indicates that these populations have moved more than just their families and possessions eastward, they have instead transplanted cultural (or perhaps even civilizational) "Germandom"—*Deutschtum*—wherever they have gone. They have not merely migrated but have instead shaped foreign space in their own image, while either displacing the native population or subsuming it under their influence.

These German exclaves are also ascribed colonial status by the framing set of inset maps, each of which contains areas circled in red, identified by the map's key as "*former* German colonies" (emphasis added). These insets depict areas in Italy, Denmark, Great Britain, Spain, and Palestine where Germans ostensibly once established "colonies" that are no longer extant. In Eastern Europe, in contrast, there are no such areas circled in red. If the German settlements depicted there are not "former colonies," then logic insists that they must be colonies of the *present.*

And indeed, the maps that follow "The spread of Germandom in Europe" portray this same concept in multiple ways, reinforcing the notion that German presence in the East represents an ongoing process of colonization that began in the distant past and continues into the present. The map labeled "German colonization in the East—The Slavic lands," for example, depicts areas of contemporary German settlement in the East and is surrounded by inset maps presenting individual "German colonies" in the region during a range of time periods. In juxtaposing multiple temporalities, the atlas portrays the German move eastward as timeless and uninterrupted. While each of the individual settlements may have had its own history of establishment and development, of growth and decline, the process as a whole is dehistoricized and elevated onto the plane of the mythic. Germans, the atlas suggests, have always been migrating and settling eastward. By following these maps with those of Africa and the Pacific, Langhans's atlas constructs the narrative of a German colonial nation: engaged in the colonization of Eastern Europe for centuries, Germans are now poised to charge into the European project of colonizing the global periphery: overseas expansion is merely the latest manifestation of an ongoing colonial project.

Langhans was neither the only publicist nor even the first to represent German history in the East as colonial history. Germans representing various expansionist interests, both overseas and in Eastern Europe, had been engaging in this practice since the eighteenth century. But Langhans's atlas appeared at the beginning of a period in which representations of the German "colonial East" found their greatest density of occurrence and achieved their most powerful effect: by the mid-1920s, certain aspects of this colonial construction had become so widely circulated—and so widely accepted by the general population—that they created the foundation for a social consensus claiming Germany's right to acquire additional state territory in the East. In the chapters that follow, I examine the contours of this colonial discourse, the political and cultural contexts in which it found its footing, and the visual and textual strategies employed to bring it into representation. This study allows me to explain how a colonialist paradigm initially developed to describe Europe's relationship to the overseas spaces it colonized was adapted to conceptualize the relationship between Germans and their neighbors right next door.

The discursive reinvention of Poland as colonial space developed in tandem with a set of material practices that, if not entirely colonial by definition, nonetheless reflected the ideals of territorial expansion and racial subjugation attending the period of European high imperialism: various eastward extensions of the Prussian/German border were strategically envisioned and carried out, while policies of cultural attenuation (i.e., under the auspices of the Kulturkampf) and population displacement (i.e., within the parameters of the inner colonization campaign) were implemented vis-à-vis the Poles. While such practices are not necessarily in and of themselves colonial according to contemporary theoretical paradigms, they were nonetheless clearly positioned as such within the discursive frame I investigate here. One can reject the categorization of specific material practices as "colonial," but such a rejection neither accounts for nor erases the presence of the colonial discourse that so prominently attended these practices.

It is therefore necessary to differentiate between two different phenomena: on the one hand, there is material colonization, which involves various forms of economic, political, and/or cultural subjugation of a native population by a foreign minority entering their space. On the other, there is discursive colonization, a historically situated process that repositions a specific relationship between self and Other into colonial categories. Discursive colonization comprises three elements: first, the creation of a colonial subjectivity for the (would-be) colonizer-self, a process exemplified by Langhans's portrayal of the Germans as a historically colonizing Volk. Second, discursive colonization requires the construction of the Other as a legitimate object of colonial intervention. In the chapters that follow, I will explore the strategies employed in portraying the Poles as primitive and ahistorical, lacking the ability to achieve progress without external intervention, and threatening German space with the proximity of their atavistic tendencies. The third element of discursive colonization narrates the relationship between self and Other in colonial terms; the Germans, as colonizing Volk, are naturally positioned to bring order and progress to the wild and primitive Slavs—indeed, according to Langhans, they have been doing so for centuries.

While material and discursive colonization are two separate processes, they are fundamentally interlinked because the latter is prerequisite to the former: material colonization does not occur as such where the discursive groundwork has not been laid. Without the conceptual apparatus introduced by discursive colonization, would-be material colonization remains mere territorial expansion. In his typological overview of colonialism, Jürgen Osterhammel considers the wide and disparate set of historical relationships conventionally categorized as "colonial" and then seeks to identify shared features distinguishing them from noncolonial forms of conquest. He finds himself faced with a difficult task, because, approached structurally, the definition of colonization is at best a fuzzy set: certain forms of economic exploitation, native enslavement, colonial settlement, and/or violent military conquest certainly occurred in each instance, but never in the same combinations to the same degrees; each case was unique. When we compare the colonial experience in Jamaica with that in Hong Kong, for example, the differences would seemingly outweigh the similarities.[5] Osterhammel ultimately determines that it is the discursive element that links these disparate cases together: "modern colonialism is not a form of rule that can be described in structural terms alone, but also a specific *interpretation* of this relationship."[6] This interpretation is one envisioning the self-Other relationship in colonial terms, and it can only arise as the product of a historical process of discursive colonization.

Discursive colonization thus asserts itself as a historical process with its own traceable development and historical reality: just as one can research the structural events constituting the material colonization of a foreign territory, one can trace the discursive process whereby this territory and its inhabitants came to be understood in colonial terms. In the case of European relationships with territories of overseas conquest, these two processes were conflated because the first coherent sets of narratives emerged out of just this colonial context. This is also true where the colonial relationship was itself indirect. Susanne Zantop has shown, for example, that Germans imagined their own relationship with South America in colonial terms despite the fact that other European nations were responsible for the material colonization of the continent. In the fictional narratives she investigates, Germans often criticized the misdeeds of their fellow Europeans in South America, but they did not question the existence of a fundamental distinction dividing the civilized European core from the primitive global periphery. Instead, Germans narrated themselves into this dichotomy, positioning themselves in competitive alignment with the European colonizers.[7] In the European worldview, there was no alternative conceptual frame in which to position South America.

In the case of Polish Eastern Europe, in contrast, we can identify and interrogate the process of discursive colonization because there were alternative conceptual frames available, and because, within this set of alternatives, German discourse underwent a significant and traceable shift.[8] In earlier centuries, "Poland" had been understood as terrain housing a neighboring European nation—one even seen as quite powerful in the sixteenth and seventeenth centuries. But by the end of the eighteenth, Poland had weakened, becoming the object of its neighbor's expansionist desires. Over the course of the following century, as first Prussia and then Germany annexed and administered territory previously belonging to the Polish state, a new paradigm gained ever stronger footing: "Poland" became conceptually repositioned as the eastern frontier into which Germans were destined to expand, analogous to the North American Wild West. Over the course of the later nineteenth and early twentieth centuries, narratives of German colonial conquest in the East were steadily introduced and gained in popularity. While many of these were set in the present to engage contemporary themes, a significant number turned to reexamine the past of medieval eastward settlement, or *Ostkolonisation* (a term that refers specifically to the medieval and early modern time periods). Although medieval German settlers had not perceived themselves as collective agents of a German colonial project,[9] their stories were later retold to claim this status on their behalf. Langhans's atlas thus presented a cartographic frame onto which these narratives could be mentally mapped.

Discursive colonization is a process able to reinvent its object in colonial terms and to harness this reinvented history to serve the rhetorical needs of the present. In the case of Poland, discursive colonization was an instrumental move typically pursued to facilitate one of two key political agendas: there were those, like Langhans, who sought to present an image of the Germans as an essentially colonizing Volk for the purpose of supporting contemporary German endeavors overseas, and there were those who depicted the East in colonial terms in order to promote the cause of German eastward territorial expansion. While the narratives of the first celebrated the hardships and triumphs of medieval *Ostkolonisation* in order to create the sense of a mythic German colonial calling, the second located their narratives in the present and represented the desired eastern space and its inhabitants as primitive and in need of civilizing intervention. To a large extent, these two agendas were mutually supportive: tales of medieval settlement were not only used to portray the Germans as an inherently colonizing people but also to establish a precedent for eastward expansion in the present; meanwhile, contemporary interventions in the East underscored the notion of a German colonial essentialism with proscriptive implications for overseas expansion. Such moments of argumentative alignment supported the process of discursive colonization.

The discursive colonization of "Poland"[10] is similar to the discursive phenomenon Edward Said introduced as "Orientalism"; both terms describe processes of constructing and delegitimizing the Other in discourse located at the nexus of knowledge and power. But there are important differences in the ways we apprehend these respective processes: although Said argues that discourse affected material practice, he ultimately conflates these two aspects under the aegis of his term, presenting Orientalism as a way of dealing with the Orient "by making statements about it, authorizing views of it, describing it, by teaching it, settling it, ruling over it." Said thus suggests a melding of material and discursive practices that is defied by the German-Polish case. Here, the relationship between discourse and practice is rather one of a dialogical back-and-forth, where new discursive strategies arose (or were indeed consciously developed) in response to specific historical exigencies: the discursive colonization of Poland was more instrumental in function and more persuasive in intention than the Orientalist model suggests. Furthermore, Said understands Orientalism as an already existing, all-encompassing social "institution" entrenched in such an authoritative position that "no one writing, thinking, or acting on the Orient could do so without taking account of the limitations on thought and action imposed by Orientalism."[11] My focus on discursive colonization, in contrast, apprehends this discursive construction in its process of becoming, and thus captures moments of internal inconsistency and contestation when there was no certainty that the colonial paradigm would ever achieve an authoritative position as institutionalized knowledge. Discursive colonization thus describes a time when colonial definitions, meanings, and identities were contested and susceptible to defeat by competing discourses.

Given the multivalent discourse on Poland, it becomes imperative to clearly articulate the parameters of the discourse that I understand to be colonial. I do not merely refer to a set of characteristics mapped onto the self (the German as civilized and powerful) and the Other (the Pole as primitive and weak) but, more important, to the way in which the relationship between this self and other is constructed.

In his book *The Colonizer's Model of the World,* J. M. Blaut examines English and French colonial historiographies dating from the period of high imperialism at the turn of the nineteenth to the twentieth century, where he finds a consistent ideological pattern structuring European (or "Western") justifications for colonialism. The "colonizer's model of the world" rested upon a specific vision of global human geography; the mental map it constructed became so dominant in European thought that Blaut refers to it as a "belief."

> This belief is the notion that European civilization—"The West"—has had some unique historical advantage, some special quality of race or culture or environment or mind or spirit, which gives this human community a permanent superiority over all other communities at all times in history and down to the present.
>
> The belief is both historical and geographical. Europeans are seen as the "makers of history." Europe eternally advances, progresses, modernizes. The rest of the world advances more sluggishly, or stagnates: it is "traditional society." Therefore, the world has a permanent geographical center and a permanent periphery: an Inside and an Outside. Inside leads, Outside lags. Inside innovates, Outside imitates.
>
> This belief is *diffusionism,* or more precisely *Eurocentric diffusionism.* It is a theory about the way cultural processes tend to move over the surface of the world as a whole. They tend to flow out of the European sector

> and toward the non-European sector. This is the natural, normal, logical, and ethical flow of culture, of innovation, of human causality. Europe is the source of most diffusions; non-Europe is the recipient.[12]

Blaut shows that this belief rests upon an imaginary division of the world into two fundamentally different realms: on the one hand, an "Inside," a European or Western center distinguished by the ability of its inhabitants to generate new cultural, technological, and societal innovations; and, on the other, an "Outside," a non-Western global periphery whose inhabitants lack this ability. Seen through this ideological lens, the periphery remains in a static, primitive state outside of the time of historical progress unless it receives infusions of innovations transferred from the center. Peripheral populations are not imagined to be engaged in their own struggle to improve their modes of existence, because they lack the prerequisite ability to envision progress. In other words, the inability to innovate is equated with the lack of will to innovate, which also suggests resistance (or inability) to change. Therefore, while some inventions and ideas may diffuse from the center into the periphery by such peaceful means as itinerant trade and migratory settlement, others will only be successfully introduced by the violent forces of military conquest, enslaved labor, and population management.

The diffusionist worldview thereby justified colonization in two ways: first, where Europeans fashioned themselves "bringing progress" to non-European populations, colonization could be presented as a moral imperative. The establishment of schools and hospitals, the introduction of European medicine and hygienic practices, and the reorganization of social and economic institutions thereby functioned as outward signs validating the belief in the colonizer's responsibility to bring about change. Second, the diffusionist belief could be mobilized to draw attention away from such (putative) concern for colonized populations and justify instead the exploitation of their natural resources. If the "natives" were inherently unable to generate the technology necessary to extract, process, and market their natural resources, then it was only right that the Europeans step in to take on the task themselves.

Given the ramifications for European wealth, power, and identity, it is of little surprise that the discourse surrounding European colonization featured ubiquitous statements denying the colonized the fundamentally human capacity to innovate. Although modern colonization took a wide variety of forms in the different geographical contexts in which it was practiced, this trope remains a constant, and unites these myriad events within a shared European worldview, if not a shared European project. The natives of Asia and Africa, of

Australia, North and South America were all represented as existing in static states of (non-)development that justified and perhaps even demanded European intervention. We find this trope directly articulated and, more tellingly, unstated and assumed in all manner of texts addressing the colonial situation: political tracts, scientific inquiries, literary texts, etc.; and we see the detailed compensatory maneuvers undertaken in cases where this assumption came under challenge. Edward Said recounts a relevant episode from English colonial history: in the face of growing criticism of colonization, the English statesman Arthur James Balfour held a speech in 1910 insisting upon England's right and responsibility to maintain its colonial holdings in the "Orient." These civilizations posed a special problem for the diffusionist paradigm, because the powerful ancient Asian and Middle Eastern empires—and the innovations they introduced—were elements firmly entrenched in the European narrative of world-historical progress. Balfour acknowledges this history but then deftly negates its importance by identifying all Oriental innovations as products of a distant past, and by arguing that the Orient had ultimately fallen due to its inability to bring forth (i.e., innovate) any viable forms of self-government.[13] This failure of the past explains the developmental stasis of the present, while also accounting for a state of development perceived to be currently more advanced than those found in other world regions that purportedly never underwent such a creative phase.

The case of the Balfour speech highlights the extent to which the diffusionist worldview was adaptable: in this case, by accounting for past civilizational greatness in the Orient by allowing for the locations of Inside and Outside to change over time. The seat of human innovation may have once been located in regions further east (i.e., in the ancient Middle East), but it had shifted to the West at the beginning of the modern era and now even included those eastern regions of North America inhabited by Europeans.[14] This new "West" was the new locus of human ingenuity, the new Inside. The "colonizer's worldview" was based upon the construction of a dichotomous world, and the mental map attending it could be adjusted as necessary.

Such conceptual flexibility was advantageous in maintaining rhetorical supremacy, but it also introduced an anxiety of impermanence, particularly for the Germans, who saw themselves at the edge of the new European Inside. Where was the border between Inside and Outside located? Was it static or shifting? The anxiety was twofold: first, to the extent that the Outside was imagined to reside just across the border in Slavic Eastern Europe, its proximity was experienced as a threat, especially given the East-West directionality of civilizational migration. Throughout the period in question, Germans repeatedly expressed this concern through references to threatening images of flooding, of German space being inundated with atavistic elements arising in the East that would sweep over German space, destroy its civilization, and drive it back into a primitive state. Against such east-west flows, barriers needed to be erected, the border maintained and monitored.[15]

Such invasion anxieties were exacerbated by the absence of a clear geographic border readily articulating the imagined distinction between Inside and Outside. Even when there was a consensus that such a border ran between Germanic Europe and Slavic non-Europe, it was never exactly clear where such a line might be drawn on the ground. There was an expansive frontier upon which German and Slavic populations and their localized domestic spaces had overlapped and intermingled for centuries. This transitional space extended far across the eastern plains, and one could therefore imagine the border to Outside to be located quite far away. But, at the same time, as Vejas Liulevicius has shown, this frontier was also seen to extend backward into Germany's predominantly Polish eastern borderlands, which led to a great German anxiety that the border to the Outside might actually be located within German space itself.[16]

The ambiguity surrounding the demarcation between self and Other was, in turn, exacerbated by an anxiety surrounding the respective strength and efficacy of cross-border flows. If we imagine a map of the world separated into an Inside and an Outside (regardless of where we draw the border delineating the two), the model of Eurocentric diffusion would be represented cartographically by a series of arrows originating in European space and extending various distances across the surface of the globe. These vectors would symbolize the movement of European innovations into non-European space: the more new inventions and ideas transferred over the border by such European agents as merchants, explorers, and colonists, the greater the density of arrows, and the further these agents traveled, the longer the arrows would extend. Travel, trade, and communication directly at the border would have been a daily occurrence, the presence of arrows thus quite dense, but the longer the distance from the border, the fewer the traveling agents. The arrows would therefore form a graduated distribution pattern with its highest density directly at the border between German and Polish space and then gradually thinning as the eye followed their paths eastward.

On the one hand, this diffusionist gradient explains why non-European space was not imagined to be homogeneous in the colonizer's model of the world but was instead differentiated by its degree of proximity to Europe: diffusions originated inside of Europe, crossed over the border into non-Europe, and then penetrated as far as the mediating agents traveled into this space. Adjacent, non-European space benefited from more frequent and more concentrated diffusions than did space at a more distant remove. Therefore the Slavs could be imagined to be just as incapable of autonomous innovation as the natives of Africa or the Americas, but their state of civilization would nonetheless be more advanced because they had benefited from European diffusions over a much longer period of time and over a much shorter distance of separation.

On the other hand, as Thomas Serrier has argued, this spatial proximity and temporal duration were themselves the source of a certain anxiety because they seemed to suggest a certain sense of German impotence.[17] If Slavic space had become more developed than overseas space due to the efficacy of diffusions originating from the Inside, then this indicated that it was indeed possible to transform Outside space through diffusion. Assuming this potentiality, the continuing existence of a frontier space directly adjacent to Germany became increasingly difficult to explain. Shouldn't one expect that adjacent space would have long since been transformed into German space of the European Inside? Shouldn't German space be ever extending its border eastward? The inability to point to such a successful civilizing extension of the Inside into the periphery was connected to lingering doubts about Germany's colonizing capacities.

Such insecurity was addressed by strengthening the narrative of Slavic Otherness and stressing the Slavs' inherent inability and unwillingness to learn, develop, and progress—and perhaps even their belligerent resistance to such change. In this regard, the German construction of the Slavs resembles that of the colonized Africans, as a brief comparison of two literary passages suggests. The first is taken from Gustav Frenssen's 1906 *Peter Moors Fahrt nach Südwest* (Peter Moor's journey to Southwest Africa), a novel set during the German war against the Herero in 1904. In this scene, the German soldier Peter Moor is sharing a campfire with a group of settlers who have joined the troops, and they discuss whether, in the sense of traditional Christian teachings, the Africans can be considered to be the "brothers" of the Germans. They are in agreement that this is not the case.

> These [Africans] are supposed to be our brothers? Let them become our brothers after a century or two! Let them first learn that which we would have invented ourselves [*Sie mögen erst mal lernen, was wir aus uns selbst erfunden hätten*]: damming water, building wells, and planting

> corn, building houses and weaving clothes. After that, they can perhaps become our brothers.[18]

The implication of the settler's speech is that the Germans have introduced a range of technological innovations to the Southwestern steppe that the African natives had been unable to invent themselves. This critique thus negates the Africans' right to self-determination on grounds hovering between moral judgment and racist presumption: either the Africans are morally inferior and too lazy to bring about necessary innovations or they are inherently unable to do so due to inferior mental capacities—either way, the German presence is legitimized and the Herero desire to oust them rendered contemptible.

We see this same rhetoric mobilized against the Poles in a text written some fifty years prior to Frenssen's. In Gustav Freytag's 1855 *Soll und Haben* (Debit and credit)—a novel whose setting never leaves Central Europe, but which, in chapter 1, I argue to be the German colonial novel par excellence—the young German protagonist travels into the Polish periphery with his paternalistic employer. En route, he is lectured about why the Poles' desire for an independent state is illegitimate.

> There is no race more lacking in that which it takes to better themselves, and less able to use their capital to improve their state of humanity and *Bildung,* than the Slavs. . . . It is remarkable how unable they are to generate that . . . which produces civilization and progress, and which can lift up a bunch of scattered farmers into a state.[19]

The Poles desire independence, but, as was the case with the Herero, their demands are rejected by the German colonists (an identity explicitly claimed by the Germans in both texts), who reach the conclusion that the Poles are not capable of self-management. Neither the Herero nor the Poles are able to "generate," "advance," "produce," or "invent," and both are dependent upon the Germans to introduce social, technological, and cultural advancements. In both cases, such a construction is introduced in order to justify the continued dominating presence of the Germans.

Beginning in the mid-nineteenth century, we begin to see an accumulation of narratives—both belletristic and historiographic—in which the German-Polish relationship is described in colonial terms. In novels and history books, political speeches and scholarly publications, German authors depict Germans and Polish Slavs as existing on two sides of a fundamental civilizational divide: on one side, Germans generate technological innovation, cultural enrichment, and historical progress, while, on the other, the Poles tend toward an unchanging state of primitive nondevelopment, ahistorical inertia, and chaotic barbarism. Only German interventions into Polish space change the dynamics of this dualism, but Polish inferiority constantly defies their efforts.

The discursive colonization of the German-Polish relationship was a process originating at least as far back as the Polish Partitions of 1772–95, when Prussia, Russia, and Austria undertook their trilateral divisions and annexations of Poland, erasing this once-powerful state from the European map.[20] For over a century, "Poland" would exist as a set of three annexed territories and would not reappear as an independent state until after World War I. In the course of the partitionings, Prussia took possession of the region of Posen, as well as large portions of East and West Prussia. This territory included the urban centers of Posen, Thorn, Danzig, and Bromberg, an extensive stretch of the Vistula river, and the surrounding arable farmland. In the third partition of 1795, Prussia even gained Warsaw—a city it held for twelve years until Napoleon reorganized the borders of the partitions, taking land from Prussia to create the so-called Congress Kingdom of Poland under Russian control.

In his influential work *Inventing Eastern Europe: The Map of Civilization on the Mind of the Enlightenment,* Larry Wolff recounts the rhetorical strategies employed by Frederick the Great and his successor to justify these territorial expansions. It was not so much that the Poles were backward or underdeveloped, but instead that their space was marked by the absence of rational ordering; its "nonsensical disordering and inversion of eighteenth-century ideas about society, politics, demography," etc. positioned the Poles as unworthy of self-governance, perhaps even as unable to manage this task.[21]

These early explorations of colonizing rhetoric feel tentative, perhaps because they were met with strong opposition from within the German community. Many felt that Prussia was acting immorally and tyrannically against a fellow European nation that, although temporarily weakened, was nonetheless taking important steps towards addressing its internal troubles.[22] Recent scholarship has made Georg Forster's derogatory pronouncements on Poland's "*polnische Wirtschaft*" (Polish mismanagement) quite well known.[23] Equally important, however, were his contemporaries who celebrated Poland's 1794 constitution as Europe's most enlightened, and who supported Tadeusz Kościuszko's uprising of the same year as a heroic and justified act of self-defense.[24]

This contestation over the meaning of "Poland"—and ultimately over its location on the Inside or Outside of the European center—continued throughout the nineteenth century. Prior to German unification in 1871, one typically viewed Polish space through a lens colored by one's sentiments toward Prussia. Those championing the extension of Prussian power tended to participate in the discursive colonization of Polish territory for two reasons: first, because it justified Prussia's continued hold on its Polish partition, and second, because a colonial Poland demonstrated German expansionist prowess. Meanwhile, those hoping to curtail Prussian power stressed the identity of the Poles as a civilized nation while characterizing Prussia as their tyrannical occupier.

Proponents of these competing stances were less invested in the actual plight of the Poles, and much more motivated by the ways in which differing constructions of Poland could be mobilized to support their respective German domestic agendas. This political-rhetorical dynamic is perhaps best evident in the responses to the Polish November Uprising of 1830–31, when the Poles attempted to free themselves from Russian rule in "Congress Poland." Prussia and its supporters quietly supported the Russians, whose defeat would have had serious ramifications for Prussia's own claims to power in Polish Prussia. German liberals, meanwhile—particularly those hailing from the southwestern German states—organized to support the Polish revolutionaries while calling for the reinstitution of the Polish state. This political *Polenbegeisterung* (pro-Polish enthusiasm) lasted for about two years and found cultural expression in the publication of over 300 poems addressing the heroism and suffering of the Poles under foreign tyranny. Participating in the production and circulation of these *Polenlieder* became a way of performing one's liberal identity; they were set to music and sung on the street, in cafés, and at the Hambacher Fest of 1832—the climax of the prerevolutionary liberal movement.[25] Within this pro-Polish campaign, the Poles were lauded as the "fellow brothers" of Germans in their common struggle to achieve national unity and liberty, and Prussia was equated with Russia as a selfish and cruel tyrant squelching the national aspirations of its heroic subject population.

This period of German-Polish solidarity was short-lived; by the end of 1832, the storm of protest had calmed, and by 1835, the Poles seemed all but forgotten. In the years that followed, pro-Polish sentiments underwent a dramatic reversal as former supporters of Polish independence realized that they were involved in a territorial conflict of interest: any reinstatement of an independent Poland threatened to diminish the size of the aspired German state, which was to include Prussia's Polish partition.

Over the course of the 1840s, the question of Germany's future territorial identity—and, hence, location—became central to the revolutionary agenda. In 1848, when the German National Assembly was tasked with drafting a constitution for the envisioned German state determining its laws and political structures, it also had to reach a final consensus about *where* this state would be located. The ensuing debate focused on several areas at the periphery of the German Federation, including Schleswig, Posen, and Istria.[26] At stake in each case was the very identity of the envisioned German state itself: Was it to be an ethnically or a politically defined entity? Should its aim be greatest ethnic homogeneity or largest territorial expanse? While each act of border-drawing necessitated a negotiation of these questions, the demarcations were the most problematic in the case of Prussia's Polish territories, because, in the province Posen, 500,000 Germans and Jews lived among some 800,000 Poles who wanted this region to be included in their own envisioned independent Polish nation-state.[27]

The delegation at the assembly had difficulties in addressing this territorial question, in part because they had inherited a non-geographic conception of the German nation. During the early nineteenth century, the cartographic jumble of German lands had shifted its borders and power structures so frequently that "Germany's" primary referent ceased to be spatial. Instead, Germans turned to concepts of the "cultural nation"—*die Kulturnation*—and underwent "an internalization of *Deutschland* into a spiritual entity for which all territorial, if not spatial definitions [were] suspended."[28] In 1813, Ernst Moritz Arndt famously wrote that Germany extended "as far as one hears the German tongue"[29] and thereby gave voice to the notion of "Germany" as a cultural space that hovered over the map of Europe without being affected by its political borders. Two decades later, however, Arndt was among the first to reject his previous model as intangible and thus politically dangerous and to insist upon a "grounded" agenda for German action. In his 1831 pamphlet "Polen, ein Spiegel der Warnung für uns" (Poland, our mirror of warning),[30] Arndt addressed the Poles' demand for a reinstated Poland and argued vehemently against the masses of Germans he thought to be naively supporting their cause. Arndt warned that German and Polish goals were mutually incompatible by identifying specific German territories that would have to be relinquished were the Poles to achieve their aims. Where Arndt's 1813 conceptualization of Germany had obligingly hovered over the map of Europe as a deterritorialized entity, his "Deutschland" in 1831 was firmly grounded in cartographic space.

The two sides of the German National Assembly's famous Poland Debate reflected the early and late voices of Arndt, and ultimately sided with the latter: the final traces of *Polenbegeisterung* were swept from the table to make way for a new "egotistical" era of Prussian-German power and territorial interests.[31] The debate lasted for four days[32] and centered around a fundamental ambivalence surrounding "Poland's" status within the shifting European order: Were the Poles a nation among other European nations, perhaps weaker but nonetheless worthy of national independence and self-determination? Or could a compelling reason be found to exclude the Poles from the category of state-building nations? This question had ramifications for Germany's border, but it was also important because it called into question the underlying premise of the liberals' drive to national unification: if the legitimacy of the German demand for a nation-state was based upon the premise that every nation deserved its own independent and united state, then how could it be legitimate for the Germans to act in a way that would deny this right to the Poles?

The Poland Debate presents a fascinating record of rhetorical trial and error as representatives searched for a set of criteria that would justify their desire to include Polish space in the German state. Disparate approaches make the debate initially appear quite unfocused, but ultimately, common ground emerged with the assertion of a colonial binary separating Germans and Poles. The Poles were not a valid nation, it was argued, because they did not belong to that group of humanity able to achieve progress on its own. Destined to remain un(der)developed without external intervention, Polish space would be best served by bringing it under German guardianship. Once this colonial model was introduced, it framed the ensuing discussion such that even those statements made by Poland's most ardent supporters came to affirm its validity. For example, Arnold Ruge, representative to the Assembly from Breslau, gave one of the strongest speeches in support of Poland's right to exist, but nonetheless claimed that, in the period following the Polish Partitions, all forms of development in Polish space had been introduced by Germans.

> It is an honor for Prussia that a higher civilization—albeit not in its entirety—has been conveyed into [Prussian Poland], it is an honor for the German nation that German industriousness and German *Bildung* have been introduced there; and it would be a disgrace for the German nation if the forms of full and total freedom were not also brought to Poland.[33]

Despite Ruge's intention to support the Poles, he nonetheless positions Prussia and the German nation as the source of higher civilization, industriousness, and *Bildung* in Polish space. He thereby reaffirms the diffusionist model that formed the basis of consensus for the Assembly's final deliberations.

The most famous speech of the Poland Debate was delivered by Wilhelm Jordan, a native East Prussian elected to the National Assembly while based in Berlin, and it both solidified the diffusionist construction and sharpened its consequences for the German-Polish relationship. Jordan was identified as a liberal, but when it came to the question of Germany's territory and the German-Polish relationship, he exhibited none of the moral ambivalence beleaguering other members of his cohort. The Poles, for Jordan, were unquestionably inferior to the Germans—they didn't have as much "human content," as he put it[34]—and Germans therefore had every right to claim the Polish territories.

> Our right is none other than the right of the mightier, the right of conquest. Yes, we conquered, the Germans conquered Polish lands, and these conquests were gained in such a way that they can no longer be given back. They were, as has already often been said, not so much conquests of the sword as conquests of the plowshare.[35]

It was, in other words, through the act of spreading their land-use practices that Germans had conquered territory in the East. For liberals uncomfortable about Prussia's role in the Polish Partitions, Jordan's argument offered the reassurance that Polish space had come under German control not through questionable acts of politics or warfare, but through a long history of peaceful German "colonization."[36] This form of territorial expansion is presented by Jordan as an organic expression of the German Volk and therefore more legitimate—and more permanent—than any state-driven annexation ever could have been. Eastward expansion had been a "natural imperative" and was now irreversible; the Germans, Jordan proclaimed, needed to develop a "healthy Volk-egoism" (*einen gesunden Volksegoismus*) and see their right to the colonized space in the East as a historical given.[37]

Jordan's speech is important for the language it introduces—the term *conquest by plowshare* appears in several of the subsequent speeches and broadly circulates in public discourse throughout the following century—and for the diffusionist model it asserts. As the debate ensued, Jordan's speech became its central point of reference and served as the basis for a consensus decision to maintain German control of the Polish space in question. In speech after speech, the German-Polish relationship was sketched out in diffusionist terms with Poland recast as an achievement of German innovation. By the end of the Poland Debate, Poland had been reinvented as German colonial space.

In the decades that followed, the colonial model of German-Polish relations established in the Poland Debate provided the language and frame of reference to address two additional concerns, namely, the question of German status within a global colonial order, and the related search for a prescriptive stance on German emigration practices. Since the late eighteenth century, German publicists had lamented the lack of German-owned overseas colonies.[38] Prior to German unification, this discussion was guided by nationalist aspirations for a Germany that could assume a place among the family of European imperial powers.[39] This was less a desire for large geographical expanse than for a colonial identity that could only be gained in a relationship with a non-European Other. In 1840, the economist and publicist Friedrich List gave expression to this relationship, which he already describes in the language of diffusionism.

> That the civilization of all nations, the culture of the entire globe is the mission of humanity can be seen in the invariable laws of nature by which civilized nations are driven by an irresistible force to transfer their productive energies onto less cultivated lands.[40]

In the binary that List establishes between civilized and uncivilized lands, it becomes clear that he doesn't consider all peoples as equal agents of "humanity," that this category applies more, or perhaps exclusively, to those endowed with the ability to spread "productive energies." Individual Germans had been involved in European projects of exploration and colonization from the very beginning of such endeavors, and, in these roles, had been involved in List's "mission of humanity," but the question was now one of a nationally identified role in this process. Establishing Germany as a civilizing nation would require the ability to claim a specific relationship with lands deemed uncivilized, a relationship in which Germans could narrate a transfer of innovation and progress into this other space. Wilhelm Jordan's notion of "conquest by plowshare" provided just such a narration of Germany's relationship with lands in the East—one that would become ubiquitous in the following decades.

The second issue was related to the first, and involved the desire to gain control over the flow of German emigration and use it to support a set of national priorities. In response to changing economic conditions and the population shifts accompanying them, the 1840s had seen a mass emigration from German lands that would continue into the 1870s. Many supported what they considered to be a release of the pressure exerted by an economically displaced population and encouraged emigration with publications offering advice on the choice of destination and how to best plan for one's "adventure."[41] However, there were also many who argued that emigration had negative ramifications because German immigrants were dissolving into the European populations abroad and investing their colonial energies to the benefit of other nations.[42] In 1842, the Society of German Rulers and Nobility for the Protection of German

Immigrants in Texas was formed with the intent to coordinate settlements that would remain loyal to the German homeland and serve as guaranteed trade outposts. By the mid-1840s, however, the Mexican-American War had put a damper on such plans, and attention increasingly turned to the possibility of routing emigration toward Central and Southeastern Europe, or, as the influential liberal periodical *Die Grenzboten* (Messengers from the border) suggested, to those "enormous stretches of land . . . , the marshland, the forests that are either unused or completely unprofitable, the uncultivated lands and abandoned villages that await plow and sower in Pomerania, not to mention East and West Prussia. This is the space that has to be taken into consideration when discussing colonization."[43]

There was, however, the fundamental problem of convincing German emigrants to exchange their planned destinations on the North American frontier for those in the East that, as the *Grenzboten* complained, didn't "offer the imagination the same allure of the otherworldly as did America."[44] The most prominent response to this problem mapped iconographic elements of the Wild West onto the eastern territories, thereby constructing a "Wild East" on the Prussian-Polish plains. If the American West was attractive to potential emigrants because they imagined it as a space where they could exercise free will and autonomous agency, or even because they entertained fantasies of proving their mettle against hostile "Indian" forces, then mapping these potentialities onto eastern space enhanced its attractiveness.

The scene was set during the Poland Debate, when Julius Ostendorf, a liberal Westphalian, argued against conquest based upon warfare but, like Jordan before him, recognized "the right of conquest by the plow, which was also exercised by the free North American vis-à-vis the native Indians."[45] Ostendorf's analogy equated German interventions in the eastern Prussian territories with the colonization of the North American frontier, and positioned the Pole as equivalent to the Indian. In the same year, an anonymous writer for the *Grenzboten*—now held to be the author Gustav Freytag[46]—began propagating this image of a Polish "Wild East" with the article "Beobachtungen auf einer Geschäftsreise in das Großherzogthum Posen" (Observations on a trade expedition to the Grand Duchy of Posen). Written under the pseudonym "William Rogers," the author takes on the persona of an American cowboy recounting his adventures in the Prussian East. This perspective allows him to look at a group of Poles and "see" Indians.

> In the light of the setting sun, they looked like a beautiful painting executed by the hand of a master. But may I never again shake the hand of an

> honest man if in this very moment they didn't appear to me as tribe of wild Indians, as a herd of Pawnee Loupes out on the grassy plains of the Missouri, good for border skirmishes, for novels and tragedies, but unfit for survival.[47]

In rendering the Poles equivalent to a "herd of Pawnee Loupes," the narrator casts Germany's neighbor in the role of a non-European *Naturvolk (*primitive people), which he then identifies as a structural antagonist existing merely for the sake of European advancement: it is the Europeans who will prove their intellectual strength by manipulating the "noble savage" in their literary and philosophical ruminations, and it is the Europeans (Germans) who will prove their mettle by expanding the frontier border against the resistant force of the Indians (Poles). Independent of these antagonistic functions, the Indians (Poles) have no reason to exist, and indeed lack the human faculties necessary to ensure their continued survival. The *Naturvolk* become an integral component of the primitive terrain that the European sets out to cultivate. But, whereas the landscape will be brought into a higher state of culture, rationality, and productivity, the native population must be pushed back, eliminated from this space. Their increasingly distant border skirmishes are necessary to mark the progressive stages of European advancement, but they can play no positive role inside of the space thus conquered.

This equation of the Pole with Indians and noble savages was a common trope in preunification German discourse, perhaps most prominently in the works of Gustav Freytag.[48] After 1871, however, the Pole became repositioned within Germany's new cartographic and constitutional reality: although the decision was made to adopt the model of Lesser Germany (the *kleindeutsche Lösung*), Prussia's eastern provinces were nonetheless incorporated, despite their predominantly Polish, Catholic populations. No longer vaguely populating the ambiguous terrain of the German eastern frontier, the Pole now indubitably inhabited specific areas of concretely defined, German political space.

This Polish presence exacerbated Bismarck's sense that religious and linguistic minorities maintained transnational loyalties and thus threatened the internal cohesion of the fledgling German nation-state. The Kulturkampf—with its specific repressive measures targeted at the Polish language and the Polish Catholic Church—was Bismarck's first response to this perceived threat and can be seen as the attempt to Germanize the Poles to better assimilate them into the body of the nation.[49] When these antagonistic policies were found to have led instead to the political mobilization and strengthening of the Polish minority, the Kulturkampf's "politics of culture" was replaced with a "politics of space and population management" designed to bring German control over previously Polish areas by displacing the Polish population.[50]

This second phase was initiated in 1885 with Bismarck's expulsion of some 30,000 ethnic and Jewish Poles across the border into space governed by Russia and Austria.[51] It continued with the "inner colonization" campaign introduced the following year, a government-funded project designed to purchase large estates from Polish landowners and parcel them into family-sized farms that would be settled by ethnic German farmers recruited from the western regions of Germany. The inner colonization campaign was launched just two years after Germany took its first colony in Africa, a concurrence that should not be overlooked. Despite the fact that Prussian Poland and German Africa were governed by different laws, administered to different effects and with different intentions, it is nonetheless the case that these two projects were ideologically linked, constituent parts of an overarching German imperial project.[52] German discourse of the late nineteenth and early twentieth centuries positions both within a global structure of center and periphery, and identifies the Germans as the agents of historical change in both cases.

In the first half of the 1880s, for instance, a series of articles appeared in the conservative monthly *Preußische Jahrbücher* (Prussian almanac) advocating German imperial expansion. Now that Germany was united, it was time for the nation to take its rightful place within global colonial structures; a European center was expanding into the periphery, and Germans should participate in this process. Interesting for our purposes is the way in which Eastern Europe was brought into conceptual alignment with overseas colonial space within this argumentative frame.

> Now that we Germans have united into a powerful nation after such a long period of fragmentation, are we supposed to close the borders of the land we inherited and forego the campaign for domination and acquisition taking place outside? Are we too weak to do what the English, the Dutch, the Russians, and the Americans are doing, and what the French are at least trying to do? It is simply a proven fact that the civilized peoples of Europe [*die Kulturvölker*] are conquering most of the races of the rest of the world, and it would be a highly sentimental weakness to regret this fact as unjust violation of other peoples. This campaign is fully just, and not only the campaign of the English against the Zulu Kafirs, but also of the Germans against the Czechs, the Germans against the Poles, and also of the English against the Irish.[53]

Written in 1882, and thus just prior to the launching of the inner colonization campaign, the article already links German eastward expansion with the larger European project of bringing civilization to non-Europe. Its author, Ernst von der Brüggen, even sees a special place for adjacent colonization; he will later name Russia the "greatest colonial power in the world" despite its lack of overseas possessions.[54]

At the end of the following decade, the historian Karl Lamprecht also articulates the advantages of adjacent colonization for a nation, but he positions Germany, not Russia, as the leader of the practice.

> We are, as far as I can see, the only large civilized nation that contains this absolutely unique and dramatic opposition between colonial space and metropolitan space [*mutterländischem Gebiet*] in direct combination and that has to incorporate this opposition within itself.[55]

Lamprecht argued that Germany's colonization in the East was the source of a national rejuvenation that would strengthen its bid for overseas colonies: "The real Greater Germany" would emerge once the "peaceful productivity of the motherland and the predominantly warlike resources of the colonial lands [were] brought together to balance each other out."[56]

While Langhans, von der Brüggen, and Lamprecht are all approaching the question of Germany's eastern "colonization" with different sets of political and strategic priorities, their arguments evince a clear set of discursive commonalities. Each claims that Germany derives strength (and perhaps even exceptional status) from its history of eastward colonization, that its experiences in the East place Germany on par with the colonial activities of its European neighbors (or perhaps even ahead of them), and that they provide Germany with the legitimacy of experience necessary to pursue additional colonial acquisitions overseas. In the decades prior to World War I, references to colonization in the East—be it medieval *Ostkolonisation* or contemporary inner colonization—served the purpose of establishing a colonial identity for the Germans both as legitimate members of the European Inside and as rightful participants in the project of bringing European civilization to the world's periphery.

World War I introduces a crucial change in these discursive patterns, because Germany loses control over its territory in the East and, with it, the narratives grounded in its possession. Upon losing the war, Germany was dispossessed of all of its overseas colonies and forced to cede approximately 13 percent of its continental expanse.[57] Most of this relinquished territory became part of a new, independent Polish state created under the auspices of U.S. president Wilson's peace agenda, which called for the creation of independent nation-states for each of the major ethnic populations in Eastern Europe, and which resulted in the formation of eleven new countries after the war.

Although the Germans were greatly fractured along political lines, the postwar population was united around the issue of regaining this territory lost in the East.[58] A wave of irredentist propaganda was unleashed in both the domestic and foreign spheres presenting arguments for the return of the previously German lands. Much of this described the nation's loss of the eastern provinces in terms analogous to the body's loss of an amputated limb and depicted the new border as a bloody, gaping wound that refused to heal. But there were problems with translating such emotional experience of loss into politically effective arguments capable of swaying international opinion. The main problem for the irredentist agenda was the ethnic distributions in the contested spaces, where Poles constituted undeniable local majorities—the key issue in determining Europe's new state lines. Unable to claim the lost territory with arguments based on the state of affairs in the present, Germans increasingly turned to colonial narratives of the past to justify contemporary land claims. "Poland" only exists, they argued, due to centuries' worth of German colonial labor, which had taken a wild, primordial landscape and cultivated it, bringing civilization to both land and inhabitants. Without this German intervention, the Poles would still be living in a barbaric wasteland, and therefore, although the Poles might currently populate this space in greater numbers, the space was nonetheless inherently German.

In 1921, the medieval historian Karl Hampe introduced his history of German eastward migration and settlement in the Middle Ages: *Der Zug nach dem Osten* (The drive to the East).[59] Hampe paints a picture of the medieval world in which Germans from all regions of the motherland streamed eastward, bringing the light of higher culture to dark lands lacking all signs of civilization, cultivation, or culture. He depicts the Germans brutally defeating the native Slavs they encountered and establishing villages and urban centers where there had once been only swampland and primordial forest. Most important, the Germans left their cultural imprint on the landscape by introducing German architecture and agricultural land-use practices. Thus, in addition to ascribing a colonial identity onto the Germans, Hampe's narrative of colonization in the East emphasized the ways in which Germans had stamped German identity onto the space itself.

Published in the early postwar years as the German population struggled to come to terms with the catastrophic aftereffects of war and defeat, Hampe's tale of the past "spread of Germandom" offered Germans an alternative, triumphant narrative. The völkisch-populist book was therefore quite successful: by 1939, it had seen five editions, and Hampe's subtitle—"the German Volk's great colonial achievement [*kolonisatorische Großtat*] in the Middle Ages"—had become a common catchphrase. Many publications celebrated Hampe's narrative of German medieval colonization, often citing adaptations of Hampe's title in their works.[60]

Hampe describes a medieval world already divided by a fundamental civilizational inequality separating a primitive "East" from a civilized "West." The West had developed politically, economically, and culturally to such an extent that it had been able to synthesize its civilizational order into the organized structure of the Holy Roman Empire. In the process, the West had produced a large, industrious population in growing need of more land and natural resources. The East, in contrast, had been unable to develop; both the population and the space it inhabited had remained trapped in a primitive state that only colonial intervention from the West had been able to transform.

> The vast plains of the barren East remained untouched by higher culture, sparsely populated, poor in production and trade, rich in raw materials. These differences gave rise to the necessity of an exchange between East and West, and it was naturally the Western bearers of culture [*Kulturträger*] who penetrated into the East, which became colonial territory [*Kolonialland*] for them.[61]

Hampe's image of medieval Europe was anachronistically structured according to the colonial economics of the capitalistic present: we are asked to imagine a world that—centuries before the first signs of industrialization—had already found itself divided into the space of industrial production, on the one side, and the space of natural resource exploitation, on the other. Hampe also insisted that the German "drive to the East" was aggressive, often violent, and that it played out over racial lines. During the initial contact, as Hampe describes it, "the sword had played the major role, ruthlessly cutting out space amongst the heathen Wends (even if not as thoroughly decimating them as was previously thought)," a first phase that was followed by the arrival of German farmers who

> in as far as they didn't stumble upon abandoned land or make land available through the ruthless expulsion [*rücksichtlose Vertreibung*] of the native occupants, usually claimed the larger and better parts of the village

> marches for themselves, while the Wendish population sank into oppressive serfdom or even harsher forms of servitude.[62]

Hampe repeatedly refers to the "terrible sword" of the Germans, which not only subjugated the Wends but also "wiped out large stretches of the Baltic Prussian population" and pushed other Slavic groups further back into the frontier march.[63] Such tales of slaughter were hardly politic in the early 1920s—the Allies had justified stripping Germany of its overseas colonies by referencing their history of colonial brutality there. Hampe's unabashed glorification of violence is thus all the more intriguing: one might bemoan the loss of a perished Volk, Hampe submits, but one should also recognize that such "racial struggles" accompanied "the entire colonial history of mankind. . . . When all is said and done, the superior culture has the historical right to defend itself against opposition."[64] We see that this very notion of violence itself served to inscribe a colonial identity upon the Germans: Hampe's introduction of seemingly gratuitous episodes of violence brought the eastward settlement into conceptual alignment with colonial violence committed overseas and thus rendered the German eastern settlements more unambiguously "colonial" in the strong sense of the term.

The Drive to the East thus contextualizes German medieval settlement within the conceptual frame of the global colonial project. If colonization was about conquering primitive landscapes and taming uncivilized populations, then surely the Teutonic Knights' Christianization of East Prussia, the German conquest and cultivation of previously underdeveloped lands, and the founding of medieval cities and fortresses across the otherwise "empty" eastern plains positioned Germans as significant contributors to the project.

Yet it was not merely German colonial identity that was at stake at this particular juncture but instead the cartographic map of German space; Hampe's book was popular because its discursive colonization of the medieval past could be mobilized to legitimize German land claims in the present.

Germany's Wild East traces this history of the German discursive colonization of Poland from the mid-nineteenth century to its high point after World War I. Through an examination of the discursive process as it played out in the public arenas of politics and the press, literature and film, propaganda and education, I hope to draw attention to the following. First, to the larger concept of Eurocentric diffusion as it was applied to Polish space, and the ways in which this spatial construct positioned Poland in the non-European Outside. Second, that this positioning served two main agendas, that of creating a colonial identity for the German nation, and that of legitimizing various German interventions and expansions into Polish space. Third, that Poland's location adjacent to Germany posed a specific set of conceptual problems within a colonial frame, but that, ultimately, the construction of Eurocentric diffusion proved flexible enough to accommodate them and to position Poland as Germany's adjacent colony.

Chapter 1

Constructing German Colonial Space in the East: Gustav Freytag's *Soll und Haben* as Colonial Novel

> Every nation has the Kipling that it deserves: the Germans had their Gustav Freytag.
>
> Jean Améry[1]

Deutschland, aber wo liegt es? Locating "Germany" after 1848

In the aftermath of the failed attempt to create a united German nation-state in the late 1840s, the question of Germany's location in the world loomed large.[2] To a certain extent, this question was cartographic in nature: according to which criteria could the rightful borders of the nation be drawn? Contemporary maps of Europe didn't offer any concrete answers and vexed their readers instead with a motley collection of kingdoms, duchies, and principalities of various shapes, sizes, and degrees of territorial uniformity—a colorful patchwork perhaps, but not a reassuring image when viewed in its broader geopolitical frame: France, England, and Russia all appear as solid blocks of uniform color, as organized spaces of integrated political and economic power.

This cartographic disunity reflected a set of relational concerns: where did Germans stand with respect to the peoples of other European nations? What was the role and status of "Germany" in the global arena?[3] This question was intimately connected to the ongoing process of European imperial expansion. In a world rapidly dividing into a dual system of imperial cores and colonial peripheries, the status of German-speaking lands was at best ambiguous. France and England appeared as solar centers surrounded by their colonial satellites, and they expressed imperial power in an ability to orchestrate global circulations of naval and trading fleets, colonial raw materials, and metropolitan processed goods. Was a non-united Germany destined to observe from the sidelines? Finally, in a world in which Europeans constructed their global superiority through narratives of colonial diffusion—of spreading cultural and technological innovations to the world's non-European periphery—did Germans also have stories to tell?

Gustav Freytag's enormously popular novel of 1855 provides its readers with a set of reassuring—and programmatic—answers to these questions of German identity.[4] The novel tells the story of Anton Wohlfart, a young man who migrates to Breslau from the Polish border of Silesia to apprentice in T. O. Schröter's import-export firm for colonial wares. Anton works his way up the company ladder, learns the value of the bourgeois work ethic, and ultimately marries his employer's sister, thereby becoming a partner in the firm. *Soll und Haben* was a best seller for over a century and introduced generations of readers to a European colonial project in which Germany was a valuable participant. This colonial subjectivity depended in large part upon the simultaneous rendering of Poland as the space of German colonial endeavor. We therefore follow Anton Wohlfart as he temporarily takes leave from Schröter's firm to spend time in Poland as a self-proclaimed German colonist. In Poland, Anton discovers land that is largely barren and unstructured in its boundlessness, and a population that is largely childlike, uncivilized, and prone to violence. In what I argue to be the German colonial novel par excellence, Anton creates an island of German order and prosperity in this sea of chaos, and thereby expands the borders of German space.

Soll und Haben is conventionally read as a bildungsroman depicting the spiritual shaping of its hero and celebrating the German *Bürgertum* he represents. The novel shows this class embodying a set of values, among them the insistence upon stability, solidity, and security, that allows its members to consolidate their strength and resources and expand their sphere of power and control. In the course of his development, Anton comes to internalize these values; his ability to successfully transfer them into Polish space proves his value as a member of the German bourgeois collectivity and ultimately leads to his elevation to an esteemed position within it.

But if the text is viewed through a slightly different analytical optic, and the focus of attention shifted from the main protagonist's personal narrative onto the way space is both organized and constituted in the novel, it becomes apparent that *Soll und Haben* also tells the story of the *Bildung* of the German nation. Where it no longer seemed wise to entrust the unification of the diverse German polities to the political sphere, *Soll und Haben* offers an alternative: a German bourgeois socioeconomic order that would be unaffected by administrative borders, yet nonetheless act spatially, steadily growing to incorporate all German regions into its quasi-organic network. The result would be a geographically continuous, internally cohesive, and hierarchically organized spatial order that could form the integrative foundation for collective action and collective identity. And, as a model of quasi-organic spatial extension, the imagined bourgeois order would also provide the mechanism for German colonial expansion. Freytag's text positions the Bürgertum as both best equipped to unite Germany and best able to locate the nation on the world map as an integral member of the global colonial project.

Soll und Haben presents the readers with three main social groups positioned in opposition to the German Bürgertum: German aristocrats, urban Jews, and ethnic Poles. To a certain extent, these groups are defined by their economic practices; the title *Soll und Haben* already refers to the novel's privileging of the economic order represented by the Bürgertum, and the novel contrasts their financial success with the inability of the other social groups to contribute positively to the collective "debit and credit." But while *Soll und Haben* can certainly be read as a tallying ledger, it also presents the reader with a narrative atlas—a collection of mental maps of an envisioned global order drafted through the codes of literary narrative. It is here that the novel's colonial import becomes most apparent.

Atlases often include maps of varied spatial frames within their covers; a road atlas may provide a continental overview of major transportation channels as well as street guides for individual cities. Similarly, *Soll und Haben* constructs several different mental maps of the world that range in scale from a world map of global economic circulation to the floor plan of a building. Through a series of analogic structures, the novel works to superimpose these maps of differing scale and focus upon one another, such that a view of any specific map also reveals the palimpsestic outlines of those lying beneath. This spatial layering is significant because the city of Breslau, the region of Central Europe, and the globe as a whole are all configured according to a shared model of modern center versus primitive periphery, and this structural congruence allows for statements made in one frame to analogously structure perceptions in the others. In *Soll und Haben,* the narrative moves easily between the various maps it constructs, silently weaving the global and the local together into an overarching narrative of world order. Be it a citywide, regional, or global frame, the German bourgeoisie is always positioned at the map's center and is shown to be best able to consolidate the order of this center such as to expand its boundaries into the space of the periphery.

In addition to its centrality, bourgeois space is depicted as integrative, easily able to interpolate ethnic Germans from other classes into its order, and possibly even able to assimilate ethnic others (i.e., Jews and Poles) into its collective. This interpolative function derives from the symbiotic relationship that the bourgeois class forms with its environment: bourgeois space is represented as space that has been infused with bourgeois values through the act of bourgeois labor. The construct is tautological because bourgeois labor is defined by the text as the infusion of (bourgeois) social values into space. The resulting buildings, fields, cities, and landscapes have been disciplined and structured to serve the needs of the Bürgertum, but these spaces have also gained the agency to shape and mold those who come to dwell in them according to bourgeois principles. In this cyclic, symbiotic relationship, space and its inhabitants are reciprocally formative: once space is conquered by the Bürgertum, the space conquers future inhabitants, and the bourgeois order steadily expands.

Through this spatial function, nonbourgeois Germans are readily integrated into the German bourgeois collectivity, but Jews and Poles are largely excluded from this process. Instead, they are pushed ever further into the peripheries of the growing German bourgeois space. On the text's mental maps, the models of center and periphery are structurally congruent: the Jews are positioned on the external margin of the German bourgeois city, and the Poles on the external frontier of the German nation. Jews and Poles inhabit the peripheries into which the bourgeois order expands, and in both cases, this process results in their physical displacement outward.

Although *Soll und Haben* has been deemed by many (including Theodor Fontane, who published an early, extensive review of Freytag's novel)[5] to be highly anti-Semitic, Jews in the text actually share many of the German Bürgertum's core qualities, and they mirror their German business counterparts down to the fine detail: they also work very hard, hold business acumen in high esteem, and structure their lives according to modern socioeconomic considerations. Yet there is a decisive difference: where the German Bürger subordinates his desire for individual gain under his concern for the welfare of the collectivity, the Jewish businessman ignores the needs of his collective to prioritize individual gain. This singular inversion of priorities reflects itself in all aspects of the Jewish habitus: Jews too create a symbiotic relationship with the space they inhabit, but it lacks the strength and stability of a collective foundation and therefore ultimately collapses into ruin.

While the Jews present an alternative—albeit negative—model of civilization with an alternative constitution of social space, the Poles are positioned as an uncivilized, primitive population (indeed, as a *Naturvolk*) lacking the ability to constitute social space altogether. "Poland" thus exists as a chaotic, unstructured expanse positioned adjacently to "Germany" in the text. Although both of these terms are frequently referenced in *Soll und Haben,* neither "Germany" nor "Poland" existed as such at the time the novel was written or narratively set; Poland had been divvied up among Prussia, Russia, and Austria in the Polish Partitions of the late eighteenth century, and Germany had yet to emerge as a unified state. Yet, despite their absence from the cartographic map, "Germany" and "Poland" categorically organize the mental maps generated by the novel. "Germany" gains shape and cohesive inner homogeneity as a structured, civilized European space most readily in its opposition to the unstructured, uncivilized, and non-European "Poland."

The text visits areas located in all three of the Polish Partitions but refers to each—even Polish Prussia—as "Poland" without any further distinction. This strategy seems to reunite "Poland" in the text's topographical imaginary, but it does so without any cartographic specificity: "Poland" hovers over the map, somewhere to the east of "Germany." Yet its function as Other serves to conceptually unite Germany as well. The civilizational inequality between "Germany" and "Poland" is so great that these two spaces seem to be separated by an oceanic divide—and this divide becomes the conceptual eastern border of "Germany."[6] The text is able to use the terms "Silesia," "Germany," and "German space" interchangeably because "Poland" gives the notion of "Germany" shape and internal coherence. As I develop my argument, I will refrain from placing these two place markers in quotation marks, but it should be understood that "Germany" and "Poland" both refer to the diagrammatic (i.e., noncartographic, and instead relationally positioned) spaces evoked in the text's imaginary topography.

In addition to locating Germany, Poland also provides the German bourgeoisie with a spatial periphery into which they can demonstrate an expansionist identity. In two major episodes constituting two-fifths of the book's overall length, the Bürgertum is shown to successfully engage in two different modes of territorial expansion into Polish space. The first of these episodes is staged on the conventional world map of global economic flow: raw materials produced in the colonial periphery are imported for consumption in the European center, and the fruits of European production are shipped out for sale in the colonies. Poland is interpolated into this network through its production of raw materials that are imported into Europe and through its dependence upon the processed goods it receives in return. In the first Polish episode, the circulation of global economic flows is threatened with stoppage due to rebellion in Poland, where local insurgents have violently attacked one of Schröter's trade convoys, captured his goods, and prevented their movement back into German space. As I will detail below, Schröter and Anton travel into Polish space, rescue the convoys, and establish bases for ensuring future security and profitability. Their brave acts help to establish a mercantile order that provides a basis of stability in a landscape mired by political and social unrest; they thereby expand the boundary of European colonial trade further into the global periphery and secure Polish goods for the world market.

If this first episode positioned Germany at the center of a global system of colonial trade, the second turns to the question of settlement colonization and again features the German bourgeoisie as agents of territorial expansion. The scene is set on a map of the peripheral frontier; Poland is cast as a primitive and unordered space into which Anton arrives as a "colonist" bringing civilization and order. Occasionally, the term *colonist* appears as a synonym for *settler* (*Ansiedler*) in the text,[7] but more frequently and conspicuously, German "colonists" in Poland are referred to as *conquerors* (*Eroberer*) who wrest control over foreign terrain by investing their physical labor in cultivating the land, and who protect their holdings against the native population through the use of armed force.

The novel presents this relationship between German and Pole in terms adhering to a colonialist model of diffusionism: the text emphasizes that the Poles are unable to develop or achieve civilizational progress on their own, and it narrates a long history of German improvements introduced into Polish space, all undertaken by businessmen or their occupational forerunners: medieval traders and merchants. The text claims German responsibility for technological innovations in agricultural and architectural practice, systems for organizing primitive space into politically and economically viable units, etc. This relationship of diffusion positions Germans as members of the civilized European center, as participants in the process of spreading European civilization into the global periphery.

Reading *Soll und Haben* as an envisioned atlas allows us to see that, whether the map is of the city, the nation, or the continent, the diagrammatical structure remains the same: the German Bürgertum consolidates its hold on the center, expands into the periphery, and incorporates the space it encounters into its spatial order.

Locating Germany in a Global Topographic Imaginary

In the wake of the spatial turn in literary and cultural studies, a number of scholars have returned to Gustav Freytag's novel to interrogate its complex spatial constructions. The marked difference between depictions of German and Polish space has featured prominently in these studies. In her insightful investigation of Freytag's imagination of the Polish East, Izabela Surynt analyzes the textual practices through which Polish space is rendered "distant" and "*unheimlich*" in *Soll und Haben.* She identifies a "topos of uniformity and endlessness (borderlessness)"[8] in depictions of eastern landscapes that provide German agents with the opportunity to exercise and prove their ability to discipline space. By placing "boundary stones, border posts, bridges, and fences," Germans take that which cannot be organized by the eye (*das Unüberschaubare*) and impose structure and control upon it: "The inscription of the landscape with visible signs is a process of spatial appropriation enacted in the ascription of meaning; at the same time, these markings also establish structures of dominance in that they bring new objects into the space, name and nationalize them, and thereby create a new map of the developed space."[9] It is a cyclical process of mapping one's own creation that naturalizes territorial claims.

In a similar vein, Niels Werber sees the landscape of the text divided into Deleuzian categories of smooth and striated spaces, a distinction that Ludwig Stockinger usefully articulates in terms of poetic space in an increasingly prosaic world. In other words, where a bourgeois order steadily brings more and more territory under the dominion of its rational ordering system (thereby rendering it "prosaic"), the only spaces left for the individual to engage in creative, heroic action lie on the external periphery of this bourgeois realm, in "poetic" (or, in Deleuzian terms, "smooth" space).[10]

I take inspiration from these investigations of space in Freytag's novel and would like to build upon the models they introduce by positioning them within two additional conceptual frames. First, each of these models rests on a binary system (smooth/striated; prosaic/poetic; bounded/unbounded), which I place in the discursive context of global imperialism, where I find them to gain enunciative potential: these dichotomies create the precondition for German narratives of territorial expansion. Second, however, I would also like to complicate the binaries themselves: German space is not simply represented as striated or bounded; but as striated or bounded in multiple and mutually incompatible ways. The city of Breslau is portrayed as a heterotopos, a space in which there is no single logic behind the social production of space. Instead, multiple social groups (Jews, aristocrats, the Bürgertum) mobilize competing spatial logics in their bid for social and economic control. Analyzing the contested interplay between various constitutions of space allows for a clearer articulation of how the novel positions the bourgeoisie as the rightful stewards of the German national project.

Reducing the text's spatial constructions into binaries also limits one's view of the multiple, often overlapping spatial frames mapped in the text. To begin with the question of a global colonialist topography, there are (at least) two different mental maps—or diagrammatic flow charts—in the text, and they address the colonial question within two independent but mutually supporting conceptual frames: colonization as "global trade" and colonization as "civilizational diffusion." While the novel is able to locate Germany within each of these colonial projects, it must sketch two different mental maps of vastly different scale and focus in order to do so. Let us consider each in turn.

For many Germans, "colonization" was a category evoking dynamic images of the global circulation of exotic products and raw materials: to have colonies was to participate in this economics of production, distribution, and consumption. *Soll und Haben's* mental map of largest scale casts the European colonial enterprise in such economic terms (rather than the national-political terms of territorial acquisition). This frame allows Germany to be positioned as an integral part of the global network: to the extent that colonization is about trading in colonial goods, the text argues, Germans can participate equally despite not owning overseas colonies.

Having arrived in Breslau and taken his post at Schröter's colonial import-export firm, Anton positions himself at the center of the global map.

> We live in the middle of a colorful web of countless strands connecting people to each other, over land and sea, from one corner of the globe to the other. Each and every person is thereby connected with the whole world. . . . When I set a sack of coffee on the scales, I tie an invisible knot between the young woman in the Brazilian colony who picked the beans and the young farmhand who drinks the coffee for breakfast.[11]

T. O. Schröter's colonial import-export company is the nerve center through which a complex set of global flows and economic transactions is routed. Other imperial powers are only visible as faint outlines on this map, as they are never mentioned by name in the sections on global trade. Furthermore, Schröter's firm never shows the need to engage in any way with the European countries whose colonies produce the goods in which the company trades. Schröter is veritably unaffected by the lack of German overseas colonies; his offices are characterized by the constant hustle and bustle of trading deals, and his storehouses are full of products from every corner of the globe. Anton stares in awe at the cornucopia of wares.

> Almost all of the lands of the earth, all the races of humankind had worked and gathered in order to produce this mountain of useful and valuable goods. . . . A Hindu woman had woven these bast mats, that box had been painted with red and black hieroglyphs by a hard-working Chinese, that cane bale had been tied by a Negro from the Congo in the service of a Virginian planter. . . . And unfamiliar shapes rose like monsters out of the chaos: there behind the open barrel filled with an orange mass—it's palm oil from the east coast of Africa—rests a misshapen animal—it's suet from Poland that has been poured into the whole hide of a cow . . . and in the opposite corner the baleen of an enormous whale towers above a pile of elephant teeth.[12]

Anton spends hours gazing at the exotic goods, a repository symbolizing German colonial access. Upon entering the firm for the first time, Anton walks into the loading terminal and watches workers hauling heavy loads of goods to and from the waiting shipping caravans. In the midst of the workers, Anton sees a businessman orchestrating the flow of action who appears to him as "a sun around which the casks and workers and wagoners were in orbit."[13] Germans might have dreamed of acquiring a colonial empire that, like the British empire, was so vast that the sun would never set upon it, but when understood in economic and not proprietary terms, the text argues that this goal has already been achieved by German businessmen.

It is significant that Schröter's storehouse includes a conspicuous contribution from Poland; the presence of the suet among the collection of colonial goods casts Poland into the category of those "lands and races of the earth" that produce goods for colonial trade. This early suggestion that Poland is located externally to the European center is consistently enhanced over the course of the novel, largely through the strategy of mapping a Wild West iconography onto Polish space. In constructing a "Wild East"—a wild frontier populated by a primitive, lazy, and unproductive race—the text creates the structural basis for German colonialist narratives.

In the first Polish episode, an uprising has broken out in Galicia,[14] and Polish insurgents have captured a caravan of Schröter's goods, threatening his company with great financial loss. The businessman has decided to travel to the Polish border in an attempt to resecure his property and has granted Anton permission to join him on the potentially dangerous journey. In preparing for this trip, Anton reveals much about how he envisions the nature of the space he is about to enter.

> He went to his room, noiselessly packed his travel bag, hauled out his damask pistols . . . and threw himself half undressed onto his bed. . . . "Good," Anton thought. "We're going to travel into enemy territory where we'll battle the scythe-bearers and force them to release our goods." . . . He was about to set out on an adventure. . . . He was pleased.[15]

Anton's frame of reference vacillates ambiguously between Wild West "cowboy-and-Indian"-based adventure tales, on the one hand, and anachronistic images of European peasantry, on the other. Entertaining visions of a lawless frontier where he'll be able to brandish his flashy pistols to good effect, Anton adapts this image to reflect his expectations of adjacent external space. Anton readily envisions his own role in Poland as that of a cowboy, but his positioning of the Poles as "Indians" is not quite as straightforward.

The Polish "scythe-bearers"—irregular troops of peasants armed with bayonet-style mounted scythes—were a visual icon German readers had become acquainted with during the period of *Polenbegeisterung* (pro-Polish enthusiasm) in the early 1830s. At a time when German liberals celebrated the Polish November Uprising, the scythe-bearers were seen as a symbol of nationalist conviction, the willingness of those at the grassroots level to fight to the death for their cause.[16] In Freytag's text, however, we see this image inverted into an object of derision; Anton not only positions scythe-bearers as "the enemy" but also imagines them as disorderly rabble lacking legitimate political or nationalist aims. The ensuing narrative affirms Anton's preconceptions as the Poles engage in seemingly random acts of violence and destruction.[17] Attacking caravans of covered wagons on the open steppe, the "scythe-bearers" take on the role of marauding Indians on Germany's adjacent frontier.

Soll und Haben is not unique in its depiction of the Poles as analogous to Indians; this trope had become widespread in mid-nineteenth-century German discourse.[18] Whereas Indians themselves had often been cast as dignified noble savages in the literature of the earlier Enlightenment and Romantic periods, the analogy drawn in the case of the Poles was always to this noble figure's savage counterpart: the negative stereotype of the wild, dangerously warlike, and stateless primitives on the North American frontier.[19] While this analogy initially served the purpose of delegitimizing Polish aspirations for independent statehood, in *Soll und Haben* it also serves to position Poland as Germany's frontier for colonialist expansion.

Intertextual references are typical for the bildungsroman, for in demonstrating the power that literature exerts upon the protagonist within the fictive narrative, the novel can claim a socializing function for itself. Anton is seen reading several times in *Soll und Haben,* where he shows a particular predilection for adventure tales, the kind of books that allow him to escape from his surroundings "by listening in on the roar of the lion and the croaking of the bullfrog on some tropical island or another."[20] While most of his reading material remains unidentified, two books are specifically noted: James Fenimore Cooper's *The Last of the Mohicans* (1826, translated by Heinrich Döring in the same year),[21] and François-René de Chateaubriand's *Atala* (1801). Each of these popular texts from the early nineteenth century depicts a fictive episode during the colonization of North America. But while both narratives are located in a liminal zone between land that has been conquered and "civilized" and the wilderness that extends beyond it, the nature of each text is quite different, and we learn much about Anton by observing his different reception of each.[22] Anton dismisses Chateaubriand's romantic tale—in which Indians appear as enlightened noble savages—as "tasteless."[23] Cooper's tale, however, in which Europeans face violent and shifty natives in a tale of frontier warfare, is much to Anton's liking. Book 2 of *Soll und Haben* opens with Anton intently reading this adventure tale of "cowboys and Indians."[24]

The text shows Anton projecting this fantasy onto Poland; as he silently packs his bags, it is as if he already imagines himself on the adventure for which his pistols would be the appropriate accoutrements. Anton's fantasy easily adapts a Wild West iconography to fit his eastern destination and even inflects his perceptions of his surroundings upon arrival at the Polish border. There, he sees the band of "savages" that has captured Schröter's caravan wagon led by "a brown fellow with a dangerous appearance."[25] The phenotypical darkness of this figure—his brown skin and black hair—will be repeatedly referenced in the text and generalized upon the Poles as a group, rendering them visually identifiable as members of another race, iconographically derived from the American "Indian," and semiotically linked with the colonized subjects of worldwide European imperialism.

Schröter rejects the cowboy scenario that Anton has conjured, and greatly frowns upon the pistols, but the ensuing narrative upholds Anton's vision. In both Polish episodes, Anton will face life-or-death situations in which the use of his weapons becomes necessary, most notably in a scene in which he frees Schröter from the murderous hands of saber-wielding Polish bandits.[26] Anton's imagination of Polish space as the Wild East is vindicated by this Cooperesque scene, and Schröter's later admission that Anton's actions had indeed saved his life translates the vision into authorized fact.

Schröter and Anton are eventually able to secure the release of their captured caravan, but Anton must remain in Krakow for several additional months to reestablish the firm's trading channels in Poland. Now, the need for armed conflict subsides, but the issue of bringing order to a land in chaos remains. Anton is successful in establishing a new framework of economic order in a region that had otherwise lacked such social structure. He anticipates that it will take years to establish channels clear enough to enable the free circulation of goods into and out of this periphery, but he has been able to lay the necessary groundwork.

The trip to the frontier has provided Anton with a useful self-narrative of successful adventure, and he returns to Schröter's firm a changed man. In his own self-assessment, he is more masculine, and he expects his employer's sister, Sabine, to concur. Recalling the moment when he intervened on Schröter's behalf, Anton finds that "since that swing of the Slavic saber . . . he had become a man in whose strength and composure a woman could certainly place her trust."[27] The narrator affirms Anton's self-assessment by providing a rare moment of omniscient access to Sabine's thoughts: "He had become a new man in her eyes."[28]

The narrative immediately juxtaposes this scene of Anton's masculine arrival with news of his best friend's demise in America. Anton receives a letter from Fritz von Fink, a former employee of Schröter's who has left the company to take over a family business in the Wild West. Fink has become involved in his uncle's land speculation scheme, tricking incoming settlers out of their meager savings by selling them nonarable marshland. Anton is not surprised at Fink's behavior—such "unbridled speculation . . . is only too common over there"[29]—a sentiment indicative of the text's consistent rejection of North America as the proper destination for German emigration.

Fink's adventure undermines the image of the American Wild West as a space of manly action and personal development. Instead, it emerges as a corrupting landscape in which the powerful become swindlers and the weak become their destitute victims. For Germans, economic exchange in America is divorced from national duty or service, and the landscape has been robbed of its romance—all of the Cooperesque elements of frontier bravery, courage, and resolve (and, therefore, the potential to prove one's masculine identity) have been mapped onto Polish space instead.

In this first Polish episode, *Soll und Haben* has sketched a map marking the global flow of colonial goods into Schröter's firm, positioning it at the center of European colonial trade. But it has also shown the German Bürgertum involved in *expanding* the boundary of this European realm of economic control further into the global periphery. Through their efforts in establishing a viable trade outpost in the Polish Wild East, they have brought Germany into alignment with the European center and positioned Poland as part of the global periphery that must be disciplined into serving the needs of European global hegemony.

Positioning Germany as the Origin of Colonial Diffusion

In depicting the growth of bourgeois space, *Soll und Haben* does not present us with a static image of space but instead presents dynamic change over time. Movement is traced by the trajectories of various human agents as they move over the surface of the text's mental maps. Content and form are changed by their itineraries: human agents either shape their surroundings according to their will or pass over the landscape without leaving a trace; they either silently cross over various borders and boundaries, actively shift them, or passively allow themselves to be restrained by them. Jews, Poles, German aristocrats, and the German bourgeoisie all move through space differently.

If we imagine a trajectory through space as an arrow on a map, we can see that the arrow itself ascribes an identity to both its point of origin and its point of arrival. The arrow narrates an identity between these two spaces and positions them with respect to each other. As Anton "ties the knot" between the producer and consumer of the coffee imported by Schröter's firm, he literally imagines the trajectories of the coffee's trade routes as strings that he creates into a network: like spokes on a wheel, all of the imagined arrows either originate or terminate at the hub, where Anton holds the strings in his hands as the reins of the international trade he has harnessed. The envisioned network of global trade routes positions Germany at the driving center of colonial commerce.

The circular, global hub-and-spokes diagram traces the trajectories of goods, but a second image emerges when we consider the movement of people. Polish goods are transported from Poland into Germany, but Poles themselves never cross this border. The text erects an invisible barrier that is impermeable to them, and we never see any ethnic Poles in Germany. This exclusion allows the text to accentuate a vast series of unidirectional flows originating in Germany and crossing into Poland. This diagrammatical flowchart is sketched in the very first sentence of the novel: "Ostrau is a small town not far from the Oder, well known—even into Poland—on account of its secondary school and its sweet gingerbread."[30] This seemingly innocuous "wafting" of oven scents and educational reputation establishes a dynamic of diffusions that structure the German-Polish relationship in the text.

In a series of lengthier passages, such flows become more purposeful;

German colonial activity in the East results in the transfer of German innovations into Polish space. The diffusionist narrative, we recall, depicts the introduction of innovation into a space whose inhabitants are themselves incapable of generating new social, cultural, or technological advancements. In *Soll und Haben,* this construction of Poland is reinforced on multiple textual levels: commentary delivered by the characters, authorized by the narrator, and enacted within the narrative all position Poland as a space out of which innovations do not independently arise.

As Anton and Schröter travel to Poland to rescue the caravan, Schröter delivers a speech on the Poles.

> There is no race more lacking in that which it takes to better themselves and less able to use their capital to improve their state of humanity and *Bildung* than the Slavs. . . . It is remarkable how unable they are to generate that class [the *Bürgertum*] which produces civilization and progress, and which can lift up a bunch of scattered farmers into a state.[31]

Schröter describes the Poles in terms of a fundamental inability to produce progress from within. His claim of racial difference divides Germans and Poles into different human categories in a passage so quintessential that it is used in the *Grimm Dictionary* to provide context for the word *race: "with a scientific tone: races of humans, of peoples (völker): there is no race so lacking in the ability to progress as the slavic."*[32] Anton internalizes this lesson from his mentor and, later in the novel, passes it on to the young farmer Karl Sturm. Anton exhorts Karl to stay in the German colony he has helped build in Poland.

> Everything that the surrounding Polish landowners have become . . . —and every Taler that they have to spend—they have acquired due to German activity. Their wild herds were domesticated through our sheep, we build the machines with which they fill their casks of spirit, the value of their bonds and properties is based upon German credit and German assurances. Even the weapons with which they try to kill us were made in our factories or were delivered to them by our companies. We won true dominion over this land not through political scheming, but by peaceful means, by our work. And that is why he who stands here as a member of the Volk of the conquerors acts cowardly if he now leaves his post.[33]

Anton's speech is noteworthy first for the extent to which it reiterates the argument delivered by Wilhelm Jordan during the Poland Debate of 1848. In attempting to justify the inclusion of Polish Prussia in the envisioned German nation-state, Jordan had also argued that Germans had conquered Polish space by peaceful means; it was not the violence of the gun but the labor of the plow that brought Germans their rightful dominion. *Soll und Haben* brings the discourse of the Poland Debate into narrative form, where it radicalizes the diffusionist model presented there. The Poles, according to Anton, have done nothing on their own. The Prussians, as he explains to Karl, gained control over Polish lands, and then civilized them: "They carved drainage ditches in the moor, planted men into empty space and produced a race that was as hard, industrious, and ambitious as they were themselves."[34]

The novel's narrator builds upon Anton's version of the story by recounting the history of Rosmin, the town nearest to the settlement that Karl and Anton have cultivated in Poland. The narrator's lengthy rendering of this history begins with a description of German medieval *Ostkolonisation* that sounds very much like tales of Europeans' first contact with primitive native populations as described in early travel narratives. Germans traveled into eastern space laden with bright and shiny objects for trade: shawls and colorful clothing, necklaces of glass and coral beads, etc. They exchanged these objects with the native, who "enjoyed what others had invented for him" and who, in return, could only offer that "which the landscape delivered him," such as wolf skins, honey, and grain.[35] German tradesmen ultimately settled in Rosmin permanently and introduced German settlement culture: they built their houses around a central market square (commerce, not religion, is privileged in this narrative), and they imported German law. The effects on the landscape were permanent, the narrator asserts: the settlements remain what they always were: "the markets of the great plains, the places where the fruits of Polish fields are traded for the inventions of German industry."[36] For hundreds of years, the narrative suggests, the dichotomy between German advanced culture and Polish primitivity was upheld.

Colonial settlement may not conventionally be considered a bourgeois undertaking, but *Soll und Haben* depicts this class leading this process of territorial expansion as well. Again, it is their ability to infuse space with stability, solidity, and order that renders them the crucial vanguard agents of the colonial project. These values are expressed in a pivotal scene in the novel, when the young Bürger *in spe* Anton Wohlfart explains his role as a colonist in Polish space. When questioned as to his motivations for working in such a difficult environment, Anton gestures over the surrounding landscape and explains.

> I stand here now as one of the conquerors who, for the sake of free labor and human culture, have taken control of this land from a weaker race. We and the Slavs: it is an old struggle; and with pride we find that formative

> culture [*Bildung*], the desire to work, and economic strength are on our side.[37]

It is, in other words, a set of bourgeois values that provides the Germans with the ability to expand into foreign territory—and the legitimacy to do so. With this performance of "territorial conqueror," Anton Wohlfart positions himself within two different discursive traditions, both important for the novel's model of German colonial expansion into adjacent space. On the one hand, Anton portrays himself as the rightful appropriator of foreign lands within a conventional colonialist logic. He justifies territorial aggression by asserting an inherent superiority over the native inhabitants—in this case by claiming membership in a human race stronger than that of the conquered. Wohlfart thereby casts himself in a role familiar from popular colonialist narratives; his conquering of foreign territory aligns with tales of the Spanish Conquistadors in South America, of the great surveying expeditions of the North American frontier, or of Victorian cartographers charting the interior of the African "dark continent."[38]

On the other hand, however, Anton is not speaking from some distant, unfamiliar land, but instead stands on acreage located less than 250 miles away from the Lower Silesian village into which he was born. In all likelihood, this "conquered territory," which is located in the Prussian province of Posen, lies even closer to the Prussian center of Berlin than Anton's hometown had (because the arm of Lower Silesia extends quite far to the east and partly encircles the Posener province). Anton has merely crossed an internal Prussian administrative border into adjacent, ethnically Polish space.

His speech, with the reference to the "long struggle" between the neighboring Germans and Slavs, reveals a position "close to home" and structures his narrative within temporal and spatial frames characterized by durative and proximal contact. This context of adjacency is problematic for Anton's colonial self-fashioning because it threatens to alleviate the possibility of constructing the fundamental difference between self and Other prerequisite to a colonial worldview. If the Germans and Poles have been in contact with each other for centuries, then we would expect either that the stronger party would have already overcome the weaker or that the differences between the two communities would have been erased over the course of time.

The novel resolves this problem through a two-pronged strategy; first, it renders the inferiority of the Slavs a reflection of their essential, unalterable nature: *Soll und Haben* will show that the diffusion of Western civilization has only led to a partial mimicry of its external trappings while leaving the underlying, primitive Slavic nature unchanged. Second, the novel suggests that, despite this essential Slavic inferiority, the Germans, under aristocratic leadership, had reached a deadlock with the Poles; the arrival of a new bourgeois German element is the factor that will change this equation and shift the balance. As Anton argues, it is the bourgeois virtues of *Bildung,* labor, and wealth that will allow the Germans to finally conquer Eastern space, not weaponry. Over the course of the novel, the Poles will engage in several violent attacks, and the Germans will turn to their weapons in self-defense, but it is their ability to infuse the land with their German bourgeois identity that ultimately allows them to create new German space and to win the "long struggle" against the Poles.

Becoming Bourgeois through Spatial Bildung

In order to become an agent of this spatial expansion, Anton must first internalize a set of bourgeois spatializing practices that he can subsequently impose upon the landscape in the East. Anton's path of development is therefore marked by moments in which he engages with the question of how different spaces are organized, and how these differences reflect differing sets of social values.

At the beginning of the novel, Anton travels from his hometown on the Polish border into Breslau. As he undertakes the last leg of his journey to the city on foot, Anton chances upon the estate of the aristocrat Baron von Rothsattel; he wanders into the garden and admires the property. When Anton's presence is discovered by the baron's young daughter, Lenore, the two spend the afternoon together in an encounter brimming with romantic cliché (an encounter that will lead to a long period of sentimental attraction for the aristocracy, which Anton will have to overcome). At the end of this episode, Lenore brings Anton back to his path by rowing him over a pond at the border of her family's estate.

> The rowboat landed near a grove of trees, and after turning towards him one last time, the young girl disappeared behind them. Through an opening in the park, Anton saw the manor-house lying before him—it rose elegantly over the landscape. . . . "So solid, so noble!" said Anton.[39]

Anton has just met a young woman who will continue to be the object of his desire for many years to come, yet his spontaneous outburst of admiration does not refer to her but instead to the space she inhabits. Anton is so enamored with this aristocratic world that, upon reaching his destination in Breslau, he immediately sketches a picture of the Rothsattel estate: drawn on the best paper he can afford and framed in gold, Anton hangs his picture of aristocratic space on his wall as his sole contribution to the decoration of his living quarters.[40]

Anton thus begins his journey of development under a seductive spell; aristocratic space presents him with a façade of social distinction, leadership, and stability. Over the course of the novel, he will come to see the reality underneath and to understand that the way in which the aristocrats constitute social space counteracts the needs of the German national collective. As a result, he will distance himself from the Rothsattels, replace his aristocratic flirtations with bourgeois solidity, and become an agent of bourgeois expansion by bringing these values into the periphery. This development in his identity comes as the result of an educational process (*Bildung*) in which he internalizes the bourgeois spatial logic imbued in his surroundings at Schröter's firm. This course of events is cued at the very moment Anton enters the building: his initial set of adjustments is described as a negotiation with the *space* of his new residence.

> In the first few weeks, Anton had trouble getting used to the new world into which he had been set. The *building,* the *household,* the *firm* were so anciently solid and grand, that they would have impressed even a cosmopolitan of much more experience.[41]

Although Anton has traveled from his small town to the city of Breslau, the "new world" to which this passage refers is not that of the hustle and bustle of city streets—indeed, the text will never show Anton encountering traffic, or crowds, or the lure of new forms of urban economic consumption. The passage also doesn't indicate that Anton had to learn new job skills, come to terms with a new set of duties and responsibilities, or adjust to his interactions with a new cohort of business colleagues. Anton arrives in a completely new setting but feels only the effect of the *space* he has entered.

At Schröter's, all of the unmarried employees are required to reside on the premises and thus spend most of their lives in a disciplined realm where they are subject to observation and correction. The intimate details of their daily lives are watched over, discussed, and criticized both by the patriarchal Schröter and by the community of fellow workers. Anton adapts well to these new surroundings; he embraces its values and responds to its disciplinary practices. He grows into a symbiotic relationship with the building—he will later speak of having cast the roots of his life into its very walls—and his growth is figured as an ascension through its hierarchical spatial order.[42] His job promotion brings him the right to have his own desk; because his employer comes to value discussing business matters with him, Anton's seat at the dinner table shifts ever closer to Schröter's; and Anton moves into larger and more refined personal quarters as a result of his good relations with fellow colleagues.

While Anton makes his way through this space of the bourgeois center, the novel offers a contrasting narrative of education in the city's Jewish periphery. Veitel Itzig, Anton's former classmate from Ostrau, travels to Breslau on the very same day as our hero, and their paths cross along the way. Veitel also hopes to find his fortune in the big city, but instead of seeking employment in the bourgeois milieu (which might not have granted him entry—there are no Jewish employees at Schröter's), he heads into the twisted side streets of the Jewish quarter.

Although Anton later celebrates industriousness as a German bourgeois value, the text shows that Veitel too works very hard; he puts in longer hours and works under much more difficult circumstances than Anton, and he ultimately becomes an independent and wealthy businessman. It is, therefore, not ultimately a question of work ethic per se that distinguishes the German Bürger from the Jew, but the way in which each constitutes the relationship between his work and his community. Breslau provides the text with the opportunity to contrast these two different systems of work and exemplify their consequences. The Jews and the German bourgeoisie are, to a certain degree, recent additions to the city, and they each occupy spaces that they inherited from a premodern past. The Jewish quarters at the riverside used to be occupied by the guild of cloth dyers; the Jews moved in after the guildsmen moved on to another neighborhood. Similarly, Schröter's building is quite old; although the text doesn't indicate how Schröter's family came into its possession, it is clear that the building was not initially constructed to house the import-export company.

Although Schröter's firm is geographically and conceptually distanced from Jewish space in the imaginary topography of Breslau, a closer look at these two realms reveals that they share a common set of traits that they inherited from this premodern time. The Jewish quarter is depicted as a nonrational organization of space: this is a world where the streets are crooked, where secret rooms are accessed through adjacent wardrobes, and where back stairs mysteriously disappear into the river. Schröter's building is described in surprisingly similar terms; it too is characterized as incoherently ordered.

> The building itself was an old, irregular structure with side wings, small courtyards and back houses, full of enclosures and small sets of stairs, of

> mysterious passageways where no one would suspect, of corridors, alcoves, deep wall cupboards and glass encasements. It was a thoroughly unnatural construction on which centuries had worked to make it as difficult and unintelligible as possible.[43]

Both the Jewish neighborhood and Schröter's firm reflect their origins in a premodern era, but they are differentiated by the ways in which their inhabitants have since acted upon the structural inheritance. At Schröter's, the building has been brought under the discipline of hierarchical order and economic rationality. Herr Pix is tasked with maximizing the building's storage potential, and we see him taking stock of each available nook and cranny, building storage units and separation walls to increase Schröter's capacity.[44] The building is thereby steadily rationalized to serve the needs of the company. In the Jewish district, Löbel Pinkus's boardinghouse also serves as a storage facility of sorts: Veitel discovers a secret room accessible both through a false wall in his wardrobe and by a door through the wall of the adjacent building; this room stores a stockpile of stolen goods that will be smuggled into Russia.

Each of these storage systems represents a symbolic accumulation of value-laden practices. Living in spaces shaped by these respective values, Anton and Veitel develop very different characters and priorities. In this bildungsroman, then, *Bildung* occurs between space and individual, where we understand the term in its various senses of "to form, to shape," but also "to cultivate, to educate," and lastly, "to build up, to accumulate." Space is created through the accumulation of formative cultivating practice; individuals come into being in these spaces, are shaped and educated by them, and continue the cycle by externalizing the *Bildung* they have received through space.

Anton ascends through Schröter's hierarchically ordered world because he is willing to subordinate his individual desire for personal gain in order to strengthen the economic and moral capital of the collective. Anton's loyalty, integrity, and hard work add to the value of the firm and fortify its interests against those of other groups. Anton is punished for transgressions by being shunned from the collective, and rewarded for positive contributions by being bound ever firmer to the space of the firm.

Veitel's experience in the Jewish underworld is directly analogous, but he is shaped by a value system organized around personal gain without concern for the collective. Veitel internalizes these values to the detriment of those around him. He gains improved living quarters by threatening to report his landlord's hidden goods to the police; and he gains a job promotion and even a seat at his employer's dinner table by threatening to financially ruin him otherwise.[45] It appears as if every business deal he undertakes serves to temporarily benefit Veitel while permanently weakening both the Jewish and the national collectives.

As a result, the Jewish businessmen are unsuccessful at their bid to spatially expand. Early in the novel, Veitel tells Anton that he plans to use his business skills to gain control over the Rothsattel residence, a scheme in which many of the novel's Jewish figures participate. But just as they lie and deceive Rothsattel, they lie and deceive each other, such that, while Rothsattel indeed loses his estate at the end of the novel, it comes into the hands of a buyer from outside of the Jewish community. Where it is "every man for himself," the text argues, each man ultimately loses. Not only do the Jews not succeed in this spatial expansion, at the end of the novel they have lost territory: all of the main Jewish figures are either dead or in prison, and Pinkus's boardinghouse is sold to an "honest dyer." A businessman, in other words, has expanded into Jewish space, and the bourgeoisie has expanded its urban center into the periphery.

In addition to its tendency to expand, bourgeois space also has the ability to grow by integrating outsiders—at least those outsiders who are members of the German Volk—into its realm. Schröter's firm becomes the home of Anton, who hails from a petit bourgeois background, but also of the wealthy aristocrat Fritz von Fink and the working-class Karl Sturm. All come to internalize bourgeois spatializing practices. The experience of inhabiting bourgeois space is thus depicted as transformative.[46]

Fritz von Fink, Anton's closest friend throughout the course of the narrative, first arrived at Schröter's firm after a wild adventure in the Americas. As a young boy, his uncle brought him to "Newyork," where he was spoiled by a life of wealth and carousing free of all responsibility ("the worse I acted, the more money I got"). After his family found him living as a rancher they brought him back to Europe and placed him in Schröter's hands. Fink initially intended to stay at the firm only long enough to calm his parents' nerves, and he dreams of returning to life in unbounded space, where he will be able to "ride from early morning until noon without crossing a border marker of my property."[47]

But as much as Fink has tried to maintain his aristocratic autonomy in the house, he has nonetheless come to internalize many of its values. The transformation isn't complete, as evinced by his subsequent escapades in America, but it has been significant (and ultimately gives him the will to extract himself from the land speculation schemes). Fink himself recognizes this: "I will have your house to thank," he tells Schröter before his departure for the Wild West, "if I maintain some of the respectable aspects of German nature."[48]

The text stresses the positive function of bringing German members of the aristocratic and working classes into German bourgeois space, for here, they absorb the values infused into their surroundings. It follows logically that there are negative ramifications for transplanting oneself away from this space, for one, of necessity, is drawn into alternative symbiotic relationships to spaces infused with lesser values. Schröter indicates this to Anton during their first trip into Polish space. The two men discuss the German population in Galicia: "good, honest people," Schröter says, "but all of them are immigrants—the upstanding bourgeois sensibility doesn't have a foothold, and is only seldom passed on to the next generation. What they call a city is only a shadow of ours, and their citizens have little of that which makes the industrious bourgeoisie the leading class of the state."[49] Schröter's conclusions are confirmed when he meets his agent in Krakow, who has come quite unglued by the revolutionary chaos breaking out around him and has abandoned all of his commercial duties. "When a businessman allows himself to be more distracted than absolutely necessary, he commits an injustice to civilization, an injustice that can not be redressed" is Schröter's repulsed assessment of the situation.

The agent has been living in Polish space on his own and shows signs of having "gone native": he wears the decorative badge of the Polish revolutionaries to guarantee his safe movement in Polish territory and is ready to retreat at the first sign of threat. The agent's situation serves as a contrast to Anton's subsequent colonial undertakings in Posen, where he is part of a larger German community that is able to present a united front against the Polish insurrection, provide protection for its members, and maintain a German cultural identity.

Yet, when Anton returns from this second journey to Poland, Schröter is skeptical that he has remained true to his bourgeois values.

> An unregulated desire tempted you into a situation that . . . must be unhealthy for anyone who lives in it. You have [worked] in a landscape where one's conscience often has a greater tolerance, and where social relations are not as rigidly ordered.[50]

Schröter has not considered that, upon entering Polish space, Anton would not simply be the passive object of spatial *Bildung* (as he had been in Schröter's firm) but would actively externalize his own will onto the landscape, infuse it with his own values, and shape it according to his own image. Anton fought restlessly with the space in Poland and found consistent victory. He faces Schröter with this conviction: "[I am proud] that I have been tested and that I no longer act out of instinct and habit like a boy, but according to my convictions, as a man. In this year, I have gained a trust in myself that I didn't have before."[51]

Diffusionary Topography: Aristocrats in Eastern Regressive Heimat

We have seen that the German bourgeoisie is able to expand its center into both the urban Jewish and nationally adjacent Polish peripheries, but Jews and Poles aren't the only groups undergoing displacement; the German aristocrats are also expelled from the nation's core. Aristocrats constitute space in a noncontinuous manner. Their world consists only of punctuated islands of aristocratic landholdings, separated from the nonaristocratic space surrounding them and linked together in a supranational network that ignores political and ethnic boundaries. While this spatial logic was in harmony with the fragmented German political landscape, it was the exact antithesis of the continuous and hierarchically ordered space needed by the envisioned nation-state.

Paradoxically, while the landed aristocracy historically have made their fortunes off the land that they owned, in the world of Freytag's novel, they are the least concerned with actual physical space. As represented by the Rothsattel family, the German aristocrats have lost touch with their natural connection to the land. While the Jews and the bourgeoisie are distinguished by the kind of work that they invest into space, the aristocrats are distinguished by an overall inability to work at all. When it comes to their landholdings, the Rothsattels exemplify an inability to invest value into space, and it is this inability that now makes them weak and vulnerable to the expansionist tendencies of competing social groups. Veitel's teacher of economic "black magic," Hippus, understands how to exploit Rothsattel's weakness: one need only bring the aristocrat into a situation that would necessitate the work of infusing space with value. Once Rothsattel has been convinced to build a factory on his property, his demise is certain, because the success of the project would have demanded his constant supervision, his investment of labor. Unable or unwilling to provide it, Rothsattel will lose his estate.

The text is not contrasting industrial and agricultural modes of production but instead, two different ways of spatializing production. In an extended passage, the narrator celebrates the modern (i.e., nonaristocratic) farmer: he knows how to subject the verdant force of nature to his wise sense of will: "He is the priest who tends to stability, breeding, and customs—the most important virtues of a Volk."[52] This modern farmer infuses space with values and is thus closely aligned with the German Bürgertum. He is also part of expanding the borders of Germany's global influence, because agriculture has become a global business, and the farmer's goods are now part of larger international flows of goods and capital.

Rothsattel, however, is no such modern farmer; he doesn't take any part in tending the fields that provide his crops, and he does not attend to the relationship his farmhands are developing with his space; they steal from his crops and pilfer his equipment, they only nominally work the fields, and they allow his infrastructure to fall into disrepair. If Rothsattel had enforced German bourgeois values, nurtured the collective, and developed a closer relationship with the land, his property would now be profitable, the narrator assures us, for the soil is rich, the estate has a long history of bountiful crops, etc.[53] Rothsattel has not fortified his space or invested in his land, and once he opens himself to the schemings of the Jewish businessmen, he is ruined. He loses the estate near Breslau and is dislocated into the periphery. All that is left is the piece of land he purchased in Posen, and he has hired Anton to take it into possession and prepare for his family's arrival.

Anton thus departs on his second journey into Polish space and again finds a landscape reminiscent of the Wild West.

> On a cold day in October, two men rode . . . across the plain that spread out unvarying and endless before them. . . . The wind swept sand and straw across the stubble fields with its enormous broom, the street was a wide path through the field, with neither drainage ditches nor planted trees; the horses either waded through rutty water puddles or through deep sand. . . . Muddy water collected on the ground. . . . No houses could be seen on the street, no wayfarers, and no wagons.[54]

The Polish landscape is depicted as a vast, barren "desert" (*Wüstenei*) lacking any signs of modern human intervention: the roads haven't been paved, drainage ditches haven't been excavated, and trees haven't been planted to tame the sandy topsoil. The area is eerily devoid of human presence, even though the harvested field indicates that the two men are not traveling into an entirely uncultivated space.

The situation is the same upon reaching the Rothsattel estate. Zaminsky was the previous owner; he had run the place quite recklessly and allowed the manor, the fields, and the entire economic infrastructure to fall prey to the forces of crime and "Polish mismanagement" (*polnische Wirtschaft*).[55] Anton climbs the manor's tower to survey the property.

> He looked over the edge of the wall and into the surrounding plain. . . . The sky gray, the earth discolored, the trees and shrubs near the stream without any green, and the forest, with its bays and inlets, like a wall that cut off this piece of earth from all men, from all *Bildung,* from all joy and beauty in life.[56]

Anton has the ability to pass judgment on his surroundings and to read the state of humanity from these visible signs. He thus begins his stay in Poland by literally rising above the landscape and detaching himself from it in order to objectify and discipline it with his gaze. Anton is not overwhelmed by the chaos but knows just what must be done: he must infuse this space with bourgeois spatial order: "All we need is capital, labor power, and a sense of order."[57] This space will not exert any influence upon him but will be subject to his will; as the narrator declares, "If he is a weakling, then he will relinquish his disposition under the sway of the foreign forces whose space he has entered. If he has what it takes to be a man, now he will become one."[58]

As if to drive this point home, the novel later compares Anton's ability to negotiate the the "sway of foreign forces" with that of the aristocratic Rothsattels, and again, Anton's superior position will be represented by his ability to see—to perceive the truth underlying the superficial image. Anton's bourgeois standing provides him with the strength to resist the entropic nature of his Polish surroundings, but the German aristocrats have no such base and are thus much more prone to fall under the sway of foreign influences.

Anton travels on business to meet with the nearby Polish aristocratic Tarowski family and is joined by the Rothsattels. Anton enters the domestic space of the Poles and immediately adopts a distanced, appraising stance. While the aristocrats engage in the superficial exchange of charming compliments and "French bonmots," Anton steps off to the side.

> Now Anton had the opportunity to take a closer look at the room. A Viennese grand piano stood amongst rough furniture from the village carpenter, the windowpanes showed patching, a threadbare rug lay next to the sofa on the black floor. The ladies sat around a worn table on velvet chairs. The lady of the house and her adult daughters were in Parisian toilette, but as a side door opened, Anton could see several children that were running around in the gray back room in clothing so inadequate for the cold winter that he felt sorry for them.[59]

The Tarowskis attempt to present themselves as European aristocrats, but Anton recognizes their performance as mimicry. Echoing the distanced view he held from the Rosmin tower, Anton is again endowed with the ability to survey the surrounding landscape of furniture and clothing and read the underlying reality. It is not poverty that leads the Tarowskis to cover their floor with a torn carpet, or to place an old, worn table in the midst of their elegant velvet chairs. Instead, the elements of filth, decay, and disrepair Anton perceives all around him are the signs of a wild and primitive "truth" existing underneath the deceptive façade of European finery. Although the Tarowskis attempt to present themselves as European aristocrats complete with Parisian toilette and a Viennese grand piano, they are only playing a class charade, adopting elements of an "aristocraticness" that they have observed and imported from abroad. But the Poles are unable to assimilate these diffusions into an organic unity of identity. It is a clichéd image of the colonial subject criticized for attempting to adopt the very cultural practices that the colonist assumes. In Homi Bhabha's schema, "mimicry is a flawed identity imposed on colonized people who are obliged to mirror back an image of the colonials but in imperfect form."[60] While Bhabha famously rendered this trope as "almost the same, but not white," in this case, skin color is not the operative difference.[61]

The Tarowskis call for a round of dancing, the Rothsattels readily agree, and cobwebs and laundry are pushed aside to make room for a wild round of the mazurka. As Lenore dances with Tarowski, Anton turns away in disdain: "That which naturally suited the Polish girls—the fast movements, the strong excitation—made Lenore wild, and, as Anton said to himself with disapproval, unfeminine."[62] Lenore has succumbed to foreign sway and become unattractive to Anton, whose thoughts turn to Sabine and his conviction that she would never have relinquished her German, bourgeois identity in such a situation.

With Karl's help, Anton has brought order to the estate. The two men arranged living quarters within the manor, secured the estate's livestock, and organized its workforce; and when another Polish uprising led to an attack on the castle and nearby Rosmin, Anton and Karl coordinated the defense of the property and the organization of a local German-led defense force. At the end of this eventful year, Anton looks back with pride at the fruit of his labor: "He had seen to it that new life blossomed upon an uncultivated expanse, he had helped to found a new colony of his Volk . . . he himself felt more mature, more experienced, more at ease."[63]

Anton has thus served as the agent of a new wave of diffusion into adjacent colonial space. Rosmin was the product of a long history of various diffusions introducing innovation and progress, and Anton's diffusion adds the ability to organize groups of people into hierarchically ordered collectives designed to fortify space through a subordination of the individual to the advancement of the whole.

At the end of his year in Rosmin, Anton returns to Breslau, where—after convincing Schröter that he can seamlessly reenter the symbiotic relationship he had cultivated with bourgeois space—he is fully interpolated into the firm by being made partner and being offered marriage to Schröter's sister. Having participated in expanding the German bourgeois sphere of influence over the surface of the globe through his two journeys into Poland, Anton has proven himself, and his story ends here. All of the novel's main aristocratic characters, however, remain behind in colonial Rosmin—a peripheralization with consequences for the diffusionist trajectory of the narrative.

Schröter had supported the fall of the house of Rothsattel because he sees the German aristocrats as a detriment to the health of the German nation, and Anton's efforts as counteracting their natural path toward decline. The aristocrats no longer have the potent strength (*Kraft*) to add value to their assets or infuse space with German identity. Their fall will thus make room for the rise of the Bürgertum.

> Where an individual or a family loses his potency [*Kraft*], he should also lose his wealth; the money should change hands freely, and the plowshare should move to hands better able to steer it. And the family that exhausts itself in pleasure should sink back into the ground of the Volk in order to make room for fresh potencies [*Kraft*] to arise. I consider anyone who, at the cost of others' free mobility, lays claim to an eternal privilege for himself and his progeny as an enemy of the healthy development of the state.[64]

While it is unclear what fate Schröter envisions for the aristocrats, the text presents their ex-territorialization into adjacent colonial space as a viable alternative to "sinking into the ground." In Germany, the aristocrats may represent an outdated mode of feudal economics and inherited privilege but even this backward-looking agrarian order represents progress in Poland, which is depicted as existing in a state of perpetual lag and chaotic backwardness.

The Poles, after all, are not positioned *outside* of historical time, but merely *behind* it.[65] Although depicted as a *Naturvolk* unable to achieve progress on their own, the Poles are nonetheless located within the time of the *Kulturvölker* due to their location adjacent to the source of the diffusions. Building upon Johannes Fabian's model of modern time-space distancing, Anne McClintock identifies this trope as the "invention of anachronistic space" where "geographical difference across space is figured as a historical difference across time."[66] A diffusionary global model accounts for this set of gradations. Poland is positioned in time according to an evolutionary logic of historical progress—not out of time but lagging in the time of absolutism and serfdom.

In Polish space, then, the Rothsattels' feudal order represents progress, which is exemplified in their ability to bring barren land into productive fruition. Within days of arriving in Rosmin to visit Anton, Fink discovers that he can greatly increase the fertility of Rothsattel's fields by rerouting the stream that runs across the property, a project that promises to rescue the financially struggling estate.[67] He is successful, and the narrator later describes the changed nature of the landscape: "A new potency [*Kraft*] and a new life was visible on the land, and when spring comes, a troop of laborers will spread over the Polish ground and force the soil to bear the fruit of arduous labor."[68] And while this ground may still be described as "Polish" now, by the end of the novel, there is the sense that this too will change. Fritz von Fink marries Lenore Rothsattel, and the narrator projects his future.

> His life will be an unending victorious battle against the dark spirits of the landscape; a troop of strong boys will spring forth from the Slavic castle, and a new German race, enduring in body and soul, will spread over the land, a race of colonists and conquerors.[69]

There may not be a place for the Rothsattels in the bourgeois German center, but they have a positive function to play in the periphery. In Polish space, aristocratic agrarian values regain their relevance, and perhaps for this reason, the aristocrats undergo a rejuvenation, regaining their lost connection to the land. Fink arises as the proper agent of German colonization, perhaps due to the bourgeois influences on his personal development. Raised in the aristocratic world but educated in the space of Schröter's firm, he has perhaps internalized enough of that which he referred to as "the respectable aspects of German nature" in order to prove a successful agent of German diffusion.[70] The text seems to indicate this in the "troop of young colonists and conquerors" that Fink and Lenore produce and that will grow to populate the landscape.

Less ambiguous is the situation back in Germany; all of the text's mental maps of German space show congruous developments: the bourgeois center is consolidated, its boundary expanded into the periphery. Gustav Freytag's literary world atlas has positioned Germany as a united space and a central player in the European colonial project, creating mental maps that would continue to structure German representations of Poland for many decades.

CHAPTER 2

The Black Pole and Racialized Space in German Inner Colonial Literature

The Struggle for *Heimat* in the Eastern Colony

Clara Viebig's 1904 novel *Das schlafende Heer* (The sleeping army) opens with the scene of a covered wagon traveling across a boundless plain.[1] As far as the eye can see, there is nothing but fields of grain that the narrator likens to a sea over which the winds cast undulating waves.[2] It is a landscape lacking organization and structure, the conventional, empty, or "negative space" of the colonial novel.[3] And, indeed, the family traveling in the covered wagon see themselves as being on a colonial venture: Peter Bräuer is a small family farmer who has left his home in the Rhineland to seek a greater fortune abroad, a decision he made after reading German adventure novels set in the American Wild West. Yet Bräuer travels eastward, because the advertisements of the Prussian Settlement Commission have convinced him to relocate to the Prussian frontier instead of traveling overseas. Bräuer has been granted a parcel of land in the Posener province, and he has hired a Pole to take him and his family to their new home in a budding German settlement colony.

The monotonous landscape exacerbates the Bräuers' sense that they have left the world of modern civilization behind; the train ride from their home on the Rhine had been long, but now they are forced to continue their journey on unpaved, deeply rutted roads through a landscape revealing few signs of human presence. Bräuer's wife feels weak from the heat, his young children cry as they are tossed about in the back of the wagon, and Bräuer takes out his frustrations by raining blows on the Polish driver. Depicted as speechless, apathetic, and dull-witted, the Pole offers no resistance when beaten by Bräuer: "Not a muscle flinched in the driver's blank face . . . . He just dumbly shrugged his shoulders and spat on the ground."[4] The text denies the driver the human faculty of speech as well as the will to defend his dignity, a seeming affirmation of Bräuer's point of view that this Pole is little more than a beast of burden.

It is a scene that, with a few minor changes, could easily be set in an overseas colony. Undeveloped landscapes and uncivilized natives are two of the most common elements found in colonial narratives, and the opening pages of Viebig's novel repeatedly return the reader's attention to just these two figures: the landscape is "flat, almost endlessly monotonous," a "sea of fields" cast in "eternally repeating shades of dusty green," and the driver remains stubbornly silent despite Bräuer's beatings.

Yet, ultimately, this image of Otherness is disturbed: when Bräuer's wife discovers a wayside shrine, she is grateful for this familiar Catholic sign and falls to her knees in prayer. Bräuer is surprised to see her joined by the Polish driver.

> The coachman took off his round hat and made the sign of the cross, bowing so deeply as if he were reaching for the ground with his forehead.
>
> Peter Bräuer stood next to them, dumbfounded. He looked first at his wife, and then at the coachman, and from the coachman back to his wife: Look at that—the Polack was praying too![5]

Arriving in Posen with a worldview informed by his avid reading of colonial literature, Bräuer casts the Pole into a category of otherness familiar from this genre. At first, this Otherness seems to reflect the "Manichean allegory" structuring colonialist literary representation.[6] Dehumanized in his congruence with animalistic behaviors and descriptors (the Pole as "mule"), the Polish native is initially positioned as absolute Other within a set of oppositions including superiority versus inferiority, civilization versus savagery, rationality versus sensuality, subject versus object.[7] But the moment of shared religious practice disturbs this absolute dichotomy. As Bräuer's gaze travels between his wife and the Pole, a critical renegotiation takes place: the Pole becomes both Other and self, both "*stumpfer Polack*" and fellow Catholic. Now removed from the category of absolute Otherness, the Pole gains both voice and agency; he demands a period of rest, and there are no further beatings. Yet his status remains unresolved; neither absolute Other nor identical with the self, the Pole presents an ambiguity, a disruption of the dichotomy structuring the colonialist cognitive framework.

Viebig's novel is the most well-known example of the *Ostmarkenroman* (Eastern Marches novel), a regional literature set in the ethnically mixed, eastern regions of Prussia, most prominently in the province of Posen, but also in

East and West Prussia.[8] The *Ostmarkenroman* appeared at the end of the nineteenth century alongside both *Heimat* literature and the colonial novel, and shares qualities with both of these genres. Like colonial literature, the *Ostmarkenromane* enact a relocation of *Heimat* into foreign terrain, depict the act of civilizing primitive space, and work to reinscribe hierarchies of racial and/or civilizational difference. Like the *Heimat* novel, the *Ostmarkenroman* is characterized by intimate rural settings and trivial romance plots, and offers predictable reaffirmations of traditional social values.[9]

Ostmark and *Heimat* literature share a preference for rural settings, but they each ascribe a much different identity to it. In *Heimat* literature, *Heimat* "functions as an integrated, meaningful, alternative model [to urban-based modernity], as an emotionally laden space identified in opposition to a 'political' world perceived as fragmented and therefore emptied of meaning."[10] Within this meaning-giving space of *Heimat,* protagonists find answers to their personal conflicts by turning to the harmonious logic of the landscapes surrounding them, where nature has been shaped over generations by collective wisdom and tradition. Thus, the lone figure who loses himself in contemplation before a mountain valley or forest clearing finds inspiration in nature as inflected through a regional German idiom.

In the East, however, the landscape offers no such image of an ideal, harmonious world. Instead, it is the site of an ongoing ethnonational struggle over cultural hegemony.[11] *Ostmarkenromane* are therefore devoid of passages in which regional landscapes induce nostalgic contemplation of a premodern German tradition. Instead, the landscape presents its German inhabitants with an additional adversary. Often portrayed as overwhelming and unbounded, the landscapes in the East issue a challenge, as a force of nature to be conquered, tamed, and brought under control. Protagonists of the *Ostmarkenromane* therefore seek succor in the landscape in vain. In Viebig's text, one German settler in the colony, Helene Doleschal, is worried about her husband and gazes out of her window at the surrounding landscape in search of moral insight. But the view only exacerbates her unease.

> One never saw anything except for this same monotonous expanse! She was suddenly shaken with a feeling of endless isolation. . . . She wavered in an immense space in which neither her body nor her soul could find sure footing. . . . The solitary woman shuddered with a feeling that sometimes came over her in the face of this vast sky that floated like a sea over the sea of fields, without a shore, without defining boundaries. . . . Never, never had the eternal endlessness been as clear to her as it had become here.[12]

In his study of German colonial literature, John Noyes has identified as a common trope the threat to the colonizing subject faced by unbounded space.[13] Considered in the abstract, unbounded space only exists outside the realm of socially constructed meaning (society does not exist without spatial markers). When space is depicted as unbounded in the colonial text, it is a double-sided coin. On one side, it offers the colonist the freedom to create something new, but, on the other, it provides him with no orientation and no limits against which he can measure success or completion. The colonist must acquire and internalize the faculties of spatialization in the homeland, such that he can find inner orientation once relocated into unbounded space. Should he exhaust his inner resources, then he will find himself existentially lost. In Viebig's text, Helene Doleschal's husband is indeed very troubled: he climbs the hill that marks the center of his landholdings and stares down at his house and fenced-in garden. This is the space that he has brought under control, the homestead that he will pass on to his children, an emergent *Heimat,* perhaps. But then his gaze turns in the opposite direction, where he faces nothing but an endless sea of fields. Overcome by disorientation and despair, he commits suicide.[14]

This degree of alienation presents an extreme case but is nonetheless indicative of the antagonistic relationship to space typical of the *Ostmarkenroman:* the East is an as-yet-unspatialized realm and must be structured by importing spatial models developed elsewhere. This model of an imported, constructed *Heimat* links the *Ostmarkenroman* to the colonial novel. A specific subset of *Ostmark* literature, which will be treated in detail below, shares colonial literature's fascination with stories of Germans struggling to re-create German *Heimat* against the resistance of primitive native elements.[15]

Functionalization of Stereotypes in the *Ostmarkenroman*

Ostmarkenromane are not of notable literary quality and instead often read as thinly veiled political tracts; in the worst cases, the narrative structures are reduced to merely frame a series of partisan statements. In the best, the literary genre allowed authors to present their political arguments in widely accessible, and anecdotally persuasive, narrative forms. The texts are all directly concerned with the ways in which governmental policies and cultural institutions affected German-Polish relations in the East; of particular interest are the status of the Polish population, the degree and nature of the threat it posed to the Germans, and how this threat would best be addressed. Some of the authors wrote opinionated forewords offering direct support or criticism for various political and cultural aspects of Germany's *Polenpolitik.* More frequently, however, the political messages are framed within the narratives themselves; protagonists might deliver political speeches at gatherings, didactic lectures in the classroom, or moralizing sermons to their neighbors.[16] Alternately, omniscient narrators might provide access to the thoughts of characters as they reach the key political insights the text supports, and then offer their praise at this development.

While noting the genre's political functionality, existing scholarship on the *Ostmarkenroman* tends to focus on the genre as a vehicle for introducing or reinforcing negative Polish stereotypes. The most detailed studies catalog the texts' most prominent images and rightly conclude that a set of typecast characters tend to be recycled through a rather constant set of narrative themes. But stereotype-focused research can be limiting when assessment concludes with such categorization; the identification of recurring negative stereotypes can mistakenly suggest a static, ahistorical group consciousness and can reduce a plurality of opinion into reduced categories of "positive" and "negative" stereotypes. Stereotype studies have thus become guilty of reducing entire historical periods into categories of either pro- or anti-Polish sentiment in Germany. But the situation was always more complex than such limited models suggest. German sentiments toward the Poles and Polish space were plural and contested, and always correlated with stances taken on other issues. At the turn of the century, these concerns were linked to different positions on the fundamental question of what it meant to be German: Was this a chosen form of membership based upon the decision to participate in a cultural community, or was membership racially based and thus an essential, unchangeable identity? One's answer to these questions determined how one viewed ethnic minorities residing in the German nation-state (in the first case, they could be assimilated, and, in the second, they would need to be identified and separated out). In addition, because the Polish minority was concentrated in Prussia's eastern, agrarian provinces, the Polish question was also linked to debates about how Germany might best position itself economically in the modernizing world, and the role Germany's eastern agricultural regions should play with respect to the industrializing west.

The *Ostmarkenromane* staked a range of positions within these discussions, and the genre served as an arena in which competing visions for the German East were presented in narrative form. In order to recognize the plurality of positions staked by the texts within these debates, one must note the repetition of various stereotypes and clichés, but one must also analyze how these stereotypes and clichés were functionalized in different ways within the literary narrative form.

The figure of the Polish Catholic priest (occasionally replaced by a bishop or other ecclesiastic) offers a key example of a stereotypical character functionalized in different ways to different effect. Playing a prominent role in a majority of *Ostmarkenromane,* the Polish priest is always a negative figure. He is characterized by fanatical nationalism with the goal of returning regional power to Polish hands. He even prioritizes this Polish cause over his vows to the Church, and he obfuscates his political agenda with implicit claims to the sanctity of his robes.

Although this set of stereotypical character traits remains constant throughout the genre, the *Ostmarkenromane* can be subdivided into two categories differentiated by the way in which the Polish priest enacts his fanatical nationalism. In one set of texts, the clergyman attempts to segregate members of the Polish community from their German neighbors. He organizes boycotts of German-owned stores, encourages Polish school children to refuse to speak German at school, and may even instigate violence against fellow German citizens and their property. Polish women are an important part of his plan, and the priest frequently has close female accomplices; he fuels their nationalistic passions because he knows that their fanaticism will, in turn, incite Polish men (their brothers, husbands, sons, and lovers) to ever greater acts of personal sacrifice for the Polish cause.

In a second set of texts, the priest espouses the opposite goal of muddling the boundaries separating Germans and Poles. He therefore calls upon his female Polish accomplices to play a much different role: to seduce—and hopefully marry—incoming German settlers. The project is one of intentional deracination and is based upon an understanding of race with both biological and cultural components; these texts show that when German men marry Polish women, they leave the German community and enter the Polish domestic sphere, where they lose their German identities and become "Polonized." If they have children, they will be raised in the Polish milieu as Polish-speaking Catholics. The Poles are convinced that German men can be taken out of the pool of German self-reproduction through intermarriage with Poles, and the texts anecdotally affirm this model.

Both of the antagonistic agendas engaged by the villainous Polish priests stand in opposition to the goals espoused by the German protagonists in the texts. In the first set of texts, the Germans struggle to assimilate the Polish population through a process of linguistic and cultural "Germanization." The Polish priest resists with his plans to segregate and polarize the German and

Polish communities. In the second set of texts, the Germans work to draw sharp lines of delineation and to exclude the Poles from the spaces of their communities while the priest seeks to undermine this plan through intermarriage and interbreeding. The two German agendas—assimilation and exclusion—are mutually exclusive; they reflect two different understandings of what it means to be a member of the German collectivity, two different visions for the future of Polish Prussia, and two different opinions about the course of action the government should take vis-à-vis the Polish minority. The stereotypical figure of the villainous Polish priest can be functionalized as the antagonist for either one of these competing German agendas.

I refer to these two sets of texts as "assimilationist" and "exclusionist" in reference to the strategy each espouses for addressing the Polish minority. These two strategies, in turn, correlate with two sets of policies undertaken by Bismarck to consolidate the nation in the decades following German unification.[17] Concerned that minority groups within Germany—particularly the Poles—were in the position to hinder the process of national consolidation, Bismarck introduced the Kulturkampf policies in the 1870s and the inner colonization project in the mid-1880s to weaken their collective strength. The Kulturkampf sought to "Germanize" the Prussian Poles and, through this process of assimilation, sever their ties to the Polish separatist movement. Inner colonization, in contrast, sought to segregate and displace the Polish population by bringing in German settlers to inhabit land that used to belong to Poles. Pushed out of German space, it was hoped that the Poles would retreat to areas further east in the Prussian frontier, or perhaps leave Germany entirely by crossing over the border into Russia.

These two projects both aimed for a homogeneity of the German nation. In the first case, Germanizing ethnic minorities would homogenize the population, ensuring that all areas of the state were equally loyal to the center. Homogenizing the population would thus lead to the homogenization of national space. In the second case, the trajectory was reversed: Germanizing peripheral space would either eliminate the minorities concentrated there or at least lead to their dispersion. Homogenizing national space would thus lead to the homogenization of the population. As I detail below, this second strategy engaged a distinct colonial discourse in pursuit of its aims.

Kulturkampf versus Inner Colonization

In the period of German unification, Bismarck expressed concern that Germany's ethnic and religious minorities were in the position to exert a centrifugal force threatening the cohesion of the fledgling German state. This fear applied particularly to those minorities with propensities to forge transnational alliances: Catholics (whose alleged ultramontanism would have brought a primary allegiance to the Vatican) and ethnic minorities (especially those living in border regions with breakaway tendencies). In Prussia, roughly 10 percent of the population were Poles. They were Germany's largest ethnic minority group—and they were also overwhelmingly Catholic, thus posing a potential threat on both religious and ethnic fronts.

Alarm was exacerbated by the resistance Polish representatives had expressed against the inclusion of Polish Prussia in larger German political formations. In the hope that Poland would one day be reinstated as an independent state, Polish representatives opposed including Polish regions in the envisioned German nation-state in 1848, and in the German Confederation in 1866.[18] The German border of 1871 thus imposed a national identity upon a largely heterogeneous population that was not entirely eager to be included. In Bismarck's initial assessment, however, there was a strong divide between the Polish aristocracy and Catholic clergy, on one side, and the Polish masses, on the other. If the Polish elite desired independence, it was to gain free rein over the disenfranchised Polish masses, and they were therefore using their religious and cultural power to agitate the Polish people to support a cause that was ultimately not in their best interests. Bismarck accordingly held Polish nationalism to be an inauthentic product of agitation from above and felt that a brisk campaign to "Germanize" the Polish Prussian provinces would be the most effective method of securing control over these areas.

The Kulturkampf in Polish Prussia, launched soon after Germany's unification, consisted of two parts, both of which emphasized the school system as the best site of social intervention. First were the measures undertaken to curb the public role of the Catholic Church: their traditional oversight and influence over the local public schools was removed, and dozens of bishops, priests, and other Catholic officials were imprisoned for their oppositional political activities. Second were the measures undertaken to strengthen the use of German in Polish-speaking areas. Laws were passed demanding the use of German in government agencies, the courts, public meetings, public announcements, and the schools.[19] Learning German would free the Polish masses from the one-sided Polish propaganda to which they were supposedly being subjected, while a weakened Catholic Church would lessen the power the Polish clergy held over their parishioners.[20] Bismarck expected that his plan would be successful in bringing the majority of the Polish Prussians to relinquish their Polish ties and identify with the German state.

Such an assimilationist goal would not have been imaginable had the Poles been held to be of inherently inferior physical or mental capacities, or had they been understood to represent an "inferior race." Germanization was only conceivable where German identity was defined in cultural, not racial, terms; the Poles were considered to be similar enough to assimilate because their differences were attributable to culture rather than nature, and thus subject to German cultural influence. According to this view, the Poles were, as the protagonist of Arthur Pachnicke's 1908 *Auf Posten im Osten* (Manning the post in the East) claimed, "merely Germans who prefer to speak Polish."[21]

Pachnicke's protagonist then speaks patronizingly of his "duty to raise [*erziehen*] the Poles into full Germans."[22] Indeed, much of the rhetoric surrounding the Kulturkampf used such metaphors of human development that equated Poles with children who needed the guidance or upbringing of parental Germans. Because this developmental metaphor is so prevalent in colonial discourse, it is important to stress the difference in its usage in assimilationist literature, which, while certainly prejudicial, was not colonial. In her study of colonial literature, Ania Loomba has argued that "one of the most striking contradictions about colonialism is that it both needs to 'civilize' its 'others' and to fix them into perpetual 'otherness.'"[23] Overseas colonial discourse is therefore dominated by the trope of an entrenched state of childhood projected onto entire populations—a state of childhood that resists improvement and therefore will (conveniently) require parental guidance far into the future.[24] The Germanization campaign in the Prussian East is different in that it insists upon the possibility of bringing the Polish individual to the equal level of the German and sees itself taking concrete steps toward achieving this goal. The state of childhood can therefore be overcome in the course of an individual's lifetime. In comparison to overseas populations, whose state of childhood is irrevocable and maintained over generations, the Poles are on an accelerated track to civilized "adulthood." Not Polish individuals but the Polish nation was the problem, and proponents of Germanization were ruthless in their critique of this collectivity, which they argued would never itself achieve progress.

Traugott Pilf's "Endlose Jahre" (Endless years, 1908) illustrates this conceptual divide between redeemable individual and condemned collectivity. In Pilf's short story, a German nationalist travels to visit his relatives in Posen and is appalled at the concessions in language and culture they have made to their Polish employees: "I am not contemptuous of the Poles," he explains, "but they must and they will become completely absorbed into our state; that is their fate, and nothing can change it, because they can no longer survive on their own."[25] The German nationalist appeals to a social Darwinist model in which the Polish nation is the weak competitor destined to collapse, its members absorbed into the stronger and fitter German nation.

Polish resistance, however, seemed to prove otherwise. The antagonistic measures of the Kulturkampf were not effective in increasing Polish allegiance to the German state and are largely credited with consolidating a Polish nationalist opposition movement instead.[26] Resistance to the Kulturkampf took many forms; some retreated into the intimate sphere of the family and local community where language and religious practices were not subject to control; others sought new arenas for political action in the Polish-language press, in Polish political and cultural organizations, or through the orchestrated boycott of German stores. Instead of culturally homogenizing the eastern provinces, Bismarck's Kulturkampf campaign resulted in the creation of a Polish collective that demarcated its boundaries ever more starkly in opposition to the German majority.

Anxiety aroused by the Polish opposition's strength and organization was exacerbated by demographic shifts that led to a steady increase in the size and visibility of the Polish population in Germany. The forces of industrialization were leading to an overall migration of workers from eastern agricultural regions into the western industrial sector. Both Germans and Poles joined the ranks of this westward migration, leaving vacancies that were filled by Polish seasonal workers who crossed into Germany from Russia and Galicia.[27] Tens of thousands of Poles migrated to the industrial and mining centers in Berlin, Upper Silesia, and Rhineland-Westphalia, while hundreds of thousands of Polish seasonal laborers continued to be hired to harvest the crops in the Prussian East, their numbers swelling to fill the ever greater labor gaps.[28] With Germans coming into contact with ever greater numbers of Poles, many came to sense that the Germanization project was not working.

Responding to the political pressure mounting around this demographic shift, Bismarck gave orders in 1885 for the expulsion of all nonnaturalized Poles living in the Prussian eastern provinces. These expulsions began in 1883 and reached their peak in late 1885, by which time over 32,000 people had been evicted, two-thirds of whom were Polish, one-third Jewish.[29] Although the practice continued until 1887, Bismarck's deportation policy met with significant domestic and international resistance. Germany's relationships with Russia and Austria become strained, and loud opposition from the Liberals, Socialists, Catholics, and ethnic minority factions led to a vote in the Reichstag condemning the action.[30] Bismarck attempted to defend his policy by stressing that his Germanization efforts could not work against such large and growing numbers. "We need to get rid of the foreign Poles," he argued in a speech to the Reichstag, "because we have enough of our own."[31]

The expulsions failed to change the direction of migration, and expressions of anxiety about the growing number of Poles in Germany increased. The demographic shift came to be represented as an overwhelming wave of foreigners that threatened to wash over Germany; the Poles were linguistically equated with a force of nature—a "flood" that needed to be staved off. References to a Polish (or Slavic) flood were frequent in late nineteenth-century discourse about the Prussian East and were often accompanied by calls to build "dams" and "dikes" to protect German space against the encroaching menace.[32] The discourse reflected a fear of ethnic infiltration but also gestured toward the spatial component of this metaphor; the flood was understood as a threat to German territory.[33]

The Kulturkampf policies of the 1870s had aimed to create homogeneous German national space by Germanizing the population; in the 1880s, this equation was reversed such that Germanizing *space* became a strategy for addressing a growing minority population. Bismarck became convinced by the arguments of agrarian reformers who advocated changing the organization of land in the eastern regions in order to reverse the demographic shifts that favored the Poles. The inner colonization campaign was devised as a way to change the nature of the population in the Prussian East by changing the distribution of landownership. Large estates were to be bought from Polish landowners and parceled down into smaller self-sufficient family farms that would be sold or leased to German settlers. The expansive landscape would be broken up into smaller units, and the demographics of the region would be shifted to increase the percentage of landowning Germans and to decrease the number of both Polish seasonal laborers and Polish landowning aristocrats (whom, we recall, Bismarck held to be the main antagonists of Polish nationalism). On April 26, 1886, the "Act for the advancement of German settlement in the provinces of West Prussia and Posen" was passed,[34] and a Settlement Commission (*Königlich Preußische Ansiedlungskommission)* was established to carry out its project; endowed with an initial fund of one hundred million Marks, it was commissioned to acquire large estates from the Polish gentry, to parcel this land, and to sell the resulting plots to German family farmers brought into the region from the West.[35]

Inner colonization marked a shift from an assimilationist to an exclusionist strategy, a transition reflected in the language introducing the measure.

> In some of the eastern regions of our country, the Polish nationality notoriously seeks to crowd out the existing German elements to further itself—and they haven't been without success.
>
> Such an intrusiveness into key areas of the monarchy by a nationality whose language and customs hold it inwardly distant from Prussian civic life demands comprehensive defensive measures in all areas of the government's administration.
>
> It is a matter of protecting the interests of the German population, preventing these regions from being flooded by Polish elements, and supporting the spread of German culture and values [*Geist* and *Bildung*].[36]

The wording continues to reflect a cultural model of the German nation: it is language and culture that separate the Polish nationality from the German, and the German national struggle in the East is defined by the goal of spreading German culture and values. Gone, however, is the notion that the Poles can be Germanized: they are "inwardly distant" as they "intrude" and "crowd out," and—in an application of popular discourse—"flood" the Germans. The inner colonization campaign was designed to push back a population now deemed unassimilable.

Polish resistance to the Germanization of eastern space complicated this image. Poles formed their own collective purchasing organizations, most notably the Bank Ziemski (The Land Bank) to counteract the Settlement Commission. This organization enabled them to undertake their own, competing project of land parcellation and create settlements for the large number of Poles seeking to buy property.[37] Thus, the Polish population was equipped with the means to fight the "struggle for the soil" on its own terms.[38] The fact that the Poles could leverage such economic resistance—both duplicating and manipulating the institutions of inner colonization—reflects the added ambiguity of the inner colonial situation.

Indeed, in order to make inner colonization work, it seemed that it was going to be necessary to take power away from the Poles and render their relationship with Germans more "colonial" in legislative terms. After the turn of the century, laws passed in conjunction with the inner colonization campaign intended to devitalize the Polish settlement project and bolster German strength in the region. As Hans-Ulrich Wehler has argued, these laws resulted in the exclusion of the Poles from full membership in the legal collectivity of Prussian-German citizenship.[39] In 1904, a law was passed restricting Polish participation in land parcellation, and, in 1908, an expropriation law was passed giving the state the power to seize any Polish-owned estates it found strategically useful for the inner colonization project.[40] These measures did not lead to the intended results—the Poles found ways to work around parcellation restrictions, and such great public opposition was expressed against forceful expropriation that the measure was only implemented a handful of times—but this lack of success does not detract from the fact that a two-tier system of citizenship was introduced in order to support the German inner colonial project.

Assimilationist versus Exclusionist *Ostmarkenromane*

In 1890, Bismarck was replaced as chancellor by Leo von Caprivi, whose political "New Course" introduced a short period of rapprochement with the Poles. During his short tenure (1890–94), Caprivi relaxed the policies of the Kulturkampf and sought to strengthen cooperation with Polish leaders. This New Course angered the Right, particularly when Caprivi passed measures to lift the protectionist tolls on agricultural products. Western industrialists welcomed the resulting drop in food prices because it allowed them to keep their labor costs down, but the eastern Junker were outraged at their loss of revenue. Caprivi passed the measure with help from the Polish minority faction, which resulted in rising tensions between the German landowners and their Polish neighbors. The post-Bismarck era thus saw a sharp increase in political mobilization on behalf of German interests in the Prussian East.

In 1894, the Eastern Marches Society (Verein zur Förderung des Deutschthums in den Ostmarken, known after 1899 as the Ostmarkenverein) was founded to represent German nationalist concerns in Polish Prussia. The Pan-German League (Alldeutscher Verband) had been formed in 1891 as a pro-imperialist pressure group. But the organization divided its interest between continental and overseas issues, and quickly lost sight of Polish Prussia; when they published an article in 1894 demanding that "the old drive to the East should be reignited [*Der alte Drang nach dem Osten soll wiederbelebt werden*]," they were referring far beyond Polish space to the reaches of Asia Minor.[41] While the politics of the Eastern Marches Society were similar to those of the Pan-German League, the organization focused exclusively on Polish Prussia and identified its main objectives as the criticism of Caprivi's Polish policies and the championing of German hegemony in the East.[42] The organization was also known as the "HKT" (and its members as *die Hakatisten)* after the first letters of the last names of its founders, Ferdinand von Hansemann, Hermann Kennemann, and Heinrich von Tiedemann. Although these three founders were among the largest landowners of the region, the majority of the organization's members were not the German farmers, estate owners, or colonists whose interests the Eastern Marches Society professed to represent. Instead, membership largely comprised the German civil servants, schoolteachers, and Protestant pastors brought in to administer and minister in the East.[43]

The Ostmarkenverein functioned most prominently and effectively as a propaganda organ shaping nationalist and conservative opinion regarding Germany's eastern regions.[44] The society introduced its journal, *Die Ostmark,* in 1896 and sought to influence the coverage of the "Polish Question" in other German nationalist papers, most successfully in the *Posener Tageblatt.*[45] In 1906, an additional journal was launched with the support of the society: *Aus dem Posener Lande: Blätter für Heimatkunde* (Local history gazette from the Posener country) provided its readers with articles on the history, culture, and ethnography of the region.[46]

In addition to its aggressive propaganda campaign in the press, the Ostmarkenverein worked to bolster a stronger nationalistic identity among the Germans living in the Prussian East. The organization sponsored various nationalistic cultural events, supported presses publishing literature pertinent to their cause, and donated large numbers of books to regional libraries.[47] This number exceeded 100,000 books annually after the turn of the century, and, although we can assume that not all of these were *Ostmarkenromane,* we know that the organization held the genre to be an important tool in generating support for its agenda.[48] In 1913, an announcement was posted in *Die Ostmark* offering a generous sum of money for the best new novel "in which the problem of the Eastern Marches is addressed in German patriotic terms and that will paint in true-to-life colors the land and people of the Eastern Marches and either the difficulties that await our fine German pioneers in the East or the accomplishments achieved in the past through German industriousness and stubborn determination."[49] The production of *Ostmarkenromane* had sunk after 1910, and the organization's attempt to intervene so generously on its behalf is indicative of the importance they attributed to it.[50]

The Eastern Marches literature is a genre circumscribed by content, and not by literary form, and thus includes short stories, dramas, and verse in addition to the novel that was its mainstay. Approximately 80 novels set in the province of Posen have been identified, and, when the entirety of the Eastern Marches is considered (including East and West Prussia and all literary forms), the number of texts exceeds 300.[51] The literature can be divided into a small set of thematic subgenres;[52] texts set in the historical past usually depict either the medieval *Ostkolonisation,* such as Margarete Gottschall's *Nach Ostland wol-*

len wir reiten! (Let's journey to the East! 1909),[53] or scenes from the Polish uprisings of the nineteenth century, as does Hugo Behrens's "Die polnische Gefahr" (The Polish threat, 1905).[54] Texts set in the present, which are the focus here, depict either the Kulturkampf (assimilationist) or the inner colonization campaign (exclusionist).

Assimilationist Eastern Marches literature (whose most notable author is Carl Busse, joined by Ernst Below, Max Berg, Erich Fließ, Elisabeth Grabowski, and others) deliver narratives in which language laws, anti-Catholic measures, and other Germanizing strategies are shown to have the potential to successfully assimilate ethnic Poles into the German national collective. These narratives are typically set either in the urban center of Posen or in small towns (as opposed to more agrarian settings), and the main protagonists are drawn from the merchants, teachers, and other civil servants whose activities structure public life in such communities.[55] The titles of Carl Busse's *Die Schüler von Polajewo* (The Schoolchildren of Polajewo, 1901) and *Das Gymnasium zu Lengowo* (The High School of Lengowo, 1907) are indicative of the settings and themes of this first group of texts, which highlight the role of state institutions in Germanizing Polish subjects in ethnically mixed localities.

In Lengowo, the support for the Germanization campaign expressed by the newly arrived schoolteacher, Dr. Holst, represents the assimilationist agenda.

> Do everything to support the province. A university, high schools, elementary schools, garrisons, railways—keep up the good work! Not since the beginning of time has any Volk ever defeated another. Conquered—yes! Defeated—no! But the higher culture always defeats the lower. In this case, the higher culture is German.[56]

From Dr. Holst's perspective, to overcome the Polish nation is to incorporate its members into the German collective through aggressive cultural assimilation. The weapons in this struggle are state institutions and technological modernization, and individual Germans in the Eastern Marches are its foot soldiers; it is their duty to protect the integrity of the German culture and establish its dominance. The government's Kulturkampf policies enforcing the use of German in state institutions were doing their part; individual Germans needed to do theirs by refusing to learn or speak Polish, and by policing the Polish community for infractions of the language laws.

The resulting narratives are often relentlessly chauvinistic and feature seemingly obligatory passages extolling the virtues of the German language and culture. But there is a flip side to this coin: while Polish culture is depicted as vastly inferior to the German culture, individual Poles are not necessarily reduced to their membership in it. Instead, they are depicted successfully entering the German collective to become full and equal members within it. Germanization is shown to have taken place over the course of history, from the earliest days to the very present. The landscapes of these texts are populated with Germans who have Polish last names, such as Lengowo's school rector Thomas Brodnicki. The decision to use this naming strategy is a way of telling the story of Germanization as a long-established, ongoing process. These untold stories from the past form the backdrop for narratives featuring the transformation of Polish protagonists into loyal German subjects in the present.

The Prussian military functions prominently in this regard: Polish men who move through the ranks of this institution are invariably converted into loyal German subjects. In Traugott Pilf's short story "Raureif" ("Hoar-frost," 1908) the narrator introduces the young, optimistic, and successful Sergeant Wladislaus Patelski as "a good example of how a man of solid Polish stock could be transformed into a good German through his time as a soldier."[57] Patelski came from a poor village located near the estate of a Polish landowner. Returning home while on leave, we see evidence of Patelski's Germanization both in his ability to speak German (commented upon approvingly by the narrator) and in the nature of his gaze as it passes over the landscape; Patelski is offended by the backwardness and decay of the Polish dwellings where he spent his youth, and he praises the Settlement Commission for bringing fresh, motivated Germans to improve the region. Feeling a lack of connection to his former Polish home, Patelski cuts his visit short to return to the garrison.

More dramatic is the metamorphosis undergone by Jan Kochanowski in Max Berg's *Am Alten Markt zu Posen (*On Posen's old market square, 1907). Kochanowski is enlisted into the Prussian military, where he enjoys a successful career. When he returns to the city to take over his father's store, he employs the virtues of discipline and hard work to save the business from the lingering effects of his father's chronic mismanagement (*polnische Wirtschaft*). Not only does he reject the fanatical nationalism of his sister (who has fallen into the clutches of a villainous Polish priest), but he infuriates the local Poles when he marks his growing wealth by displaying successively larger portraits of the Prussian monarchy in his home.[58]

In this group of texts, the model of the national collective reflects Herder's understanding of the relationship between culture and identity. In his *Ideen zur Philosophie der Geschichte der Menschheit* (Reflections on the Philosophy of the History of Mankind, 1784–91), Herder places culture at the center of human organization. If the Volk was "a people bound together organically by language, religion, education, inherited tradition, folk songs, ritual, and speech," then an individual's membership in this collective could arguably be learned.[59]

Herder also rejected the notion of distinct races: "In short, there are neither four or five races, nor exclusive varieties, on this Earth. Complexions run into each other: forms follow the genetic character and upon the whole, all are at last but shades of the same great picture, extending through all ages, and over all parts of the Earth."[60] Assimilationist literature adopts this model by presenting the Germans and the Poles as similar in physical appearance. Both German and Polish characters tend to have midrange features in these texts—dark blond or brown hair (as opposed to black or flaxen blond) and brown eyes (instead of black or blue)—and their skin tones are rarely commented on.[61] Where neither Poles nor Germans are readily identifiable based upon visible signs of "race," the barrier to the successful "dissolution" of the Poles into the German nation is reduced.

A sense of fluid racial continuity across a German-Polish spectrum is enhanced by dismissing the presence of Slavic features as ambivalent signs of identity. Characters may have high cheekbones, wide and flat foreheads, or square-shaped skulls, but these physiognomic characteristics are rarely held to be adequate to determine a person's "true" identity definitively. The claim that a given forehead was "broad" or cheekbones were "high" was usually contestable, and herein lay the value for the assimilationists. The narrator of Carl Busse's *Das Gymnasium zu Lengowo* describes Dr. Holst as possessing

> a not very handsome, but nonetheless intelligent face with somewhat Slavic features. Maybe there was a shot of Polish blood in him.
>
> His cheekbones protruded a bit. But it may have just seemed so.[62]

While initially asserting the legible presence of "somewhat Slavic features," the narrator then distances himself from this reading: the visible signs are indeterminate, subject to the vagaries of perception. And they are ultimately unimportant. Dr. Holst is a fervently pro-German character in a text promulgating the "Germanizability" of individual Poles. The fact that his own identity remains unresolved leaves open the question of whether he might not himself be the product of past assimilationist pressures. The possibility that he might originally be of Slavic origins suggests the positive potential of an aggressive assimilationist program.

Where assimilationist texts depict Germanization as a set of measures targeted at *the population,* exclusionist texts feature attempts to Germanize *space.* These texts are set almost exclusively in the agrarian milieu where farmers and landowners are engaged in the project of inner colonization. Clara Viebig wrote *Das schlafende Heer,* the most well-known novel of this subgenre, which also includes texts by Annie Bock, Paul Oskar Höcker, Albert Liepe, Arthur Pachnicke, and others.[63]

Exclusionist *Ostmarkenromane* all engage the question of inner colonization in the East, and each espouses the same set of overall goals: to bring as much land as possible under German ownership and to contain the Polish population either by excluding it entirely from German space or by rendering it subservient to a dominant class of German landowners. These texts may engage some level of interest in certain aspects of the Kulturkampf agenda, but when they do, they show it as a means of further excluding the Poles instead of assimilating them. While Poles in assimilationist texts learn German, for example, in exclusionist texts they are either unable or unwilling to do so. The disciplinary measures of the Kulturkampf therefore don't serve to bring Poles into the fold but instead to render them the permanent objects of derision. The assimilationist literature portrays the Poles as developmentally inferior to the Germans but identifies this inferiority as situational, a result of their political and cultural history, and thus subject to change. Exclusionist texts, in contrast, present essentialist arguments, insisting that Polish developmental inferiority is inherent to the Poles' nature or racial makeup. The assimilation of the Poles into the German collective is thereby placed out of question, and the claim is instead made that the rightful relationship between German and Pole is that of colonizer and colonized.

Race, Miscegenation, and the Black Pole

In his study of German literature set in the Slavic East, Uwe-K. Ketelsen argues that there is little difference between the colonial discourse employed in German Southwest Africa and in the "Saxon East." "The colonial discourses draw from different pools of images for landscapes and inhabitants, but the content and internal structures remain constant; there is little difference between Southwest and the Baltics. . . . That which the narrator has [the protagonists of] Friede H. Kraze's colonial novel *Heim Neuland* experience in German Southwest, 'he' could easily have them experience—mutatis mutandis, of course—in the narrative worlds of the 'Saxonian East.'"[64] To a certain extent, I agree with Ketelsen but argue that the nature of this "mutatis mutandis" must be more carefully explored. The exclusionist Eastern Marches literature is indeed a colonial literature (I will thus refer to it as "inner colonial literature"), but it addresses a different colonial situation than does overseas colonial literature, and a different set of issues is therefore at stake.[65] Within the literature of the Eastern Marches, we have found two subgenres that disagree about the essential nature of the Poles: one asserting the assimilability of the Poles, the other insisting upon their exclusion as a racially separate and inferior group. Within the body of German colonial literature set in Africa, we do not encounter a similar tension, because, within this literature, there isn't any real disagreement about the fundamental Otherness and inassimilability of the Africans. Consequently, we could compare an overseas colonial text with an inner colonial text and find significant discursive overlap; both may depict the ordering of unbounded space, the disciplining of natives, etc., but when we place these texts back into the contexts of their respective genres, we find that each text engages in a significantly different conversation.

The main difference is introduced by the implications of the geographic adjacency attending inner colonialism. In overseas colonial literature, texts proceed from an unquestioned assumption of difference: the colony is already seen as an unambiguously non-European space populated by non-Europeans. This collectively shared perception of essential difference explains why there is no assimilationist discourse vis-à-vis the Africans; the discussion instead revolves around the ways in which Germans should organize their relationship to Africans given this assumed difference. In the inner colonial text, in contrast, the colonial landscape is geographically adjacent to the *Heimat* and the differentiating categories of race and space must first be constructed.

In nineteenth-century European scientific and philosophical discourse, one of the central concerns was the explanation of human diversity.[66] Many argued that several different species, races, or varieties of humans existed, but there was ongoing disagreement about the method one should use to determine the identity of the different human groupings (should one measure skull sizes? grade skin color?), and consequently, there was disagreement about how many such groupings there were. In the late eighteenth century, for example, Johann Friedrich Blumenbach, considered by many to be the father of physical anthropology, initially proposed four varieties of man, then extended this number to five. Immanuel Kant found four different races, and Joseph-Arthur de Gobineau, perhaps the most well-known racial theorist of the nineteenth century, later decided that it was only three.[67] Important to note, however, is that, regardless of how many human groupings theorists posited, the distinction between the white European and the black, sub-Saharan African existed in all of their models. Gobineau adds "yellow" as the third element to this "black-and-white" scheme, and other racial theorists distinguished Americans, Polynesians, Australians, etc. But as soon as any concept of difference is introduced, black and white are present as the external frames of the spectrum.

The problem for inner colonial discourse was, accordingly, twofold: the establishment of racial difference extending over the Eurasian continental expanse and the assertion of a firm delineation separating Germans from this Otherness in the East. Germans traveling to Africa went by sea, which resulted in a punctuated racial and spatial experience: they left "white" Europe and arrived in "black" Africa after crossing over the nonspace of an expansive oceanic divide. Germans looking eastward, however, faced graduated difference: they could perhaps imagine the "yellow" Asian on the other side of the continent, but what about all of the populations in between? Where was the border between self and Other? An anonymous author in the *Grenzboten* explains the problem.

> Let's assume a common humanity. . . . But let's also assume that the idea of humanity is only realized partially and in gradients in different races and peoples [*Völker*], such that there are quarter-humans and half-humans and full-humans, and many variations within each category. The Mongols indeed stand as far away from us as Chamberlain describes; the Negroes and Malays are not quite as distant; the Negroes are described as giant children by those who have studied them; but we will have to acknowledge the non-Aryan branches of the Caucasian family as humans who share in humanity in the highest sense of the term, and we must acknowledge that it is possible to reach an understanding with them about the most important questions and the most sacred issues, such that we can share common cultural assets with them. However, it remains a fact that none of these *Völker,* not even the Germanic [*germanisch*] or half-Germanic, enjoys the same abundance of noble capacities as the German [*das Deutsche*].[68]

The author unhesitatingly asserts a gross distinction between groups he identifies as "Mongols" on one side of a spectrum and Germans on the other. Much more work is necessary, however, to determine the boundary between the German self and the *adjacent* (be it Caucasian, Germanic, or half-Germanic) Others. The author finds it necessary to cede them status as fully human but then struggles to maintain a conceptual border that separates them from the German

Volk. The insistence upon an unequal distribution of nebulous "noble faculties" indicates the degree of anxiety present in such considerations. If the Mongols are positioned as the absolute Other, and the Slavs are the last people separating them from the Germans, where is the border between the two?

Inner colonial literature seeks to alleviate this ambiguity by positioning the Poles on the other side of an unambiguous racial divide, where their equal membership in humanity can be denied. The first step in establishing this difference involves the depiction of Germans and Poles as visually distinguishable. In inner colonial texts, a chromatic polarity between dark and light physical features identifies the Poles as *nonwhite.* Where the assimilationist texts feature German and Polish protagonists sharing midrange features, inner colonial texts polarize the spectrum of chromatic options. One might argue that one or the other of these two approaches was truer to the "real" distribution of physiognomic features across the German-Polish genetic spectrum, but this would be missing the point. Instead, it is important to question why—in two different sets of texts distinguished by their different ideological views on German-Polish relations—two different sets of choices were made about how to represent the Poles. Inner colonial literature blackens the Polish physiognomy, while assimilationist literature paints Poles in shades of brown: midrange features facilitate the Germanization and assimilation of Poles, while blackness erects a barrier to such shifts in identity.

Different representational strategies are used to address different classes of Poles in inner colonial literature. Peasants are often portrayed in deindividualized groups and described as having a dark skin color resembling either North American "Indians" or "Gypsies." "The men looked reddish brown," one narrator said of Poles working the fields, "copper, like the Indians."[69] In the first encounter between Germans and Poles in Viebig's text, Peter Bräuer's wife looks out over the fields, sees the female Polish laborers, and gasps in horror.

> Were those Gypsies? She anxiously looked over her blond-headed children—they say that Gypsies steal children![70] . . . Frau Kettchen's blue eyes surveyed the brown women . . . suddenly one of the brown women walked right up to the wagon.[71]

This steady juxtaposition of blond, blue-eyed features with the "darkness" of the native population is an overburdened strategy in Viebig's text and in inner colonial literature as a whole; the relentless repetition, the need to constantly reinscribe chromatic difference, reveals an anxiety of racial containment—the light versus dark, blond versus black dichotomy must be constantly reinforced, for the distinction it hopes to discipline always threatens to collapse.

Aristocratic and ecclesiastic Poles are distinguished from the Polish masses in the inner colonial texts by pale complexions framed by jet-black features. Annie Bock's 1898 *Der Zug nach dem Osten* (The drive to the East) offers a typical example: the narrator follows the gaze of a German representative of the Settlement Commission as he musters the guests at Felix von Graach's dinner table. His attention is captured by a "slight man with black hair, black eyes, a black mustache, a clean-shaven chin and cheeks, and conspicuously small hands with which he held his knife, fork, and spoon with almost ladylike daintiness while eating."[72] Even before we learn that this man's name is Kornatschewski, the repetition of the adjective *black* and the attention to his delicately decadent features has identified him as an outsider among the blond German farm employees at the table—and also as a Polish aristocrat. This Pole's black features might merely be an arbitrary set of attributes were Kornatschewski alone in possession of them, but the text proceeds to enforce a strong polarization between black and white—between black and blond, straw-colored, or flaxen hair; between black and blue eyes; and between dark and light skin. Polish figures in the novel become categorizable due to their blackened features, be they articulated in detail as in the above case of Kornatschewski or reduced to a generalized adjectival: "the black Kascha stepped forward."[73]

The impact of this spectral polarization becomes clearer upon consideration of the alternative within this organizing dichotomy: a "whiteness" that exceeds the visually perceptible while claiming an innate connection to the divine. When Felix von Graach enters the chambers of his sister-in-law, Ella, the text offers the reader this first glimpse of her from his point of view.

> At a large table near the window sat a young, blond woman. . . . On her rich, ash-blond hair, on her almost transparent, delicate cheeks, on her simple white dress, and on her fine, diligent hands lay the reddish-gold radiance of the sun, enveloping the entire image almost like a halo.[74]

Von Graach contemplates Ella's spiritually transcendent beauty in tones of blond, white, and gold. The purity and cleanliness of this whiteness is associated with Ella's modesty (her dress is simple), and with her work ethic (her hands are "diligent" because she is embroidering a tapestry for the church).

Similarly, when Helene Doleschal makes her first appearance in Clara

Viebig's novel, the narrator describes her approaching image in exalted terms from the point of view of the Bräuers (who are still on their initial trek into Polish Prussia): "Light was the hat and the garment, light was the face, and the tresses were like wheat at harvest time."[75] "The light of the morning shone golden" through the surrounding fog, "because a friendly figure stood in the middle of it, a woman with blond braids and light-colored eyes and—she spoke German."[76] While Helene Doleschal's ethereal white appearance makes the Bräuers see her as a divine messenger, her whiteness does not have such positive connotations for the Polish seasonal workers; they think that they are seeing a ghost walking through the fields, and they run away in fright.[77]

The Polish shepherd Dudek is infuriated by the presence of the Germans, whom he repeatedly refers to as the "white invaders [*weiße Eindringlinge*] with yellow hair," or the "pale invaders with bloody hands."[78] The fact that Dudek marks the Germans as "white" reinscribes the text's construction of the Poles as nonwhite, for his invectives are cast as acts of Othering. Even from the Poles' own point of view, the text suggests, Germans inhabit a role analogous to that of overseas colonizers: as white invaders into nonwhite space.

The strategy of blackening Polish features introduces a racialization underpinning further acts of dehumanization, beginning with the assertion of parity between Poles and animals. *Either* Black Poles are rendered interchangeable with animals, or their behaviors are likened to those of animals. Peter Bräuer, as we saw above, saw fit to treat his Polish driver like a mule; similarly, Felix von Graach gives his horse a Polish name; when a Polish day laborer—"the black Wanda"—is called into the courtyard, it leads to some confusion: "Not you, good girl, no, not you," he comforts his horse, "this time they were talking about another Wanda."[79] Von Graach makes little differentiation, and neither does his whip, which is interchangeably applied to both Pole and packhorse. In Viebig's text, all Poles working for Germans are rendered in animalized terms; in a closing scene of the novel, Poles who have been hired to work in the west are loaded onto the back of a wagon: "the women crouched on their bundles . . . dull-witted and mute like livestock being loaded."[80]

A brutish irrationalism correlates with this dehumanized status and often expresses itself in the form of mob violence. Scenes of irrational Polish hordes were crucial to the narrative in Freytag's *Soll und Haben;* the culmination of Anton Wohlfart's colonizing activity came when he organized the Germans into militias to protect German space from the senseless violence of the Poles. We see strong echoes of this narrative in inner colonial literature. In Viebig's text, a drunken Polish mob throngs at the gates of Doleschal's estate, beats the German farm inspector to the verge of death, and thirsts for more violence.

Only when Doleschal's young son offers Easter eggs do they disband. The mob could not be brought to reason but is collectively distracted by the promise of children's treats offered by a figure they can directly identify with—a child talking to children.[81] But the mob later recoalesces to unleash its violent energies in a reincarnation of the 1819 "Hep Hep" riots.[82] The Jews only escape certain death by fleeing into the fields.[83]

Unlike the Poles in the assimilationist texts, the "childlike" Poles in inner colonial literature do not progress beyond this developmental state. Their irrationality, unleashed in violent attacks on both Germans and Jews, introduces a sense of urgency to the "parenting" actions of the Germans. If the Poles can't be raised into collective adulthood, and their collective immaturity is a threat to the peace of the community, then steps must be taken to discipline and contain them.

The problem with this parental role is that the Poles aren't just racially inferior—they are also racially contagious. In inner colonial literature, a recurrent theme is the degeneration of the German colonist as he becomes, or threatens to become, "Polonized." Uwe-K. Ketelsen finds that, in texts depicting German settlement in the East, the motif of aggressive expansion into the space of the Other is joined, even replaced, by that of the need to protect the self against the threat of "*Ver-Fremdung*" (becoming Other). "On almost every page," Ketelsen finds, the German protagonists must "battle to resist becoming overwhelmed by Slavic slovenliness, tendency to disorder, and inclination to take the path of least resistance."[84] Identifying this process as the "inner corrosion of one's own sphere of values," Ketelsen doesn't discuss the reproductive aspects of this Polonization. The literature makes it clear, however, that characters that become Polonized pass this identity on to their children, which introduces a quasi-biological component to the deracination.

In one of the first studies of German colonial literature set in Africa, Joachim Warmbold argued that a main source of narrative conflict in this genre was generated by the motif of *Verwilderung* ("going wild") or *Verkafferung* ("going native" or "going Kafir," where *Kafir* is a disparaging term for a black South African).[85] In several of the most well-known German colonial texts, including several authored by Hans Grimm and Frieda von Bülow, white German men travel to Africa, set up farmsteads in sparsely populated areas, hire black servants, and take on black mistresses.[86] This movement of the individual from German space into African space always leads to the psychological, physical, cultural, and/or racial degeneration of the German individual. The domestic environment shapes identity.

The *Deutsches Kolonial-Lexikon* (German colonial lexicon) of 1920 defines *Verkafferung* this way.

> The sinking of a European down to the cultural level of the native . . . An isolated life on the plains, constant contact with coloreds, but especially the intermarriage with them, leads to this regrettable degeneration of white settlers. Once a European has gone native, he is lost to the white population, because even where he is of personal intelligence, he has lost one of the most essential advancements of his home culture—an energetic will and the ability to adhere to a given plan. . . . This threat should not be underestimated, and the surest way to prevent it would be to facilitate marriages to white women.[87]

In each of its usages in this passage, the word *European* is grammatically coded as male. This gender specificity is consistent with the German literary narratives, in which *Verkafferung* is a distinctly male phenomenon that is indeed alleviated by the presence of white women. Through their reproductive role in the domestic sphere, German women serve as transferable embodiments of *Heimat.* They reconstitute this space upon arrival in the colonies, offering men a physical, psychological, and cultural reproduction of home.[88] The women serve as a permanent connection to the German collectivity and aren't themselves susceptible to the degenerative influences of their surroundings.

This role of the German woman is the same in inner colonial literature; while men are responsible for Germanizing the greater landscape, German women are responsible for the domestic, reproductive sphere of the home. Polish women perform the equivalent role in the Polish domestic sphere, creating a space in which Polish values are reproduced. Analogous to the native vectors of *Verkafferung* found in overseas colonial literature, the Polish woman becomes the primary agent of German deracination, and she is aware of her power. Almost every inner colonial text features a Polish woman exerting seductive force upon a German male protagonist, usually as part of a calculated plan orchestrated by a villainous priest. The title of Albert Liepe's *Die Spinne* (The spider, 1902) refers to the sinister plot of Kasimir Lokjetek, a Polish priest who convinces his sister to seduce the German arriving to take possession of the nearby estate. Agreeing to the plan, she becomes a spider spinning a dangerous web.

> And now decorate yourself for battle! The German should enjoy himself in the house of the Polish priest. The entire charm of our race should caress him; we will envelop him in a soft, gentle web of friendliness and kindness, and, bit by bit, suck the German poison from his veins and fill him with the noble juice of Polishness.[89]

This division of roles is steadfast: with rare exception, Polish men do not marry German women in the Eastern Marches literature.[90] Heinrich von Treitschke provided figures suggesting that this pattern was reflected in the marriage statistics of the period and argued that it was indicative of a national weakness.

> We are still the Volk that has the least power of national resistance. This is even true in relation to our Polish neighbors. Here too, women play an enormous role. One must pay attention to the marriages that take place. In Posen, it is usually the case that the woman is Polish and the man German. . . . The mother tends to be Polish, and that is the decisive factor.[91]

Since the female is the racial determinant, this marriage pattern results in a path of deracination that is only traveled in one direction: from German to Polish. Inner colonial literature thereby gives expression to a collective anxiety about German national virility, and does so in decidedly gendered terms.

Of even greater concern than the threat of "going native" was that of miscegenation, for the resultant hybridity undermined the categorical dualism between colonizer and colonized in a more fundamental way than "going native" did; the man who "went native" indicated that the line between self and Other could be easily crossed, but the existence of individuals with mixed parentage threatened to erase the line itself. The history of European colonialism is, therefore, in part the history of the struggle to maintain this line by carefully cataloging transgressions of it. In 1825, W. B. Stevenson published an often-cited table listing twenty-three different categories of racial admixture.[92] The table identified twenty-two ways in which a person could be *not white,* each of which could be traced back to the original act of border violation, when white and black intermixed to create the first hybrid in the chain.

In the adjacent territories at the turn of the century, this degree of racial differentiation was not present. There were no charts labeling individuals according to the racial identities of their grandparents and great-grandparents, no equivalents to Stevenson's "Mulattos, Quarterons, Quinterons, and Zambos" in German inner colonial discourse. Characters of mixed or ambiguous German-Polish parentage appear frequently, but their hybridity only lasts for one generation and is not passed down to future offspring; instead, it resolves itself into one identity or the other following set patterns based on gender.

When these characters are male, they are typically the novels' main protagonists, and their mixed parentage provides the central narrative conflict.

Both Annie Bock's 1898 *Der Zug nach dem Osten* and Valeska von Bethusy-Huc's 1903 *Hans der Pole* (Hans the Pole) tell the story of young men who are members of the landowning aristocracy and the sons of Polish mothers and German fathers. Their childhoods had been dominated by the stormy temperaments and impulsive pleasure-seeking of their Polish mothers (while the acute financial negligence and will to leisure of their fathers testified to their Polonization). Now, as young men crossing the threshold into adulthood, they find themselves in situations in which their Polish allegiances are being challenged by an awakening German identity. For male characters, German-Polish hybridity expresses itself as a state of temporary indecision.

Both Felix von Graach and Hans von Walsberg had left home to join the Prussian military, which exerted the same Germanizing force upon them as it did upon the Poles in the assimilationist texts; they develop a loyalty to the German state, along with German values and ethics. At the beginning of each of the novels, the son is called home to oversee the sale of his family estate after the death of his German father, and both of their Polish mothers complicate this task. The military pressures Hans to support inner colonization and sell his property to Germans. When they discover that his mother has clandestinely organized Polish buyers, Hans loses his career. Felix von Graach, meanwhile, has been hired by the Settlement Commission to oversee the parcellation of his family's former estate. But when the commission discovers that Felix's Catholic mother has been converting the incoming German settlers with the help of her fanatically nationalistic priest, Felix too is fired.

In these texts, the aristocratic Polish mother represents a sentimental tie to the naive past of childhood. In order to cross the threshold into (a German-identified) adulthood, the hybrid male must permanently denounce his mother, extinguish the Polish aspects of his character, and begin life anew as a German-identified man. Hans struggles with his Polish identity and spends several years drifting with Polish nationalists in Paris. As their revolutionary activities become increasingly irrational and violent, Hans escapes and finds his true self in an ordered, German life of hard work on his own small farm.

> The German blood of his father must have been more powerful in him than the Polish instincts of his mother. Her soft, fantastical, sensuous laughter and song echoed to him from his childhood memories: he had translated this into real life—and found it worthless. And now he gazed longingly towards his old fatherland. German home, German customs, German reliability—how sweet this all sounded.[93]

These male hybrid characters each present an embodiment of the regional conflict on the German-Polish frontier, and their lives serve as allegories for the Germanization of the mixed region. An ambiguous, hybrid identity was possible for the region in its historical youth, but national maturity now calls for homogeneity. Just like these protagonists, who are unable to successfully integrate their conflicting German and Polish identities, so too must the region fully relinquish its ties to a Polish-inflected past. Hans's mentor stresses that "the time when one could be Polish-German or German-Polish is over, and now you have to show your colors!"[94] The German-Polish hybrid casts out his Polish heritage as part of the past he must overcome to achieve progress, thereby providing an allegorical narrative for the hybrid regions and their paths into the future.[95]

Female hybrids occur just as frequently in inner colonial texts, but they play much different roles than their male counterparts. These women aren't the main protagonists but lurk instead at the margins of the narratives, and at the margins of German space. The hybrid female's outward appearance typically suggests a German identity—against a backdrop of black Poles, she stands out as blond—which facilitates her access to German space. But her external façade conceals a true underlying Polish identity, and she is therefore particularly valued by priests orchestrating deracination campaigns. Functioning as Trojan horses of a sort, these women are better able to cross the border into German space and successfully seduce German men. Themselves the products of past boundary transgressions, hybrid women threaten to further corrode the border between self and Other in the German settlement colonies.

Both Naska Jarezka in Annie Bock's *Der Zug nach dem Osten* and Stasia Frelikowska in Clara Viebig's *Das schlafende Heer* set out to seduce the texts' male protagonists. In Bock's text, Felix von Graach tries to stave off the advances of his housemaid, Naska, but repeatedly notes the physical similarities between her and his sister-in-law, Ella (whose whiteness was discussed above): their hair is of the same blond color, which causes Felix to confuse them.[96] In love with Ella, Felix repeatedly releases his sublimated feelings for her in physical encounters with Naska. Felix's mother works with her priest to encourage this relationship, hoping that Naska will bring about her son's ultimate Polonization. Whereas the German military had strengthened Felix's German sense of duty and self-restraint, Naska causes him to lose control over his libidinal drives. When she enters his quarters making advances, both figures seem guided by their darker sides.

> He saw that the passion in this uncivilized creature was naturally without restraint, and that it couldn't be otherwise. And then a different feeling

> crept over him—as he looked down upon her clinging to him—a feeling of fear of his own self.
>
> He could have seized her and suffocated her with wild kisses, crushing her in an impassioned embrace. He frantically struggled to free himself from her, but her fingers clenched his arm like iron clamps. She clung to him like a vampire, her fervid eyes glared at him, her moist red lips trembled in passion as she bared her strong white teeth at him in enraged arousal.[97]

Felix is only able to free himself of Naska's vampiric embrace by thrashing at her with his whip, an act for which he is punished by the Settlement Commission. They find his actions "reminiscent of the justice meted by Dr. Peters down in Africa," and so Felix too loses his colonial post.[98]

There are, therefore, fundamental differences in the ways that hybridity expresses itself in the male and female cases. Felix's hybridity divides both his body and soul into two halves: he has midrange external features (brown hair and eyes) and a character that is divided into two warring halves. Naska's hybridity, in contrast, expresses itself in a mind/body duality: her external German features (i.e., her blond hair) mask a character that is unambiguously Polish. Only her dark eyes—the window to her soul—reveal the truth of the Polish identity residing beneath.

The Domestic Degeneracy of *Polnische Wirtschaft*

This same model of hybridity holds for Stasia in Viebig's text as well. Like Naska, Stasia—the only child of a Polish mother and a German father—has a rich mane of blond hair. Stasia's father exemplifies the stereotype of Polonization: he once identified as German and served proudly in the Prussian military, but when he married a Polish woman, everything changed. He became lazy, started drinking heavily, began speaking Polish, and even Polonized his name from Fröhlich to Frelikowski. As a consequence of his Polonization, his daughter has been raised Polish in a Polish household. The repetitive invocation of her blondness (she is usually referred to as "the blond Stasia")[99] introduces uncertainty regarding her true nature. When Valentin Bräuer falls in love with Stasia, this question becomes more urgent, because his parents won't allow him to marry a Pole.

The figure of Stasia embodies the fear of ambiguity attending adjacent colonialism. Her hybridity disturbs the chromatic polarization dividing "black" Pole from "white" German and suggests that the eye alone might be unable to reliably determine identity in the fluidly adjacent eastern frontier. The text resolves this ambiguity by introducing a new category of difference: racialized space. As in all of the inner colonial texts, Germans and Poles are shown to externalize their racial identities in the means by which they produce space: German space is rationally, hierarchically, and morally ordered; it is clean, modest, and well kept. Polish space is a manifestation of the opposite: it is always filthy and in disrepair; it is irrationally ordered (often erasing the line dividing human from animal) and reflects an amoral work ethic. Individual characters may be defined as racially hybrid, but the space that they produce reproduces the space of their childhoods—and it is strongly demarcated as either German or Polish. Any racial ambiguity can be clarified through this spatial dichotomy.

In her study of colonial literature, Anne McClintock has found that depictions of "domestic degeneracy" are used to introduce space-based distinctions in colonial situations "where skin color as a marker of power was imprecise and inadequate."[100] Instead of scrutinizing an individual's outward appearance for clues as to their "true" identity, one must merely enter his or her space of social reproduction, where the colonial subject becomes identifiable by the filth, backwardness, and depravity of self and space. McClintock finds widespread use of "domestic degeneracy" to demarcate space in English colonial discourse; in the case of German depictions of Polish Prussia, a specific variant of this iconography can be found in the reconfiguration of the long-standing stereotype of *polnische Wirtschaft* (Polish mismanagement).

The history of the term can be traced back to the writings of Enlightenment travelers to Poland, most notably Georg Forster,[101] but the stereotype was broadly popularized in Gustav Freytag's 1855 *Soll und Haben,* after which it gained greater currency in both the press and public discourse.[102] The Polish Germanist Hubert Orłowski has written a 500-page study on the history of the stereotype, including examples from novels, political speeches, the illustrated press, letters, memoirs, etc.[103] "Polnische Wirtschaft" was a chapter title in Albert Emil Brachvogel's popular novel of German-Polish antagonism *Der Fels von Erz* (The cliff of ore, 1872), and it was the title of a 1890 operetta, a 1928 film, and Paul Oskar Höcker's 1896 *Ostmarkenroman.*[104]

Integrating attributes of race and space under the aegis of one sign, *polnische Wirtschaft* evokes images of agricultural mismanagement, dilapidated villages, and pestilent dwellings. At the same time, it renders these as the inherent by-products of the filth, backwardness, laziness, and brutality of a Polish race that readily submits to primitive sexual urges and extremes of alcoholic indulgence. In general, *polnische Wirtschaft* describes the condition of a primitive people unable to fully manage the stresses and responsibilities of civilized life. This deficiency expressed itself differently for members of different classes: "among the wealthier classes, one identified wastefulness and frivolousness, among the 'simple people,' filth and ignorance."[105]

For examples of *polnische Wirtschaft* among the wealthy, one might turn to Freytag's depiction of the Polish aristocrats in *Soll und Haben*—the Tarowski residence was an external manifestation of Tarowski's own identity: a dilapidated building covered with a layer of false finery. The *Ostmarkenromane* draw directly from Freytag, as when Karl von Steinmann enters the mansion he has purchased from a Polish aristocrat in Liepe's *Die Spinne.*

> His gaze traveled across the room. What a strange mixture of elegance and decay, of fine taste and slovenliness! . . . the gold-pressed leather wallpaper was hanging in shreds from the walls; the parquet floor was missing several pieces, and one of the areas of the wall where the wallpaper had been torn away revealed a hole that had been stuffed with a rag.[106]

Next to this decadent disrepair, aristocratic degeneracy includes disastrous financial mismanagement; in the novels discussed above, the estates of the von Graachs and the Walsbergs must be sold off due to debt. In both cases, German landowners had married Polish women, become Polonized, and allowed their estates to fall into financial ruin.

Depictions of *polnische Wirtschaft* among the peasant population also combine elements from a standard iconographic set but are much more vulgar. Images of bodily filth are intensified by attention to fur caps and jackets that are unwashed and malodorous; hair is matted and louse-ridden, with frequent mention of "Polish plait" (a condition of matted, encrusted hair accompanied by scalp inflammation, caused by improper hygiene); children are often naked, even when the weather would demand otherwise, and Poles frequently lack shoes. Dwellings are filthy, in unhealthy states of disrepair, and typically shelter animals together with their human occupants. The peasant oven—and the bed built on top of it—feature prominently; the lazy man of the house can often be found here sleeping off his excessive vodka consumption.

After Karl von Steinmann visits the Polish aristocrats, he takes a walk through the Polish village attached to his new estate. He finds the whole scene "bleak" and demands to see the individual houses.

> The slanted mud walls had cracks and holes glued over with paper. The straw roof was in disrepair and allowed the weather free entry. . . . The

> men entered a room that was indistinguishable from a stall; they were hit by a rush of foul air.

In the next house,

> there was great commotion in the main room. A large flock of children—half naked, half covered in rags—crammed and pushed themselves in a race with two goats, and it was a miracle that the hens that were running around in the commotion weren't trampled.[107]

The children are starving, and the peasant steals wood from the estate's forest to trade for food: a well-rounded image of *polnische Wirtschaft.*

Although Viebig never uses the term directly, *polnische Wirtschaft* is rendered literally in the tavern that Stasia and Valentin operate after their marriage. The word *Wirtschaft* has multiple meanings in German; next to the abstract concept of "economic management," it also has a concrete instantiation as "a pub or an inn." Both in terms of its clientele and of the way in which its space is maintained, Stasia and Valentin's tavern is indeed a *polnische Wirtschaft.*[108] The establishment was built by the Settlement Commission, but Stasia soon "Polonizes" it; she refuses to clean, and the level of filth becomes overwhelming. Meanwhile, Stasia encourages a clientele of heavy-drinking Poles that seem at home in such a filthy space, and she loses track of their large, unpaid tabs. It is a *polnische Wirtschaft* both in its filth and in its economic mismanagement.

Domestic degeneracy—and the specific variant of *polnische Wirtschaft*—are models claiming that one can resolve ambiguous racial identity into opposed categories of spatial practice.[109] Stasia may be a German-Polish hybrid, but she was raised in the Polish domestic sphere, she has internalized this spatial order, and this is the environment that she reproduces in the tavern. There is no German inheritance in this either/or model.

Stasia is connected to three different generations of "Polonization": her paramour, Szulc, whose name is a Polonization of Schulz or Schultz, which marks him as a descendent of Germans Polonized in the past; her Polonized father; and now Valentin, destined to join the ranks of these Polonized men. He is obsessively devoted to his guileful wife; unconcerned with the ramifications for his German identity, he struggles to learn Polish, takes on a Polonization of his name (Wladek), and submits to Stasia's Polonization of the tavern. When Valentin discovers her affair with Szulc, Stasia confines herself in her father's house. Driven by desire, Valentin watches Stasia's window night after night. His midnight stalkings culminate in a hallucinatory delirium during which he is sucked down into the marshy quagmire surrounding Frelikowski's house. Dying in a primitive Polish landscape not yet subjected to modern German drainage practices, Valentin's death is attributable to more than one aspect of *polnische Wirtschaft.*

In Clara Viebig's novel, the ambivalent hybridity muddling the border between self and Other in the adjacent colony is ultimately resolved by a clear German/Polish spatial dualism: texts entertained the possibility of hybridity's racial *both/and* only to ultimately reduce it into a spatial *either/or.* The iconography of *polnische Wirtschaft* rendered even the hybrid Pole immediately identifiable; one merely needed to observe the quality of the environment an individual (re)produced. Polish domestic degeneracy also legitimized German colonial intervention: the Polish peasants were depicted living in an animalistic, barbaric state from which they were unable (or unwilling) to free themselves of their own accord, and their degeneracy was reinforced by the economic and social degeneracy of the Polish aristocrats in power. German colonization would break this reproductive cycle by taking control, eliminating Polish space, and introducing a new, German order.

But the Poles are intent upon protecting their space and expanding its borders because it provides the basis of their racial reproduction. German colonists thus operate in landscapes teeming with Polonizing interests and forces that they are often unable to recognize. This threat of Polonizing contagion rendered colonization an urgent national priority: the Polish flood was heading westward and absorbing German men in its wave of deracination. Space became the key determinate of racial identity, and colonization the only viable means of self-preservation.

Inner German Antagonisms and the Contestation over Inner Colonization Practices

The inner colonial texts all share the conceptual backdrop of a Polish spatio-racial threat that can only be countered by successful German colonization. But they proceed to stake very different positions on the question of which Germans should lead the way, and which form of inner colonization they should pursue. Through narratives of both colonial successes and failures, authors distinguish between aristocratic and bourgeois Germans, between Catholics and Protestants, between those pursuing individualistic gain and those hoping to strengthen the German nation. Inner colonial literature thus becomes an arena in which inner German antagonisms are staged as texts to make claims about who is best able to create German space in the East.

One of the most prominent theorists of inner colonization was the political economist Max Sering.[110] His work addresses a question raised by most of his contemporaries on the subject of inner colonization: Which types of Germans should the inner colonial agencies recruit and send to Polish Prussia? Sering supports the experienced family farmer, and not the "bankrupt landowners and industrialists" that have joined the ranks of the inner colonists. In the case of overseas colonization, the difficult conditions successfully discouraged inappropriate Germans from going there in the first place, but when "the colonization is to take place in the immediate neighborhood of the former *Heimat,*" the threshold for migration is too low, and the state must intervene to attract family farmers.[111] Alfred Brenning, an agrarian economist, similarly stressed the importance of attracting farmers to the East, describing their role in Germanizing the land in language drawn straight from the *Heimat* movement.

> The farmer has grown more firmly connected to his land [*Scholle*] than the large landowner. No one is more the product of the native soil [*Produkt des heimatlichen Grund und Bodens*] than he; it determines his character, his whole state of being. The soil that he cultivates is the sole object of his interest, and his worldview is rooted in it.[112]

To a certain extent, the support of the German family farmer is to be expected: the inner colonization project was never about increasing the urban German population or introducing industrial development in the East, but was instead entirely agrarian. But to support the family farmer was to engage in a discussion of class, which is articulated in the comparison Brenning makes between this group and the large landowners: while the latter has a role in reproducing the elite class of German politicians and military officers, it is the small family farmer who reproduces German space.

Such promotion of the small farmer was connected to larger political and social tensions within Germany. Unification had brought the large landowners of the Prussian East into new economic and political power constellations that now included industrialists from Germany's western regions. A central point of contention between these two groups involved the issue of food prices and the ramifications of tariffs imposed on foreign agricultural imports. Landowners wanted a protectionist tariff system to keep their crop prices high, while industrialists pressured for the opposite: reduced tariffs would lower food prices and keep sustenance-level labor wages low. In the context of these so-called food wars between the eastern landowners and their opponents, anti-Polish rhetoric came to play a significant role.

Large landowners were dependent upon hired labor to work their fields, and, given the small number of Germans available for hire in the East, landowners usually had little choice but to hire Polish seasonal laborers—the same Poles that were being characterized as constituting a "Polish flood" and a "contagious threat" in conservative national rhetoric. Inner colonization was meant to solve this "Polish problem" by replacing these Polish seasonal workers with a new population of German family farmers. There was, however, a problem with this plan: those Poles who worked the large estates did so because they were dependent upon this income. These Poles either didn't own their own farms or owned farms too small to make them financially independent. They made ends meet by working as hired hands on the large estates during the harvest and planting seasons. In contrast, the Germans introduced into the region as inner colonists were set up with land parcels large enough to provide the farmers with financial independence; they had no need to work for the large estates. In hopes of producing a new, semidependent German workforce, large landholders encouraged a parcellation process that would result in smaller land parcels, but there were few Germans interested or willing to move to plots this small.

It thus seemed that the existence of large land estates was inseparably linked to a large population of Polish seasonal workers. This equation provided leverage for agrarian reformers promoting new land-use practices: the only way to get rid of the Poles would be to eliminate the large estates dependent upon their labor. A successful inner colonial policy, according to the reformers, would increase the amount of space inhabited by small, independent German family farmers, and decrease the size and number of the large estates. Such reform plans shifted the discussion surrounding inner colonization from the question of *why* space in the East should be Germanized to a debate about *how* it should be Germanized. Potentially at stake was a fundamental reordering of the Prussian landscape—a spatial reordering that would directly correlate with a political reordering were the number of landowners really to become reduced. Within this context, both the German farmer and the Polish peasant became rhetorical figures manipulated in a conflict of interests between German landowners and their opponents. Anti-Polish sentiment (as well as a celebration of the German farmer as the producer of traditional *Heimat*) can both be linked to an antiagrarian stance: the more threatening the "Polish problem," the more urgent the need to eliminate the large estates channeling the flow of

Poles into German space. If the "Polish flood" was the problem, then the German family farmer was the answer. This constellation of positions perhaps explains why membership in the Ostmarkenverein—which backed the most vitriolic anti-Polish rhetoric—was largely composed of members of the bourgeoisie, and not of the large landowners (nor the colonists themselves).

Was inner colonization a nationalist project to push back the Polish element, or was it a liberal project to undermine the national legitimacy of the large landowners in the East? The inner colonial texts provide varying answers.

In Annie Bock's *Der Zug nach dem Osten* (1898), Felix von Graach is initially bitter at the loss of his land inheritance (which, we recall, his Polonized father had gambled away), and, when the estate is parceled, he looks down upon the incoming settlers with aristocratic disdain; for Felix von Graach, these small family farmers are a plebeian nuisance.[113] Felix's point of view, however, changes over the course of the novel. He comes to equate the aristocratic and Polish aspects of his identity and rejects both on behalf of a more bourgeois German allegiance. As he takes leave from the estate for the last time, Felix declares that large landownership is a vestige of a feudal past that must now be overcome for the sake of German progress. Graach has come to see the small family farmers as Germany's hope for the future, and the lengthy programmatic speeches he delivers to this effect on the last few pages of the text suggest that he hopes the reader has followed Graach's change of opinion.

Until Felix is finished parceling his family's former estate, he remains dependent upon hired Polish labor to work the fields. The Polish seasonal workers live in centralized housing and will be moved out of the colony once parcellation is complete. Significantly, both Felix's mother and Naska—the two Polish figures in the household—leave when he does; there is no place for them in the new German order. Felix's mother even finds that there is no place for her in Prussia and indicates that she will join a convent in Austrian Galicia. The parcellation of the estate has thus led to the elimination of its Polish population from German space.

Albert Liepe's *Die Spinne* offers a different solution. As we saw above, Karl von Steinmann purchases a formerly Polish-owned estate edged by a sickly, dilapidated Polish village. Karl addresses the problem of Polish domestic degeneracy by eradicating this Polish space; he razes the entire Polish village and builds a new settlement on the other side of his property. This village is designed to provide him with a dependent labor force; the houses are all on small plots of land that allow for little more than a vegetable garden. Karl admits that he is dependent upon the labor of these Poles and therefore allows them to stay on. But there are several conditions: Poles can only work as field hands (Germans will be hired for all other professions), and they can only live in the village he has built. In his settlement, all houses are duplexes, and Polish families must share theirs with a German family. This, Karl thinks, will ensure that Poles don't re-create Polish space. The Poles are allowed to remain in this German colony but will only be tolerated as long as they acquiesce to German dominance and accept their second-class status. Karl's farm is deemed a role model by the local chapter of the Ostmarkenverein; he has imposed German order upon the Polish landscape, rationalized this space, and thereby increased the estate's profitability. The Polish peasant population has been disciplined and contained, as have been the members of the Polish elite: the priest has been jailed for his criminal anti-German activity, and his sister, Wanda, has joined a convent.

These two texts present the reader with two different spatial variants of inner colonization: a conservative version led by German aristocrats, and a reformed version led by German farmers. The latter envisions the complete displacement of the Polish population and stresses the dangerous contagion of the Poles in order to justify this plan and render it more urgent. The former portrays a new generation of German aristocratic landowners able to rejuvenate the existing spatioeconomic estate structures. While the aristocratic and ecclesiastic Polish elite must be expelled from this space, the Polish peasants can be shaped into a useful, dependent workforce. Here, the Polish threat is less urgent, and is largely instigated by the Polish elite; once they have been removed, the Polish population becomes compliant. We see that the way in which the Poles are represented in these texts is closely tied to the model of inner colonization being promoted: the aristocratic-conservative agenda is dependent upon a less ominous understanding of Polish identity (because they must be maintained as a work force), while the reform model depicts a much more uniformly dangerous and contagious Polish population.

Clara Viebig's novel deviates from this pattern in that it doesn't ultimately present any successful narrative of inner colonization. *Das schlafende Heer* instead offers a catalog of inner colonial failures represented by a diverse cast of characters, both large landowners and small farmers. Her work was therefore criticized by its contemporaries for its lack of support for the inner colonization project and has been celebrated in recent studies for the same reason. But both assessments fail to note that, although Viebig doesn't depict colonial success, her text nonetheless offers support for future attempts. *Das schlafende Heer* depicts the region as a large, unbounded space that needed to be ordered, and shows that the Poles threatened to fill this space. The title of the novel—

"the sleeping army"—is referred to by both Polish and German characters. Both sides dream of a powerful force that will achieve power for their people in the region: for the Poles, this is an army of swordsmen that will drive the Germans out of Polish Prussia; for the Germans, this is an army of ploughshares that will spread over the region and make the landscape German.[114] The novel depicts the Poles as too poor and too weak to achieve their goal, but, while the Germans are better positioned to do so, they must first overcome their internal political and social fragmentation. Viebig's text thus points the way toward a future of German domination in the region but argues that these characters aren't going to be the ones to do it. The large landowners have all lost their connection to the soil and are purely driven by personal profit.

The Bräuers are the only family farmers introduced in the text, and they are shown to be unfit for several reasons, most notably because they are Catholic.[115] Nationality and religion were largely held to break down along clear lines in Polish Prussia: Poles were Catholic, and Germans were Protestant. We don't encounter Polish Protestants in the literature, but German Catholics feature prominently in positions that weakened the clear lines of division. German Catholics would usually find themselves forced to attend Polish churches, their children would need to learn Polish to receive religious instruction, and they would be dependent upon Polish clergy for spiritual and moral guidance. Coming into such sustained contact with Poles, German Catholics were deemed to be at greater risk of Polonization. The Bräuer family exemplifies this Catholic problem; when Valentin wants to marry Stasia, his parents have only the Polish clergy to turn to for advice, and the end result is the Polonization of Valentin and the decision of Peter Bräuer to head back to his home in the Rhine valley. Policymakers called for the restriction of Catholic settlers to regions without large German populations, because German Catholics were less reliably "German."[116]

Perhaps as significant as Bräuer's Catholicism was his desire to move to the East to achieve personal wealth instead of serving a greater German cause. When he arrives in the settlement and is asked about his motivations, his answer reveals his assumptions about the colonial project.

> I have a nice little nest egg, but in the Rhine Valley, it's nothing—there are a lot of people there that have money. But in Posen, it amounts to something, because the Polacks are poor. And I thought: it's at least enough to make a good start. When I talked about it with Valentin, he was immediately hooked on the idea. He used to read books about the Indians in school, and as for Karl May's stories—man can he write! I even liked to read them! And so we were really excited about it![117]

Peter Bräuer's German identity is compromised not only by his religious denomination, but also by his colonial naïveté. Bräuer is repeatedly shown projecting the myth of Wild West adventure (à la Karl May) onto the Polish territories. Idealizing America as a terrain of absolute freedom, Bräuer dreams of dealing with the "wild natives" (*die Wilden*) by flashing his revolver. In Posen, he complains, he must heed the state authority and established law granting the native Poles a certain (if unequal) set of political and personal rights. "Oh, if I had only gone to America, really far away, where there are still wild natives. At least there, one can mete out one's own justice!"[118]

Viebig's text ends on a programmatically optimistic note; Helene Doleschal stands among her five flaxen-haired sons, gazing proudly over the fields of the coming harvest.[119] She has raised these boys with stories about the German "sleeping army" that must be awakened to march over this landscape and make it German.[120] For these five boys, this eastern Polish region is their *Heimat,* and the reader has every sense that they will stay on to successfully manage this territory, banishing the threat of racial contagion to the space beyond that which they bring under German control.

Chapter 3

A German Dracula: Fontane's *Effi Briest* and the Anxiety of a Reverse-Diffusional Slavic Flood

Although Gustav Freytag's *Soll und Haben* is often identified as the precursor of the *Ostmarkenromane,* the writers of this genre, as we have seen, were largely unable to produce narratives equaling his unhesitant colonial triumphalism. With few exceptions—most prominently Albert Liepe's *Die Spinne*—the novels set in the inner colonial East feature depictions of colonial anxiety, setback, and failure rather than successful settlement and the diffusion of German advancements. Although this apprehensive stance might seem to disqualify the *Ostmarkenroman* from categorization as colonial literature, a closer look reminds us that it actually shares this diffident posture with many of the most prominent German colonial novels set overseas. Works by authors such as Frieda von Bülow, Hans Grimm, and Gustav Frenssen all feature German colonists in Africa struggling against the opposing natural and social forces of their surrounding environment. They are confronted with various forms of native resistance to their exercise of local power, they are under constant threat of illness and malnutrition, and their attempts to maintain a German identity in foreign space are challenged by myriad deracinating and decivilizing forces.[1]

Similarly, the inner colonial narratives set in the Prussian East depict German settlers under threat—collectively, by native resistance in the form of mob violence and organized crime, and, individually, by targeted acts of deracination, typically through seduction into the Polonizing domestic sphere of the Other.

The landscape of the inner colonial East is thus rendered the site of ongoing struggle: the eastward flow of Germans represents the introduction of technological and social innovation, the forward march of progress and order. But these civilizing diffusions are always threatened by reverse-directional flows:

the westward seepage of a resilient atavism, a stubborn primitivity, an entropic force of chaos.

The *Ostmarkenroman* depicts the East as a space of civilizational contest, of the competition between elemental forces representing progress versus regression, order versus chaos, logic versus irrationality. As a trivial genre, it often reduces the nuance of these structuring conflicts to the opposing shades of black and white. Yet even texts that don't paint this space in such broad and crude brushstrokes can be shown to reproduce the discourse of the East the *Ostmarkenroman* constructs. Theodor Fontane's *Effi Briest,* a text whose inner colonial setting in the Prussian East is often overlooked, exemplifies the ways in which this discourse is brought into representation in German canonical literature. An understanding of the symbolic landscape in which *Effi Briest* is set allows for a reading of the novel that positions it much closer to the late Victorian-era gothic invasion narrative, and thus to the imperial anxieties this genre represents.

Edward Said's Contrapuntal Analysis

When Said published *Orientalism* in 1978, he offered German studies scholars a significant provocation. Although he admits that Germans had produced important (or at least popular) scholarly studies and literary representations of the Orient during the imperial period, Said claims that these works were merely derivative in nature. In an often-quoted passage, he makes this argument.

> The German Orient was almost exclusively a scholarly, or at least a classical, Orient: it was made the subject of lyrics, fantasies, and even novels, but it was never actual. . . . There is some significance in the fact that the two most renowned German works on the Orient, Goethe's *Westöstlicher Diwan* and Friedrich Schlegel's *Über die Sprache und Weisheit der Indier,* were based respectively on a Rhine journey and on hours spent in Paris libraries. What German Oriental scholarship did was to refine and elaborate techniques whose application was to texts, myths, ideas, and languages almost literally gathered from the Orient by imperial Britain and France.[2]

At the same time that he excludes Germans from this process, Said argues that Orientalism was a hegemonic discourse in the West, such that "no one writing, thinking, or acting on the Orient could do so without taking account of the limitations on thought and action imposed by Orientalism."[3] Within his model, then, Germans—as members of that community he identifies as "the West"—were interpolated within a discursive structure introduced, shaped, and developed by those other nations who held "actual interests" in the region.

This model has been questioned on several fronts. Some reject Said's denial of organized German interest in the Orient and argue that, although Germany was not in the position to orchestrate state-driven colonization in the region prior to the late nineteenth century, German individuals were nonetheless active in the Orient as merchants, traders, explorers, scientists, engineers, etc.; German firms engaged in economic ventures there; and various German governments pursued political interests in the region.[4] Meanwhile, literary and cultural scholars have sought to correct Said's limited treatment of German Orientalist discourse by identifying a wide body of texts, both literary and fictional, in which Orientalist structures appear within a specifically German (i.e., nonderivative) idiom.[5] In this latter regard, there is increasing interest in the way in which this German conceptualization positioned "the Orient" within a larger understanding of "the East" that included Eastern Europe.[6]

A third body of scholarship applies Said's own strategy of discourse-analytic literary analysis to German texts in order to show the pervasiveness of Orientalist thought in German collective consciousness. Said's "contrapuntal analysis" allows one to identify Orientalist (as well as imperialist, colonialist, etc.) discourses in literary works that are neither set in the Orient nor have explicitly Oriental themes. The strategy brings "a simultaneous awareness both of the metropolitan history that is narrated and of those other histories against which (and together with which) the dominating discourse acts."[7] In other words, it attends to the ways in which imperialism, Orientalism, etc. are present in literary texts as the understood, if unstated, backdrops—the larger historical contexts in which the narratives are positioned, and within which they gain their social meaning. By showing that canonized German novels too reveal silent or understated economic, aesthetic, political, and/or social ties to the Orient when read contrapuntally, it can be argued that German authors were not limited to writing derivative Orientalist works (in which the Orient is the overt subject matter) but were producing texts from within a social discourse shaped and permeated by an Orientalist worldview.[8]

Theodor Fontane's 1895 *Effi Briest* is one of the German novels most commonly subjected to this form of contrapuntal analysis.[9] Its story of marital infidelity is set in a Prussian context and features no direct connection to the Orient: the setting of the plot never leaves Prussia, none of the main characters ever travels to the Orient, and there are no overt references to German imperial interests in the region. Yet the novel is replete with references to the Orient, most conspicuously in the figure of the Chinese ghost that haunts Effi Briest once she moves to the house of her husband, Innstetten, but also in the myriad meaning-laden objects and anecdotes pertaining to the Oriental East that are exchanged over the course of the novel.

These studies of Orientalist discourse in *Effi Briest* exist alongside—but seldom engage—a second body of scholarship investigating the image of Poland and the Poles (or of Eastern European space and the Slavs) in Fontane's oeuvre.[10] These readings emphasize the eastern location of the spaces visited by *Effi Briest* as well as the Slavic characters that figure in the novel. Effi spends the first years of her married life in the predominantly Slavic region of *Hinterpommern* (Outer Pomerania), a peripheral space in which she is seduced by Crampas—a "half-Pole." In this respect, the novel engages a second, adjacent East in addition to that of the Orient; this is the East of German inner colonization, of German-Polish territorial contestation, of past and future German expansionist aspirations.

Relevant to my considerations here, Said-inspired contrapuntal analyses of *Effi Briest* have overlooked this adjacent East to focus exclusively on the Orient and the mental map of German overseas colonial aspiration. Therefore, even as these studies challenge Said's dismissal of a specifically German form of Orientalist thought, they nonetheless reinscribe the validity of his West-versus-Orient global dualism and ignore the unique plurality of the German imperial context that would offer the strongest basis of challenge to Said's model. This disregard for the entirety of a German imperial experience—which was active in two very different "Easts"—has led readers to find in *Effi Briest* a one-sided "critical examination of the phenomenon of colonialism,"[11] arriving at an overall "critique of German imperialist aspirations."[12] Attending to both Easts, however, reveals that, instead of this global critique of imperialism, the text is instead suggesting a *prioritization* of German imperialist concerns: while the Oriental East may offer Germans a seductively exotic object of colonial desire, the novel argues, their real and urgent imperial responsibilities lie in the adjacent Slavic East.

This sense of colonial urgency is not generated through the traditional language of a primitive space calling for external intervention and cultivation, but instead through the suggestion that the Prussian East is the source of an atavism that threatens German civilization—an atavism that must be brought under control, and either contained or eliminated, because it threatens to otherwise infiltrate and contaminate German national space. In this regard, *Effi Briest* reveals its connection to a larger European discourse arising during the period of high imperialism: *the anxiety of reverse diffusion,* or the fear, both consciously articulated and unconsciously sensed, that the imperial center was losing strength vis-à-vis its colonial periphery.[13] The "colonizer's model" had understood the world to be structured by a set of transfers originating in the European center and diffusing outward into the periphery. These transfers were always envisioned traveling in the same, outward direction, slowly petering out as they extended ever further into non-European space, but never reversing course. However, as Steven D. Arata has shown, at the turn of the century, a set of invasion narratives appeared in which the directionality of these transfers started to shift. Now, elements were depicted originating in the periphery and crossing borders to travel into the space of the center. The mere reverse directionality of this movement was threatening, because the periphery was, by definition, less developed than the center, such that elements originating in this space "must be ancient, savage, atavistic, uncivilized, evil—black magic, vampires, plagues, 'the bogeyman,' and the like."[14] Indeed, such are the agents of terror in the fin de siècle invasion narratives, the most iconic example of which is Bram Stoker's *Dracula.* As Arata has shown, Dracula brings a series of reverse-diffusionist anxieties into representation: he arises out of the Eastern European periphery and is able to infiltrate into the imperial center unnoticed because he can pass as British, a skill he has acquired by successfully appropriating cultural and technological diffusions from this imperial center.[15] He represents the fear that, in the space of the adjacent periphery, the ability to draw lines of demarcation between self and Other may be undermined by the very success of diffusional transfer. Dracula also threatens the imperial center with deracination, because his virile bite has the power to convert his victims and their offspring into fellow vampires; his virility itself resonates with a growing sense that the processes of modernization—industrialization, urbanization, mechanization—had led to a biological weakening and degeneration of the imperial populace.

> A terrifying reversal has occurred: the colonizer finds himself in the position of the colonized, the exploiter becomes exploited, the victimizer victimized. Such fears are linked to a perceived decline—racial, moral, spiritual—which makes the nation vulnerable to attack from more vigorous, "primitive" peoples.[16]

Fontane's novel too can be read as an invasion narrative: both the Orient and the adjacent East are represented by figures that cross over borders demarcating German space and, once there, pose threats either real or imagined: the Chinese ghost and the "half-Pole" Crampas. There are significant differences between these figures that must be noted from the outset: the Chinese is an absent, spectral figure—the site onto which desires and anxieties are projected, to be sure, but a character that lacks any agency within the space of the narrative. He does not act but is only imagined into action by the novel's protagonists. Crampas, in contrast, enjoys both material presence and autonomous agency. His hybrid, indeterminate identity as a "half-Pole" has camouflaged his peripheral Otherness, allowing Crampas, like Dracula, to infiltrate both the geographic space of the imperial center and its intimate space of domestic reproduction. Both Crampas and Dracula are perceived as threats to the individual as well as the collective, and, within the context of an ostensibly weakened imperial center, both are ritually eliminated for the sake of preserving its integrity.

Crampas may not be a representative of the undead, but, as I will show below, he does appear as the embodiment of a larger discourse of symbolic threat to the body of the German nation, namely, that of "floodwater." In the 1890s, we recall, depictions of Germany under the threat of flood had gained widespread currency; both in the press and in fictional narratives, one encountered images of water, ominously rising, seeping through weakened dikes, spreading over the surrounding landscape. Perhaps imperceptible at first, the floodwater steadily claimed ever larger areas of land and threatened to drown the German nation, transforming its very nature from that of a rationally ordered cultural landscape to an irrational, nonordered, boundless sea.

> If the current flooding of Germany is not energetically restrained by state-driven measures . . . then we face not only the national loss of our eastern provinces, but also, in the imminent future, the inundation of the nationally unmixed regions of Germany.[17]

This was, of course, not an ordinary flood but a metaphorical one; for it was not elemental water but Slavs from the East who were the perceived threat—Slavs who were migrating westward, reversing the directionality of imperial diffusion, and entering German space in ever greater numbers.[18]

Effi Briest finds its setting in the landscape of this purported "Slavic threat." Fontane both chooses prominently Slavic Outer Pomerania as the primary setting for the novel and identifies the agent of the conflict driving the plot (i.e., the seduction of Effi) as a "half-Pole." By attending to the strategies through which the novel engages this cultural-historical context, a reading emerges positioning the Slavic flood within wider considerations of the German nation and imperialism.

Symbolic Geographies

Fontane's novel appeared in 1895, during the high period of German imperialism; the nation's colonies in Africa had been acquired in the previous decade, and plans for territorial seizures in China and the Pacific were already well under way. Germany, in the minds of many, had finally taken its place alongside the great European colonial powers, and support for the colonial project was widespread. But there were now multiple forms of colonization at play, such that, in the late nineteenth century, the concept of "colonial expansion in the East" held multiple meanings.[19] The coastal naval, shipping, and heavy industrial concerns championed territorial acquisitions in the Orient with particular agitation for a military and trading base in China, a goal attained in 1897 with the takeover of Kiautschou.[20] Meanwhile, proponents of the inner colonization of the Eastern Marches were striving to attract colonists and resources to the outlying, sparsely populated regions of Prussia with growing Slavic majorities. These two colonial Easts represented alternate and, to a certain extent, competing concerns within the larger German imperial project. Contrapuntal readings of Fontane's novel seeking to address the specificities of Germany's imperial history must, therefore, attend to the historical discourses of both German "inner" and "outer" colonialism.

Such a reading might begin with an overview of the mental map generated by *Effi Briest:* which spaces are brought into representation, by which means (are they visited, discussed, imagined?), and in which relation do they stand with respect to each other? Within the historical context of imperialism, relations of center and periphery are particularly significant. Where such spatial organization is present, we must identify the categories of difference employed to distinguish between the spaces and inhabitants of each: which qualities, experiences, and expectations are mapped onto center versus periphery?

Effi Briest's mental map charts out the hierarchical structure of the empire. The imperial metropolis of Berlin is positioned as the center of wealth, power, culture, and social prestige, a central hub around which a series of concentric peripheries is organized: the working-class outskirts of the city, the surrounding countryside of the landed aristocracy, the eastern frontier of the nation, and the colonial periphery of the globe. Each of these spaces gains its meaning and ascribed place in relation to the organizing principle of Berlin.

For the Prussian aristocracy (non-Prussian Germany is absent in the novel), Berlin is the central axis around which their world of meaning and reference revolves. After years spent in Outer Pomerania, Innstetten's social and professional advancement is rewarded with a promotion that brings him from this periphery to the center of Berlin, a move that he and Effi celebrate for its promise of increased social prestige. The reader shares this expectation; earlier in the text, Effi and her mother traveled to Berlin on an extravagant bridal shopping trip, and they experienced the city as the center of elegant *flânerie;* Effi and her mother moved through an upper-class world staging its wealth and power in luxurious hotel lobbies, fashionable cafés, and celebrated shopping avenues. In turn, Berlin became a commodity of sorts: while shopping for the latest fashions, attending the theater, and rubbing elbows with the metropolitan elite, Effi and her mother collected eagerly awaited news, impressions, and anecdotes that would make them the center of attention when they returned to their social circle back home.

The city of Berlin is itself organized according to a center-periphery model common to the turn-of-the-century metropolis.[21] As they plan their move to the capital, Effi is very concerned that she and Innstetten find a place to live located in the center of the city. While their new residence shouldn't be excessively expensive, it should nonetheless be "elegant" and located in the western, Tiergarten quarter surrounded by members of their class. Effi and Innstetten move into an apartment just off the famed Kürfurstenstraße and are easily integrated into privileged society.

Effi's taste of the social high life is, of course, short-lived. After Innstetten learns of her former affair with Crampas and casts Effi out of his house, the disgrace of her social fall is marked spatially as a marginalization to the outskirts of the city. Effi moves from the elegant Tiergarten quarter to a small and plain apartment in the area surrounding the Anhalter train station, where the desolate view from her window looks over the train tracks leading out of the city. This peripheralization is not only horizontal (having been relegated to the city's margins) but also vertical: she no longer lives on the *bel étage*[22] but instead on the rather pedestrian fourth floor.

Berlin's role is thus one of providing a central social referent and point of focus, spatially organizing social hierarchies and power differentials within the German center. As Germany's capital and seat of governance, Berlin also plays a dominant role organizing the nation's political and economic relationships with the global colonial periphery. However, there are marked differences between the ways in which the German relationship to overseas colonization and its relationship to the inner colonial Prussian East are represented; whereas the signs of German governmental power interests pervade—and indeed symbolically organize—the landscape of the Prussian East, they are absent in the case of the Orient, which figures instead as the object of individual—that is, noncollective—initiative and concern. In regard to the Orient, Berlin might have provided a point of coalescence in which individual desires were orchestrated into a collectively shared narration of German-Oriental relations (perhaps one furthering state-driven colonial interests in the region), but the city is instead that space in which these individual desires are rather systematically expunged. Effi expresses a strong desire to purchase Oriental objects while on her bridal shopping trip in Berlin, but her mother rejects these ideas, and there is no further mention of them in the text (which also lacks any reference to a colonial import-export industry similar to that which pervades Gustav Freytag's earlier depiction of Breslau). Similarly, the Chinese ghost (and the Oriental desires he represents) loses his haunting function when moved from the periphery into the center: a cutout image of the Chinese accompanies Effi and Innstetten when they relocate to Berlin, but it is soon forgotten, and Effi does not sense the ghost's presence while in Berlin. We recall that the Chinese man himself arrived in German space due to individual, not state, initiative: he was brought to Kessin by a shipping merchant who was not even German (his identity is left ambiguous, he is perhaps English or Danish), and there are no links connecting the Chinese to any German state-driven interests in the region: for the imperial center, he does not exist.

The adjacent East, in contrast, is very much the object of imperial concern; even though Outer Pomerania is both in Prussia and within the borders of the German state, the space is constructed as peripheral, even external, in the text, and managed as such from the imperial center.

Effi had imagined her future home in Kessin to be "a half-Siberian place,"[23] a term resonant with references to Eastern Europe as "Half-Asia" (*Halb-Asien*) popular in the late nineteenth century. This term was first introduced in 1876 by Karl Emil Franzos in his collection of short stories set in Eastern Europe and released under this eponymous title.[24] In the decades that followed, Franzos published several more volumes of his Eastern European tales, always including the term *Half-Asia* in his titles, perhaps because it sold well, but also because he was invested in this particular construction. His stated intent was to depict the culture of the Eastern Jews who lived in Eastern Europe as the product of two major civilizational influences. In the foreword to his first edition, Franzos gives this explanation.

> In the political and social relations of these lands, we find a singular intersection of European *Bildung* and Asian barbarism, of the European drive towards progress and Asian indolence, of European humanity and . . .

> wild, savage feuds between nations and belief communities. . . . [They are] neither as civilized as Germany nor as barbaric as Turan, but instead a mixture of both—*Half-Asia*![25]

Franzos's overarching argument was that the Germans should expand their sphere of cultural influence eastward into this "half-Asian" space to liberate the Jews residing there from the barbaric, Eastern, Asian influences from which he claimed they suffered. In this purported mix of Western "civilization" and Eastern "barbarism," "Half-Asia" was a large hybrid border region separating two continentally defined cultural groups, the exact location of which remained ambiguous. Prussia's own eastward expansion (i.e., the Polish Partitions) had resulted in a shared border with Russia in a region of mixed German-Slavic populations—so where did Franzos's "Asiatic barbarism" end? In the popular imagination, "Half-Asia" came to be mapped onto all non-German space in the East, including Polish regions, as one East Prussian author noted as he looked to the Polish regions in the south: "This 'Half-Asia' . . . doesn't just start at the Danube and the Don, it surely already begins on the southern border of our province."[26]

Effi's reference to "Half-Siberia" reflects this mental mapping of the East and would have signaled in the contemporary reader a liminal zone positioned outside of the spatially conceived German nation and into which the sphere of Asiatic, primitive-barbaric cultural influence extended. Therefore, while the depiction of her future home in "Half-Siberia" is partly a bid to secure a new fur coat for her dowry, it also reveals Effi's perception of the move to Kessin as a form of peripheralization. Perhaps she won't be going as far as St. Petersburg or Archangel on the White Sea, she ponders, "but I'm on the way there."[27]

Effi's expectations of "Half-Siberia" are met in the colder eastern climate, the barren, desolate landscape, and the sparse population consisting largely of Poles and Kashubes. Immediately upon entering the area, Innstetten describes to Effi the local population he has been brought in to govern.

> The rural population . . . they are a different kind of people . . . in terms of both their ancestry and their contemporary ties. Heading into the interior, one finds the so called Kashubes, of which you have perhaps heard, Slavic people that have been here a thousand years and probably even longer.[28]

These Kashubian Slavs are "a different kind of people," the natives of the outback of Outer Pomerania. They create the Slavic landscape in which Kessin is conceptually located, further isolating this town from the imagined center of the German nation and placing it squarely in the territory contested by Bismarck's inner colonization campaign.[29]

After their honeymoon, Effi and Innstetten travel to their new home in Kessin, a journey itself marked as a move from the center into the periphery: they travel first by train from Berlin to Stettin and then to the outlying station in Klein-Tantow. Since the train line ends here, they continue their journey by carriage. While technological modernity may not extend this far east, German national interests do, and the text renders these interests legible in the symbolic topography of the region.[30] Central in this regard is the crossroads at which Effi and Innstetten arrive on their way to Kessin.

Effi will cross this intersection at three significant moments in her life, and in each instance, it is marked as a symbolic threshold. The first crossing occurs as Effi enters the space of her new married life for the first time, and the last, when she takes her final departure from it. At these moments, the intersection marks the transition between center and periphery, between German national space and adjacent frontier, between Europe and "Half-Asia" (or at least "Half-Siberia"). Between Effi's two threshold crossings into and out of the periphery, she approaches the intersection during an outing with Innstetten, and he shows her the grave of the mysterious Chinese. It lies off to the side, unmarked and forgotten—a static (and, significantly, *unliving*) trace of a past tie to the Orient no longer deemed important.

In contrast, the signs marking the state interests in the adjacent East are very alive and present. First, at this intersection linking Berlin to Kessin, one can also turn left and take the road to Varzin, where Bismarck maintains his regional residence. In 1894, the year prior to *Effi Briest*'s publication, Varzin had played a significant role in articulating an inner colonial agenda in the adjacent Polish periphery, because it was the site where the Ostmarkenverein was consolidated. Following his ascension to the chancellorship in 1890, Leo von Caprivi had systematically relaxed his predecessor's Polish policies. Frustrated at a perceived power shift favoring the Poles, two large deputations of landowners and officials (from Posen and West Prussia) made a pilgrimage to Varzin to express their support for Bismarck's former anti-Polish measures. The former chancellor enthusiastically received the deputations and delivered speeches critiquing Caprivi and supporting an acceleration of the inner colonization project. Later that year, the political momentum generated by these deputations led to the founding of the Ostmarkenverein (the Eastern Marches Society), the organization most aggressive in support of German inner colonial interests in the adjacent East.

This power-political resonance is anchored by the second defining feature of the intersection, namely, the inn located there. With its name—Zum Fürsten

Bismarck (To Prince Bismarck)—this inn at the crossroads invokes Bismarck's power and unifying function in the region; crossing the threshold from the center into the periphery transpires under his gaze, under his aegis; the paths from Varzin, Kessin, and Berlin all lead to this junction, joined under the sign of *Bismarck.*

And yet, as if to directly underscore the concerns of the emergent Ostmarkenverein, this symbolic control is itself disturbed by a powerful Polish presence. For the figure who invariably stands guard in front of Zum Fürsten Bismarck is the inn's owner, Golchowski—a "half-Pole."

> In front of the inn stood a broad-shouldered man of average height wearing a fur coat and hat . . . . "Who was that?" asked Effi. . . . "He looked like a *starost.*" . . . "He indeed looks like a *starost* [answered Innstetten] and is actually something of the sort. He's a half-Pole named Golchowski, and when we have an election here or a hunting party, that's when he's really in his element. He's a pretty dubious character who I wouldn't let out of my sight and who probably has a lot to answer for. But he pretends to be a loyal subject, and when the gentlemen from Varzin pass by, he all but prostrates himself in front of their carriages. I know that Bismarck also finds him repugnant, but what can we do? We can't afford to get on his bad side because we need him. He's got the whole region in his pocket, and knows how to run an election campaign like no one else, and he's said to be quite wealthy."[31]

As someone whose endorsement is necessary to advance one's political or social agenda, this "half-Pole" is more than a nuisance—he is a menace to Bismarck, standing in the way of his easy and direct control over this eastern region. All paths may lead to "Bismarck," but Golchowski stands as the gatekeeper regulating access and efficacy. And it is apparently his hybrid, "half-Polish" identity that enables him to hold such power: he is held to be duplicitous in character and able to switch loyalties as best serves his personal power interests. With the regional votes held squarely "in his pocket," it is not only symbolically that Golchowski stands gatekeeper "zum Fürsten Bismarck."

The Desire for the Exotic Orient

Initially, Effi perceives her move into this periphery as holding the promise of a certain—albeit civilized and restrained—sense of exotic adventure consonant with her sense of moving to "Half-Asia." Effi is intrigued by Innstetten's descriptions of the region's inhabitants, but more than the Poles and Kashubes, she tells Innstetten that she anticipates "a whole new world here. All sorts of exotic things. Isn't it so? . . . A whole new world with maybe a Negro or a Turk, or maybe even a Chinaman."[32] Thus, even prior to Innstetten's introduction of the specific local Chinese figure, Effi had indicated that, for her, the Chinese represent the ultimate manifestation of the exotic, and her language reveals an almost childish sense of anticipatory pleasure at the thought of encountering one. However, when Innstetten incidentally affirms that a Chinese had indeed once lived in Kessin, and then gestures toward his grave just over the dunes, Effi's fascination suddenly shifts to anxiety. Although she does not yet know anything about the life or death of this Chinese man in Kessin, the mere thought of the Oriental figure conjures negative associations: Effi claims that "there is something sinister about Chinamen," then immediately conjures his image as a ghost, positions herself as the object of his malice, and anticipates that he will haunt her bedside at night.[33] In the months that follow, her predictions seem to come true; Effi's sleep is regularly disturbed by what she assumes to be the ghost of the Chinese; she hears the sound of his shuffling slippers in the room above her bedroom, and she senses his presence fleeting past.

Given the tendency for these apparitional visitations to take place at night, when Effi lies alone in bed, connections are often drawn between the Chinese and Effi's erotic economy. If we interpret the repeated lurkings of the Chinese as the haunting return of repressed sexual desire, the ghost is easily read as a manifestation of the Freudian "uncanny."[34] There is much to support this reading, first and foremost the frequent suggestion that Effi is pressured into repressing her sexual desire for the sake of achieving social station. Given his good looks and professional status, Innstetten seemingly presents the ideal husband, but underneath this thin veneer, the problematic nature of his marriage to Effi is readily apparent. Prior to Effi's birth, Innstetten had courted Effi's mother, and he now asks for Effi's hand without ever having met her as an adult—if not a case of misguided love-object substitution, then, at best, a choice reflecting an arbitrary, class-based spousal selection. Despite the presence of incestuous suggestion, and despite the fact that Effi does not know Innstetten, her mother coaches her to grasp the opportunity to achieve social standing: "If you don't say 'no,' which I would hardly expect my clever Effi to do, then, at twenty, you will already have achieved a position that others don't reach until their forties."[35] Effi accedes to her mother's insistence that love ranks second to social position, and the engagement is decided immediately, without any period of courtship. The text thus rapidly juxtaposes scenes of Effi divulging secrets of her mother's former lover to her childhood friends with the event in which Effi is presented by her mother as a bride to this very same man. In the incompatibility of these two scenes, the text conveys a disturbing tension underlying Effi's subsequent marriage to Innstetten, a discomfort heightened by the lack of access to Innstetten's point of view, for the text never presents or clears his incentive for pursuing marriage to Effi.

Meanwhile, the reader has been introduced to Effi as a young "child of nature," inhabited by emphatic emotions that she must learn to control: "Not so wild, Effi, not so impassioned," scolds her mother as Effi rushes to embrace her. "It always worries me to see you acting like this."[36] Effi's mother's discipline reveals a concern for her daughter's future standing within elite society, where open expressions of an impassioned nature would threaten her class membership. During the period of high imperialism, female desire was increasingly read as dangerous and subversive, which, as Anne McClintock has shown, was an Othering strategy directly linked to a larger colonialist worldview. The aristocratic, imperialistic center identified itself against a global periphery inhabited by colonized subjects marked as less civilized and thus less able to control animalistic drives. In casting the self-Other dichotomy in these terms, sexuality, even uncontrolled emotionality, gained a stigmatization that was, in turn, brought back into the metropolis to chart internal social hierarchies. Strategies by which "degenerate" sexual excess was inscribed onto the racial Other of the distant colonies came to be projected onto the urban "dangerous classes" (the working class, criminals, prostitutes, etc.) at home.[37] Strict codes of sexual conduct thus became a means of disciplining the boundaries of aristocratic identity.

As the new wife of a popular and ambitious *Landrat,* Effi must conform to aristocratic expectations of proper social decorum. That this involves a restraining and suppression of libidinal expression is reinforced throughout the text, as reflected in conversations Effi has with various members of the local gentry. Fontane's novel is filled with the disciplining gossip of aristocratic characters who carefully enforce distinctions between female behaviors they find "charming" and those they condemn as unacceptably sensual. They variously lament the lack of upbringing in children they perceive as behaving in a sexually precocious manner,[38] criticize the indecent cut of Effi's dresses,[39] etc. Effi is surrounded by the bespectacled, critical gaze of her predominantly female class elders who appraise her every move.

Even in the privacy of her own home, in her relationship with her husband, Effi's libidinal energies are subject to discipline. Innstetten is emotionally cool, adopting a rather distant and paternal stance vis-à-vis his child-bride. His "rather tired caresses"[40] fall short of the sensuality and romance Effi seems to desire. After returning from the last of their seasonal social visits, she expresses her dissatisfaction to Innstetten: "You could give me a kiss, but you never think of that. During the whole, long ride, you were frosty as a snowman. And always the cigar."[41]

Although Freud wouldn't write his *Unbehagen in der Kultur* (*Civilization and Its Discontents*) until much later (1930), it was this phenomenon of sexual repression that he hoped to account for. Freud claims European culture to be the world's most civilized, but he attributes this degree of development to the ability of white men to suppress their natural drives (Innstetten's compensatory turn to the cigar fits in well in this regard). Freud also registers the threat attending this civilizing process: that the abject element one struggles to rid from the self through repression does not disappear but looms at the periphery of the self, defining its contours and ever threatening to infiltrate through its protective border. The uncanny is the manifestation of such a repressed element—one whose strength of presence has allowed it to stage a successful return. The form it takes is typically a metaphorical or metonymical sign representing the repressed element. The Chinese—little more than a piece of local folklore prior to Effi's arrival—only gains agency once Effi has animated it with the suggestive force of her projection: her repressed desire brings the Chinese to life.

For Effi, the Chinese figure lends itself as a site of such projection due to her association of the erotic with the Orient (a term that she loosely associates with Turkey and Morocco as well as India and China). Long before she imagines the Chinese at her bedside, Effi engages the question of her own sexuality through a coded Orientalist idiom. In lieu of any direct conversation about sex or attraction, for example, Effi expresses a desire to stock her dowry with Oriental objects for her bridal bedroom—objects conveying direct erotic connotation: a Japanese screen for the bed, black with golden, long-beaked cranes, and a lamp that will cast a red glow over the room.[42] Her mother's immediately negative reaction indicates that, even in this indirect form of expression, Effi has crossed a line of propriety.

At the same time as she longingly associates the Orient with the erotic, Effi also displaces the danger that might result from acting on these desires onto the same sign. The motif of marital infidelity—and the negative consequences that threaten the women involved—runs through the entire text, foreshadowing and framing Effi's own eventual tragedy. Yet when she directly considers this theme at the beginning of the novel, Effi appears to reject any true sense of danger for herself, displacing it too onto the Orient. Early in the novel, for example, Effi and her childhood friends sink a bundle of fruit peels over the side of their rowboat.

> "They say they used to throw poor, unfortunate women out of boats and make them sink, due to infidelity, of course."
>
> "But not here!"
>
> "No, not here," laughed Effi, "that sort of thing doesn't happen here. But it does in Constantinople."[43]

Effi hereby displaces the sensually erotic—as well as the danger potentially arising from acting on it—onto a distantly imagined Orient. This displacement strategy functions as a *system-stabilizing* mechanism in the maintenance of social order, because it allows Effi to deny the presence of these elements in her own life. Of course, the repressed sexual element finds a path of return as manifested in the uncanny Chinese, but this ghost remains a merely spectral figure; while Effi often suspects his presence, he never physically enters her space (i.e., he never figures as an actual, material threat). Perhaps more significant, the apparition doesn't enter social reality: he doesn't appear to more than one person at a time, so that social consensus regarding the truth and meaning of his existence is never established. The Chinese thus exists separately for the individual characters in the novel, each of whom experience him according to their own personal preinclinations. Innstetten seems to be presciently aware of this fact as he warns Effi of the preferability of the Chinese ghost to that which he might represent: "You are free to think whatever you will about ghosts. But beware of that which is out of the ordinary [*das Aparte*]. . . . It may seem very alluring, . . . but one usually pays for it with one's happiness."[44]

The Seductive Slav

Effi, of course, will fail to heed Innstetten's warning. In entering into an affair with Major Crampas, she will succumb to that which is "alluringly out of the ordinary" (*das Aparte*); the price of this transgression will be her happiness. In this equation, Crampas has come to replace the Chinese ghost, and a closer look at the definition of *Aparte* sheds light on the ease with which this substitution could take place. The term not only refers to the "unusual and interesting" but also, in its French origin—*à part*—to that which exists separated, or *at the margins* (*abgesondert* or *beiseite*).[45] In the structure of the narrative, Crampas inhabits this position of *das Aparte;* he is not a member of the social collective but instead hovers at its boundaries, seeking admission. Representing qualities, values, and aspirations that have been rejected by the disciplining forces of the collective, he also becomes an enticing manifestation of the socially repressed. Crampas becomes threatening because he does not respect the boundaries demarcating the social spaces from which he has been excluded; he will violate the sanctity of Effi's marriage as well as the set of conventions that circumscribe and define her class and nation.

Therefore, while the Orient functions as a distant, absent, and system-stabilizing repository upon which Effi can map her socially censured desire, the adjacent East reveals itself to be the source of the *destabilizing* reintroduction of this repressed element back into the German social system. In the predominantly Slavic Prussian East, the Polish Major Crampas is dangerously *present,* engaging Effi's desire in an immediately threatening way. As he strategically plans and executes his seduction, it is Crampas who introduces the central violation and destabilization of social order around which the entire plot of the novel turns.

Crampas is a free spirit who refuses the restrictions of social convention. In stark contrast to the Germans depicted in the novel, the "half-Polish" Crampas refuses to suppress his desires, restrain his emotions, or acquiesce to the dictates of Prussian social order. In this role, he joins a host of Polish and Slavic characters that feature prominently in Fontane's oeuvre, beginning with his first novel, *Vor dem Sturm,* of 1878. Set in the Prussian East and depicting the relationship between two aristocratic families, one Polish and one German, issues of national identity play a central thematic and structuring role, particularly regarding the question of whether a Pole can ever become a loyal Prussian subject, an option the novel ultimately rejects.[46]

Fontane's engagement with Polish characters continues through such works as *Schach von Wuthenow; Unterm Birnbaum; Cécile; Irrungen, Wirrungen;* and *Mathilde Möhring.*[47] While Fontane's Polish figures are diverse and irreducible to any singular stereotype, they nonetheless share a common narrative function in his texts. Typically, they are not the main protagonists but secondary figures who manifest those behaviors and attributes the Prussians themselves are shown striving to repress. They thereby become the embodiment of "everything that the up-and-coming German petty bourgeoisie abhorred at the end of the nineteenth century as that which had no future, no security."[48] The Pole enjoys a richness of experience denied to those who adhere to social convention, and thereby alternately provokes and enthralls the main German protagonists, presenting a threat to their social order. In *Mathilde Möhring,* for example, the title figure struggles to keep her intended husband, Hugo Großman, away from his friend, the Polish theater actor Rybinski, because she fears the influence of this passionately eccentric theater actor: "Rybinski was a threat."[49] Once she marries Hugo, Mathilde further limits his contact with his Polish friend, while seeking to instill in her husband a Prussian sense of "order and discipline" (*Zucht und Ordnung*). When the married couple attends a theater performance, Hugo is distracted and spends the evening "thinking about Rybinski and envying him his life of freedom in the arts."[50] Later that evening, Hugo catches a chill from the strong wind symbolically originating in the Polish Carpathian mountains and dies from the ensuing illness. Both symbolically and literally, the text locates the Slavic East as the source of threat.

Fontane's fascination with this East and his concern with the role played by ethnic Poles in Prussian society long preceded his career as a novelist, as evinced by his reception of Gustav Freytag's *Soll und Haben* in 1855. Fontane wrote an exceptionally positive review of the novel—he found that *Soll und Haben* surpassed the English novels from which Freytag had drawn aesthetic influence, and claimed that the novel marked the dawning age of modern German realism. Within this context of overwhelming praise and literary affirmation, it is instructive to consider his differing assessments of Freytag's depictions of Jews and Poles: while Fontane strongly criticized Freytag for his excessively negative portrayal of the former, he lent his full support to the manner in which Freytag addressed the Polish question. In doing so, Fontane cites a passage central to my own treatment of *Soll und Haben* as a German colonial novel. In the scene in question, the protagonist, Anton Wohlfart, stands looking out over the fields of the German estate he manages in Polish Prussia. The narrator has consistently referred to Anton as a German "colonist," and now Anton proudly claims this identity for himself, positioning the Poles as the object of his colonial endeavors.

> I stand here now as one of the conquerors who, for the sake of free labor and human culture, have taken control of this land from a weaker race. We and the Slavs: it is an old struggle; and with pride we find that formative culture [*Bildung*], the desire to work, and economic strength are on our side.[51]

"This is not only refreshing for a German and Prussian heart," comments Fontane, "it is also just as true as it is beautiful. The Polish system (*Polenwirtschaft*) has led itself down the path to destruction; Prussia is the state of the future."[52]

In Fontane's own fictional writing, this notion of a broken Polish state being superseded by the Prussian "state of the future" is brought into representation through the depiction of Poles as fractured, stateless elements drifting among intact Prussian communities. It is as if the central Polish collectivity had self-destructed, scattering its remaining members in all directions. Fontane's Polish characters tend to have arrived at the narrative scene from some unspecified, distant elsewhere, and while, as in the case of the Ladalinskis in *Vor dem Sturm,* they may be joined by immediate family members, these families tend to be broken (Ladalinski is widowed and raises his children with the help of a housekeeper), and they are never part of an intact, local Polish community, even where the historical setting would have allowed for this. Instead, the Poles figure as permanent outsiders. The Ladalinskis are never really at home in the Prussian landscape; their ties to their new regional residence are strained, and their attempts to assimilate into Prussian society fail because, at heart, the Ladalinskis remain tied to their Polish identities and to the dream of a reinstated Poland.

In *Effi Briest,* we find that the difficulties Slavs face in their attempts to join German society are not just political but also due to heritable qualities of racial difference. When Effi and Innstetten attend the fateful New Year's party (after which Crampas's seduction will take place), Effi meets Ritterschaftsrätin von Padden, a woman whose physiognomy reveals visual signs of a Slavic lineage, which, in turn, is linked to implications of unbridled sexual excess. Von Padden thus "attempted to counterbalance what nature had bestowed on her from the heathen, Wendish side, especially in the form of prominent high cheekbones, with strict observance of the Germanic Christian faith."[53] It is unclear whether von Padden's Wendish origins leave her "naturally" inclined toward overabundant sexual desires or whether her high Slavic cheekbones arouse this suspicion in her German aristocratic peers. Either way, von Padden's social strategy involves a highly performative religiosity that finds its main expression in the ardent suppression of the sexual impulse—a suppression that von Padden is eager to discuss. She pryingly inquires into Effi's "satisfaction" in her marriage, and into the presence of any "temptations." When Effi hesitates with her answer, von Padden enjoys a moment of triumph and lectures Effi.

> The main thing, my dear young woman, is to fight. One always has to wrestle with one's natural instincts. And when one holds them down and almost wants to cry out because it's so painful, that's when the sweet angels rejoice.[54]

While Frau von Padden has negotiated a social identity based upon a celebratory self-negation of her (supposed) natural inclination toward the sensual, the Major von Crampas has evidently made no attempt to bring his own Slavic side under control. Indeed, Crampas is regarded with disdain among the Prussian aristocracy due to what they perceive as his complete disregard for the social codes regulating sexual conduct. Crampas has a reputation as a philandering ladies' man (*Damenmann*) and is therefore socially ostracized as a potential source of sexual threat—a threat that is consistently attributed to his identity as a "half-Pole." Concerned that his wife is showing too much interest in Crampas, Innstetten warns Effi of his character.

> He's one of those half-Poles, not very reliable, not in anything, actually, least of all with women. He's a gambler. He doesn't gamble at the game table, but he gambles his way through life, and you have to keep your eye on him.[55]

In the overdetermined reference to "gambling," the text evokes and refigures a common nineteenth-century anti-Polish stereotype. The "gambling Polish aristocrat" had no sense of personal or social responsibility but instead devoted his life to the pursuit of hedonistic pleasure, most often by abandoning his agricultural estate in the East and gambling away his assets at the gaming tables in Paris.[56] The degenerate aristocrat is seen as both product and cause of the *polnische Wirtschaft* that, as we saw above, Fontane judged responsible for Poland's political and cultural demise.

In evoking this stereotype, its import resonates even in the act of its negation: Crampas doesn't gamble at the gaming table, but he is nonetheless cut of the same cloth as his compatriots who do. The implication of social irresponsibility and hedonistic tendencies are merely mapped from the financial onto the sexual realm: Crampas is willing to risk everything for the sake of fulfilling his immediate desires.

In addition to violating sexual codes of conduct, Crampas also violates social codes in ways that directly disrupt the Prussian social order, even going so far as to attack the written law underlying it. Fantasizing about a seal hunt on the beach, he is reminded by Innstetten that this is against the law. Crampas is irritated: "Does everything have to be so dreadfully lawful? All legalities are unamusing."[57] Crampas is chastised by Innstetten, who reminds him that he has been trained as a Prussian officer.

> Someone like you, Crampas, who came of age under the banner of discipline and who well knows that order and discipline [*Zucht und Ordnung*] are indispensable—a man like you really shouldn't talk like that, not even in jest.[58]

But Crampas does talk—and act—in this manner, disregarding Prussian civil and social dictates in the pursuit of personal pleasure. He is *das Aparte*—the disruptive element poised at the margins of the social order, threatening to dismantle the bonds of convention that hold it together.

The Slavic Flood and the Anxiety of Reverse Diffusion

The Chinese is an unfixed and elusive figure in *Effi Briest,* experienced and interpreted in different ways by the various characters of the novel.[59] Only Effi ever claims to perceive him as an actual ghost; she is also the only one to express fear in association with the Chinese. Innstetten, in contrast, seems to use the Chinese as a story he can tell to make himself appear more interesting (as an aristocrat living in a purportedly haunted house), or perhaps to frighten Effi as a means of establishing control.[60] Effi's nursemaid, Roswitha, meanwhile, rejects the notion of a Chinese ghost altogether and identifies instead with the tragic life story of a figure she views as distinctly human: "The Chinese are people too, and in most things they are probably just like us."[61]

Who is right? The narrative voice itself refrains from any authoritative comment that would resolve this plurality of interpretation and experience. Instead, the text maintains the instability of the Chinese and leaves the reader to deduce the nature of other characters in the novel based upon their reaction to this central polyvalent figure. Due to this role, Fontane considered the Chinese to be of central importance to his text. In a letter to his friend Joseph Viktor Widmann, Fontane writes about this subject.

> You are the first to notice the haunted house and the Chinaman: I don't understand how one can see past them. First of all, the ghost is interesting in and of himself, or at least I think so, and second, as you have noted, it's not just there for the fun of it, but is instead the pivotal point of the whole story.[62]

As the Chinese figures as a fundamental absence in the text, the other characters of the novel can use him as a projection screen for their own private needs and desires, which renders these accessible to the reader. But, in serving to bring aspects of the other characters into starker relief, the Chinese loses importance as an individual; his "true" story is erased in the multiple and conflicting narrations provided by the surrounding figures. He is truly spectral, becoming the screen on which the other characters can be more clearly viewed.

In stark contrast to the text's polyvalent treatment of the Chinese is the very deliberate and univocal portrayal of Crampas, who is singularly presented as an unfaithful and disloyal profligate. This is the central, stable sign of his identity, reinforced from multiple viewpoints over the course of the text: Innstetten warns Effi of Crampas's character, and Effi repeats these ideas in a letter home to her parents. Most significantly, however, the narrator himself becomes involved, presenting an authoritative affirmation from his omniscient perspective. His voice mimics Innstetten's tone, stressing infidelity at the very core of Crampas's identity.

> He was cavalier regarding chivalrous romantic adventure, but, to the same degree, he could be a good comrade. Naturally, all of it was superficial. Helping a friend and cheating him five minutes later were both things that his sense of honor allowed for. He did one and the other with unbelievable bonhomie.[63]

Crampas's character is thus confirmed at the meta-narrative level of the text. This narratory statement not only attests to the rumors of Crampas's sexual adventurousness but also introduces a second characteristic important for an understanding of Crampas's identity: his fundamental lack of loyalty, his ability to juggle "one and the other." Crampas is repeatedly referred to as a *half*-Pole, a miscegenetic embodiment of violated national boundaries. Crampas is thereby denied the unity of identity deemed prerequisite to the development of loyalty.

In the representational economy of the text, the "half-Pole" Golchowski shares Crampas's characteristic lack of fidelity, except that it finds its expression in political instead of sexual terms. Like Crampas, Golchowski straddles the German-Polish border, performing great allegiance to the Prussian government on the one hand, and organizing the regional (Slavic) votes on the other. The main difference between these two characters lies in their identifiability. Golchowski visibly presents himself as a "half-Pole." As he stands in front of his inn wearing an iconic Polish fur coat and cap, Effi readily recognizes him as a Slav ("He looked like a *starost,* although I have to admit that I've never seen a *starost* before").[64] Crampas, meanwhile, presents no such external signs of his identity and, accordingly, moves much more fluidly through German society.

This invisibility explains why the "superficiality" of Crampas's actions is so strongly criticized by Innstetten: Crampas's motives cannot be read on the surface because this surface itself is deceptive. Although repeatedly referred to as a "half-Pole," there are no further indelible signs indicative of a Slavic identity. He does not share, for example, Frau von Padden's high cheekbones, nor does he wear Golchowski's traditional Polish clothing. Indeed not even Crampas's name reveals a Polish background: "Crampas," as we discover later in the novel, is the name of a village on the island of Rügen and therefore might even be of Scandinavian extraction.

Indeed, Crampas is repeatedly associated in the text with things that cannot be identified based upon visual perception. Most significant, his first physical encounter with Effi takes place when their carriage is stalled before an underground stream referred to locally as a *Schloon.* Shortly before Effi leaves with Crampas, an acquaintance warns her of the nature of the *Schloon:* "It's not like one can see it. And that is the worst part about it, that's the source of the danger."[65] The landscape of the *Schloon* is dangerous, because its outwardly visible signs do not reveal the true nature of what lies beneath the surface: the road appears to be safe, but quickly gives way under the weight of the carriage, because the water has hollowed out the earth below. This structure provides the guiding metaphor for the various manifestations of danger in the text, and it is therefore significant that Crampas seduces Effi at the site of the *Schloon.* After all, he shares its essential nature: outwardly, Crampas appears to be no different than his Prussian counterparts: he wears the identity of a Prussian military officer of noble lineage (his name—Major *von* Crampas—even bears the distinction of nobility). The threat posed by Crampas as a half-Pole is not legible upon the surface but lurks as the truth underneath.

And how appropriate that the threat of the *Schloon* is that of water working to undermine the integrity of the landscape—flowing through it, undetected, hollowing it out—for this is the nature of the fear expressed by the discourse of the Polish flood. This association is further suggested by Crampas's close alignment with the element of water. Not only does he seduce Effi at the site of the *Schloon* and spend much of his time with her on or near the beach, but, when he appears for the very first time in the text, Crampas arrives at Effi's breakfast table still dripping wet from the swim he has just taken in the sea.

A metaphor favored by the political Right, "floodwater" conjured images of a natural, irrational force that required an urgent collective response. The

Poles posed a silent, impending threat to the German population in the Prussian East: as an element that "both seeped through the cracks in the German defenses and flooded German society . . . the Poles constituted a Slavic flood that would overwhelm the German empire."[66]

> [We in the Eastern Marches] can tell of the loss of German land [*deutsche Erde*]. Washed under, broken up, washed away. . . . Who didn't know of them, the farms that were wrested away by the Slavic flood? Many a bulwark that used to stand on the German language border and that seemed so solid and enduring has fallen victim to the surge of the Slavic sea. And many a bulwark still braving the onslaught of the enemy is threatened with the same fate.[67]

As a response to the flood metaphor, German settlement in the East was depicted as mounting the necessary defensive dike wall to protect against Polish infiltration. Under Bismarck, this inner colonization had been supported by a government apparatus brought in from the west to govern and control the region. Bismarck's role in organizing this national defense earned him the popular title of *Deichhauptmann* (dike captain).[68]

Innstetten's temporary peripheralization was a professional strategy he undertook to expedite his advancement up the hierarchical ladder of Prussian governmental positions. Effi was willing to relocate to the East because she recognized the benefits of Kessin as "a stepping stone" on the way to a higher social position.[69] The couple expected that, after spending a few years at this distant outpost, Innstetten would be able to return to the imperial center in Berlin with a position he would have been otherwise unable to achieve so quickly.[70] As a representative of the new social group that has risen with Bismarck, "the aristocratic officialdom" (*das adlige Beamtentum*),[71] Innstetten works his way into the chancellor's inner circle and ultimately gains a coveted post in Berlin—a return to the metropolis after an expedited tour in the "colonial periphery." While in the Pomeranian outback, Innstetten joins the inner colonial governmental apparatus and, as one of Bismarck's favorites, becomes part of the defensive dike against the Slavic flood in the East. He is accordingly received by the local aristocrats as defending Prussia by his very presence: "as long as we have men like Baron Innstetten, . . . we will be all right, our old Prussia will continue to endure."[72]

But Crampas has evaded this dike system to infiltrate German society, his symbolic alignment with elemental waters a reflection of his connection to an anti-civilizational, natural force, and to a primitive sexual virility. The conflict between center and periphery is thus played out symbolically in Effi's bedroom. When Effi fails to get pregnant a second time with her husband, her doctor recommends that she spend some time at a spa. But it is unclear how this will help the situation, which seems to be rather due to Innstetten's "tired caresses" and his barred access to Effi's sleeping chambers. Meanwhile, Crampas—the virile, peripheral Other—easily encroaches upon this space.

Crampas's status as agent of reverse-diffusional threat is further indicated by a prominent intertextual reference in the novel. Crampas repeatedly refers to Heinrich Heine as his favorite poet and ultimately brings one of his poems, "Vitzliputzli," into the space of the narrative by recounting the beginning of its story to Effi: The temple of the Mexican war god Vitzliputzli has been destroyed by the colonizing Spaniards leaving Vitzliputzli homeless and in search of revenge. Although Effi cuts off Crampas before he can complete the story, readers familiar with Heine's poem would know that Vitzliputzli decides to travel to Europe and take on a new, covert identity that will allow him to spread horror and pestilence throughout the population (many readings of the poem understand this to reference sexually transmitted syphilis).[73] Heine's poem ends with the ominous image of the formerly colonized now dangerously infiltrating into the space of the colonizer.

Crampas's attachment to Heine's poem suggests an identification with its themes of reverse diffusion and sexual incursion. When Effi complains that the poem is ruining her appetite, Crampas's suggestive reply—"I . . . determine my appetite entirely in response to the menu"—echoes the sexual metaphor of biting/consuming/devouring characteristic of both Vitzliputzli and Dracula.[74]

The figure of Crampas may lack the bloodthirsty vengefulness of a Vitzliputzli or the sinister planning of a Dracula, but it nonetheless shares the structure of their narratives: a virile subject from the periphery infiltrates the imperial center. Adopting the appearance of an "insider" allows each figure to move about rather undetected, and the virility of each (whether real or metaphoric) comes to threaten the very "body" of the imperial nation.

Transferred Hauntings

The Chinese apparition haunts Effi at those moments when she is most libidinously dissatisfied: as she sleeps alone on her first night in Kessin, or when Innstetten leaves town for several days. Significantly, with the introduction of Crampas, the Chinese apparition ceases to haunt Effi. This sudden disappearance occurs because, in the moment of his seduction, Crampas usurps the function of the Chinese as repository for repressed libidinal excess. No longer repressing her sexual desire, but quite directly acting upon it with Crampas, the energies that fueled the existence of the uncanny are rescinded, and the Chinese loses his function.

Effi seems to recognize this development shortly after her encounter with Crampas at the *Schloon.*

> Once, late in the evening, she stepped in front of the mirror in her bedroom. Lights and shadows flew back and forth . . . and she felt like someone was looking over her shoulder. But she quickly came to her senses. "I know, what it is; it wasn't him," and she pointed to the haunted room above. "It was something else . . . my conscience . . . Effi, you are doomed."[75]

Effi's sense of guilt has taken the place of her past libidinal suppressions, and the Chinese ghost does not appear again in the text. Meanwhile, the role of haunting Effi has been transferred to Crampas: when Effi and Innstetten travel on vacation to Rügen shortly after her affair with Crampas has ended, Effi stumbles upon the town named "Crampas," to her great alarm.[76] The anxiety initially introduced into the text via the uncanny figure of the Chinese ultimately comes to be mapped onto Crampas. This development follows the shift from a libidinal economy of repression to one of open expression; from the haunting of the Chinese to the affair with Crampas; and from the system-stabilizing projection of the erotic onto the distant Orient to the system-destabilizing introduction of sexuality via the Polish Crampas.

Contrapuntal readings of Fontane's novel have drawn attention to the semantic resonance of fear developed around the color yellow in the text.[77] If we follow this logic, we find that this sign, too, is gradually mapped from the Chinese onto Crampas. The "Yellow Peril" or *Gelbe Gefahr* was a well-established, widely circulating construct in the 1890s. Although this version of the German phrase did not appear until after the Sino-Japanese war of 1894/95, the terms *Gelber Schrecken* (yellow scare) and *Chinesenfrage* (Chinese question) had already reached public discourse.[78]

The color yellow is accordingly introduced in *Effi Briest* in conjunction with the figure of the Chinese—Effi finds the picture of him, in which he is wearing yellow pants, in the upper floor of the Kessiner house, where all of the rooms are painted yellow. Upon returning to the Kessiner house after a longer stay with her family, Effi notices the light shining in the front hall and is frightened because the light is yellow. The presence of this color has therefore come to signal an expectation of danger and threat that Effi associates with the Chinese.

With the introduction of Crampas into the narrative, however, the source of danger shifts, and the color yellow is dissociated from the Chinese to become aligned with Crampas instead. When Effi joins Crampas for horseback rides on the beach, the yellow sand is covered with yellow flowers (*Immortellen*), and the inn where she meets him after the start of their affair is also yellow. Perhaps most significant, however, are Crampas's letters that Innstetten fatefully stumbles upon in Berlin. These love letters—the proof of Effi's affair and the cause of her subsequent banishment and early death—have turned completely yellow with age.

Of course now, the color yellow also indicates the passing of time. The letters have aged, for several years have transpired since Effi ended her affair with Crampas. Yet Innstetten, who claims to still love his wife, and to not even be particularly enraged, nonetheless challenges Crampas to a duel, kills him, and ousts Effi from his home and life. He explains to his friend, Wüllersdorf, that these steps are necessary, not for personal reasons but, instead, in order to uphold the social structure of the national collective: "One is not just an individual person, one belongs to a larger whole, and it is this whole that we have to constantly consider."[79] Through his affair with Effi, Crampas has violated the border encompassing this larger whole, and Innstetten feels compelled to travel back to the periphery to ritually reinstate it. But he nonetheless questions his decision. Was he justified in avenging an act that took place so far in the past? How far back must an event lie to be considered outside of the sphere of relevance? Innstetten articulates this question through the idiom of physical borders: "The border, the border. Where was it? Did it exist? Had it already been crossed?"[80] Perhaps Innstetten is drawn to the metaphor of a physical border because Crampas's seduction was itself a border violation—a symbolic and literal violation of the national border between center and periphery that Innstetten was stationed to defend.

Indeed, Innstetten's connection to the Polish-German border is inscribed in the phonemes of his name: "in Stettin." Stettin is the port town that lies at the mouth of the Oder river, currently on the German-Polish border. In the late nineteenth century, Stettin was recognized as the last German stronghold prior to entering eastern territory dominated by Poles and Kashubes. In Fontane's novel *Vor dem Sturm,* for example, the Oder plays an instrumental role in organizing the symbolic geography of the text. The novel is set in an eastern landscape largely identified through its relationship to this river. Von Vitzewitz's castle lies on the river's western bank, and he is obsessed with defending this border at all costs against Napoleon's encroaching army (which threatens to attack from the east) because the river represents the true border of the body of the German nation in the text.

This same mental map of the nation is deployed in *Effi Briest* on a more subtle level. Here, Stettin—and the conceptual border it represents—is evoked in the orchestration of Effi's seduction. Innstetten leaves town, temporarily abandoning his symbolic border post and thereby leaving Crampas free to act unchecked: "Innstetten had only been gone for four days when Crampas arrived from Stettin."[81] Crampas thus symbolically violates the very border between center and periphery that Innstetten has been stationed to protect.

By casting a historically resonant symbolic topography, Fontane maps out a discourse of threat impending in the Prussian east. This threat is manifested in the figures of "half-Poles": themselves embodiments of social, racial, and cultural miscegenation, the half-Poles threaten to further undermine the border between self and Other—between center and periphery—in the adjacent, inner-colonial East. Read within this conceptual framework, Crampas's successful seduction of Effi appears as more than a mere violation of Innstetten's home and marriage—it is a reverse-diffusional violation of national borders.

The Orient, meanwhile, is not materially present in the text. Effi speaks of Oriental objects, but she never holds them in her hands; she conjures images of a Chinese ghost, but it never appears in front of her eyes. By the end of the novel, the Chinese—and the "Oriental" colonial East that he represents—have been almost completely forgotten; his private hauntings have given way to much more pressing matters of the adjacent East.

As increasing attention is paid to the contrapuntal analysis of German literature of the high imperial period, it will be crucial that we remain mindful of Germany's specific imperial past and that we attend to the multiple Easts that were at play in this history. In the case of *Effi Briest,* such awareness leads to a very different understanding of the novel's position vis-à-vis German imperialism. Fontane's text does not offer a critique of imperialism per se but instead suggests a prioritization of German imperial projects. The Orient figures as a mere object of fascination, a screen onto which desires and anxieties can be projected, but ultimately a space of little import for the German national collective. The adjacent East, in contrast, is a very real source of instability. The Polish elements in the East were threatening the regional power structures as well as the identity of the border separating center and periphery. The Slavic flood was creating cracks in the German defensive dike—leaving the latter in dire need of reinforcement.

Chapter 4

"Post-Colonial" Mappings: Cartographic Representations of Lost Colonial Space in the Interwar Period

Looking back at the literature published in the decades preceding World War I, we find a complex set of representations describing German presence in the Polish East in colonial terms.[1] Gustav Freytag's early, unencumbered depiction of German territorial expansion was followed by an entire genre of German colonial novels investigating the hardships attending colonial settlement in the Wild East. Set during the period of German inner colonization, these texts depicted the threats posed by unbounded space and the anxieties aroused by ambiguous lines of racial distinction. This literature responded with an elaborate construction of racialized space that allowed perceived threats of racial contamination to be described in the concrete terms of spatial threat. The discourse that emerged was so pervasive that it structured meaning in texts not overtly engaging its themes, as was seen in Theodor Fontane's *Effi Briest.*

World War I introduces a rupture in this colonial discourse as it responds first to the confidently anticipated German eastward expansion envisioned during the war, and then to the sudden, unexpected, and devastating loss of German state territory afterward, in the wake of military defeat. In the postwar period, attention shifts from discussions of how to best administer the Polish Prussian territories to those of how to get them back into German hands. German colonial discourse undertakes the seemingly paradoxical move of shifting from an emphasis on the demands of the present to a focus on the achievements of the distant past. At the same time, the models of racialized space developed in the nineteenth century undergo transformations into widely propagated popular theories about the essential nature of völkisch space in the present. In a specifically German articulation of the "post-colonial," narratives of past colonial accomplishment come to be mobilized to justify land claims in the present.

Wartime Dreams of Eastward Expansion

> I still consider the question of the Eastern Marches to be one of the most important policy issues, regardless of the reconfigurations that the World War brings to the current Prussian state border in the east and beyond it.[2]
> —Bernhard Fürst von Bülow (1916)

The former chancellor of the German Empire penned these words in a moment of wartime optimism. Germany's eastern offensive was showing signs of success, and Germans representing a wide range of political positions were envisioning various forms and degrees of eastward expansion.[3] Large segments of the population demanded the extension of Germany's eastern border to create a new buffer zone vis-à-vis Russia, and some even advocated the inclusion of recently occupied Russian territory in this plan. In this context of military success, Germans weren't questioning *whether* land in the east should be brought under German control, but instead, *how much,* and under what conditions.[4]

In his September Program of 1914, Chancellor Bethmann Hollweg had drafted a set of war aims focused upon the consolidation of German continental power. One of the central items on his agenda was the establishment of an organized *Mitteleuropa,* envisioned as an economic and military union of the Central European region under German leadership.[5]

Further to the right, the president of the Pan-German League, Heinrich Claß, had drafted a memorandum in 1914 on behalf of his organization calling for broad annexations of land in the East for the purpose of settling Germans and increasing Germany's size and power. Claß's plan called for the incorporation of sizable regions that were to be cleared of their non-German inhabitants; Poles and Jews were to be pushed out into their own, separately designated states.[6]

Although Claß's proposals were quite radical, studies of German war aims have shown that they were merely an extension of views espoused within the national mainstream.[7] On June 20, 1915, well over one thousand people signed a petition to the chancellor demanding that Germany's eastern border be extended into Russia, and that within this region, a border strip be evacuated for the purpose of German settlement. Exemplifying the extent to which such demands reflected social leadership, this petition is known as the *Professoreneingabe* (or *Intellektuelleneingabe*) due to the 352 university professors who were among those signing it.[8]

In the language of those promoting eastward expansion, most of the rhetoric either claimed the need to protect Germany from Russian aggression with a new buffer zone or fueled the collective desire to establish Germany as a world power (*Weltmacht*) by promising a future state with expanded borders and territory and resources under its control. But there were also ways in which the prewar colonial discourse was harnessed within this new context to promote expansionist aims. In direct appeals to the German colonial imagination, the East continued to be depicted as a wild frontier inviting civilizing intervention.

> The biggest mistake of European policy has been its acceptance of Russia as a nation of equal cultural status just because it wears the façade and has the material resources of a great power [*Großstaat*]. Russia is an Asian barbarian and therefore rightful hunting ground—or, because we aren't Huns, let us say "a workshop," virgin soil in which Germany's spirit and energies can be put to use constructively.[9]

This colonial East could thus be imagined extending far into Russia. This author may have rejected the pejorative wartime equation of Germans with the marauding Huns, but he nonetheless evokes the vast expanse of territory this people conquered. Yet even among supporters of the most aggressive forms of German eastward expansion were those who doubted Germany's ability to undertake a project of such magnitude and to establish the administrative presence and population density needed to dominate such grandly envisioned acquisitions. Recalling the failure of the prewar inner colonization project to increase significantly the presence of Germans in Prussia's Polish provinces, Germany's ability to handle an even greater amount of territory seemed questionable. Opponents of expansionist war aims stressed the failures of inner colonization in their arguments, and supporters responded with ever more radical suggestions for engineering the envisioned population. One plan involved the establishment of colonial protectorates (*Schutzgebiete*) under direct German control,[10] and an even more popular option involved settling the region with injured soldiers returning from the battlefields.[11] As plans and strategies proliferated, it became clear that, whether "protective border strip," "economic *Mitteleuropa*," or even "German colonial settlement into the Ukraine," many Germans were imagining significant extensions of German control beyond their eastern borders. Of interest to us here are the means by which colonial constructions of the East came to play a role in the articulation of these annexationist desires, and, perhaps more unexpectedly, the ways in which they were reconfigured after the war in the wake of Germany's defeat and territorial losses.

Dietrich Schäfer, a professor of history at the Berlin University, was one of the most prominent voices championing German territorial annexation during the war.[12] Closely aligned with both the Pan-German League and the Eastern Marches Society, Schäfer espoused their expansionist war aims and joined with Heinrich Claß to establish a war-aims committee;[13] he also played a central role in formulating and disseminating programmatic statements in the völkisch press and was a key player in the production of the *Professoreneingabe.*[14]

In 1916, Schäfer published a map of Europe—his "*Länder- und Völkerkarte Europas*" (plate 2. *Map of the countries and peoples of Europe*). In the following two years, he released eight revised editions of the map, each updated to reflect the current positions of battlefronts and shifting borders of control.[15] The maps were explicitly designed to justify the extension of German power into the East and are significant for the extent to which they bring colonial discourse into visual representation: through unique manipulations of conventional cartographic codes, the maps present the relationship between Germany and its eastern neighbors through a set of dichotomies—order versus chaos, developed versus undeveloped, modern versus archaic—that serve as both template and invitation for German expansion. These cartographic strategies resulted in a set of visual images widely adopted by cartographic propagandists and prominently reproduced in a wide range of maps produced and distributed throughout the interwar period. They are therefore worthy of closer investigation.

Schäfer, as he indicates in the four-page brochure accompanying all editions of the map, intends to show that the lands to the east of Germany lack the ability to govern themselves, and that the Germans are both best positioned to take on this task and most deserving of the resulting territorial spoils. In his earlier writings promoting German eastward expansion, Schäfer had often asked his readers to imagine a map of the East as they followed his line of argumentation ("Whoever glances at a map of the peoples of central Europe immediately notices . . . ," "A glance at the map of language distributions shows . . ."[16]). These imagined maps would allegedly provide the objective, scientific evidence Schäfer needed to back his claims. Now that he has turned his attention to producing a real version of this imagined map, he goes to great lengths to authorize it with all of the markings of cartographic accuracy. As a result, the map presents itself as a technologically advanced and scientifically objective product authorized to prove his previous arguments about Eastern European space.

The map's large size (116 × 86 cm.), rich coloration, and density of cartographic information indicate an investment of time and resources that lend the map an immediate air of institutional authorization. On the map, the image of Europe is framed by a detailed legend, precise scale markers, systematized marginal notes and titles, all presented in scholarly, typeset fonts. Inside this set of accrediting frames, the European continent is positioned with respect to the trajectories of meridians and parallels of latitude indicative of a conventional conic cartographic projection. While the map's title only promises information about state boundaries and ethnic distributions, the map further depicts topographic features including elevations, depressions, rivers (named), and streams (unnamed); it indicates railway lines and major transportation arteries, and offers an almost illegible profusion of place-names—often translated into multiple languages. In addition, each of the map's nine editions was updated to reflect the most recent wartime shifts in state borders and military fronts. This overabundant attention to topographic detail provides a background excess of informational "noise." More important than any potential to enhance the study of ethnic distributions, this topographical information enacts a strategic textual function—it signifies scientific endeavor and exactitude at the meta-level of the text, hence scholarly objectivity, and (again, given the collective resources needed to produce such a map) larger academic consensus.

Deploying conventions of scientific cartography (and not those, for example, of touristic, illustrative, or propagandistic mappings), Schäfer imparts to his text the aura of authority that adhered to the field of institutionalized geography after the turn of the century.[17] The map thereby claims to present accurate, objective, and disinterested information reflecting an empirical "truth" about the nature of European space.[18] But the very "scientific-ness" of the map is itself merely a textual strategy employed to authorize its visual arguments; Schäfer's map manipulates a further set of cartographic codes to deliver a politically persuasive message within this authorized frame.

The first code is that of surface coloration, which is used to signify the distribution of peoples in Europe. The continent is covered with a multitude of colored fields, but there is a meaningful discrepancy between the kinds of colors used in Eastern versus Western Europe. In the West, ethnic groups are represented by bold, saturated, primary (or near-primary) colors. This choice allows each group to be readily distinguished from its neighbors. Visual demarcations are enhanced by the frequent alignment of ethnic and state borders, which results in solid black lines separating distinct pools of bright color. There are several areas where an ethnic group extends over a state border, but each case appears to be reparable by a rational process of border readjustment.

Eastern Europe, in contrast, appears as an irrationally ordered space. While the western peoples are represented as solidly inhabiting their respective territories, the ethnic groups of the East appear indistinctly dispersed and spatially indefinite. They are all represented by nonsaturated, washed-out, pastel colors neither as visually dynamic nor as readily distinguishable from neighboring colors as those used in the West. Against these lighter hues, the black lines demarcating state borders, railway lines, rivers, and battlefronts create a prominent visual jumble that adds an additional sense of chaos and disorder. This coloration pattern makes it impossible for the eye to organize the contours of the ethnic landscape, with the result that the viewer can indeed not "see" any rational way of creating order out of this chaos. Had the ethnic groups in Eastern Europe also been represented with fully saturated colors, and had the use of black lines been limited to demarcating state borders, the visual chaos would have been reduced, and while the alignment of peoples and borders would perhaps not be as clean as in the West, it would certainly be much more rational than represented here. Imagining the map as it would appear were it uniformly colored highlights the connotative function of the disparate coloring patterns chosen by Schäfer.

Like the Eastern European peoples, the Germans too are dispersed over the Eastern European terrain; however, the different qualities of coloration visually indicate that the German distribution is of a different nature. Because the colors used to depict eastern ethnic groups are indeterminate, it is difficult to see coordinating dispersion patterns—when light green splotches are scattered over areas of even lighter green and light blue, the eye cannot apprehend them all at once to synthesize them into a meaningful whole. The Germans, meanwhile, are represented by the color red, a hue often chosen by makers of propaganda maps for its visual prominence; against the light pastel color wash in the East, the network of red dots, spots, and splotches representing German distribution is easily discerned and appears as a cohesive system.[19]

The order of German space is further suggested by an almost complete lack of minority ethnic presence within the red area representing it. While the Polish enclaves in Germany's western mining districts are indicated, their light coloring renders them visually "silent."[20] Other groups, meanwhile, are erased entirely. The map's legend (plate 3) is revealing in this regard: while the existence of Kalmucks, Mordvins, and "Kutzowalachen" (Aromanians) is indicated, Sorbs, Kashubes, and Jews are all missing. These are, of course, ethnic groups that would have disturbed the uniformity of the red area denoting the German Volk. Including them would have undermined the map's central message by showing that German space too was "jumbled up" like its Slavic neighbors to the east.

On the key, we further see that the Poles are represented by a shade of off-white containing a slight tinge of grayed pink. It is a color without presence, without visual force and density, nothing more than a radically desaturated hue of the red used to denote Germans. The legend also indicates that the people represented by this color don't exist independently. The bottom entry in the second column from the left presents their color swatch partially covered in geometrically aligned red dots that the key identifies as "Polish with German admixture." This relationship of intermixture is repeated with the Rumanians, Magyars, and Latvians, and in each case the Germans are superimposed upon this other ethnic base, in a dominating gesture that is never reversed—there is no category of "German with Polish admixture," for example. In addition, no other Volk is so "intermixed"—there is no "Polish with Ukrainian admixture," or "Magyar with Rumanian admixture." The map thus presents the argument that German presence in non-German space is somehow different from all other forms of minority presence across Europe, their copresence taking a unique form that must be further explored.

This sense of German uniqueness is enforced on the map itself (plate 1). Within the confines of Germany's state borders, areas containing significant Polish populations are only represented as "Polish with German admixture." Red dots are evenly distributed across these spaces, which, according to cartographic convention, suggests that Germans are evenly distributed over the area so covered. Yet the 1910 census clearly identifies significant stretches of land in Prussia with overwhelming Polish majorities—for example, areas where German presence was below 10 percent. These differences are erased through the homogeneous distribution of the red dots, a strategy that visually overwhelms the noncolor representing the Poles and creates the impression that Prussia's Polish regions are uniformly under German control and thus firmly anchored within the German state. Within German state borders, then, the presence of the Poles is silenced, and the diversity of population distributions reduced to an image of German-dominated homogeneity. The effect of this strategy is enhanced by the fact that it is not used in the depiction of any other areas of intermixed populations. Were the ethnic minorities of all states in the East subsumed under homogeneously distributed dots representing the majority population, then the map would appear to affirm the validity of state borders rather analogously to its representation of the West.

On the outside of the German state border, the evenly distributed red dots give way to localized clusters of red splotches that analogically represent specific areas of German presence (or, perhaps, dominance? The map leaves this issue vague). The border between Germany and Poland ("Congress Poland," although under Russian control, is represented as an independent entity on the

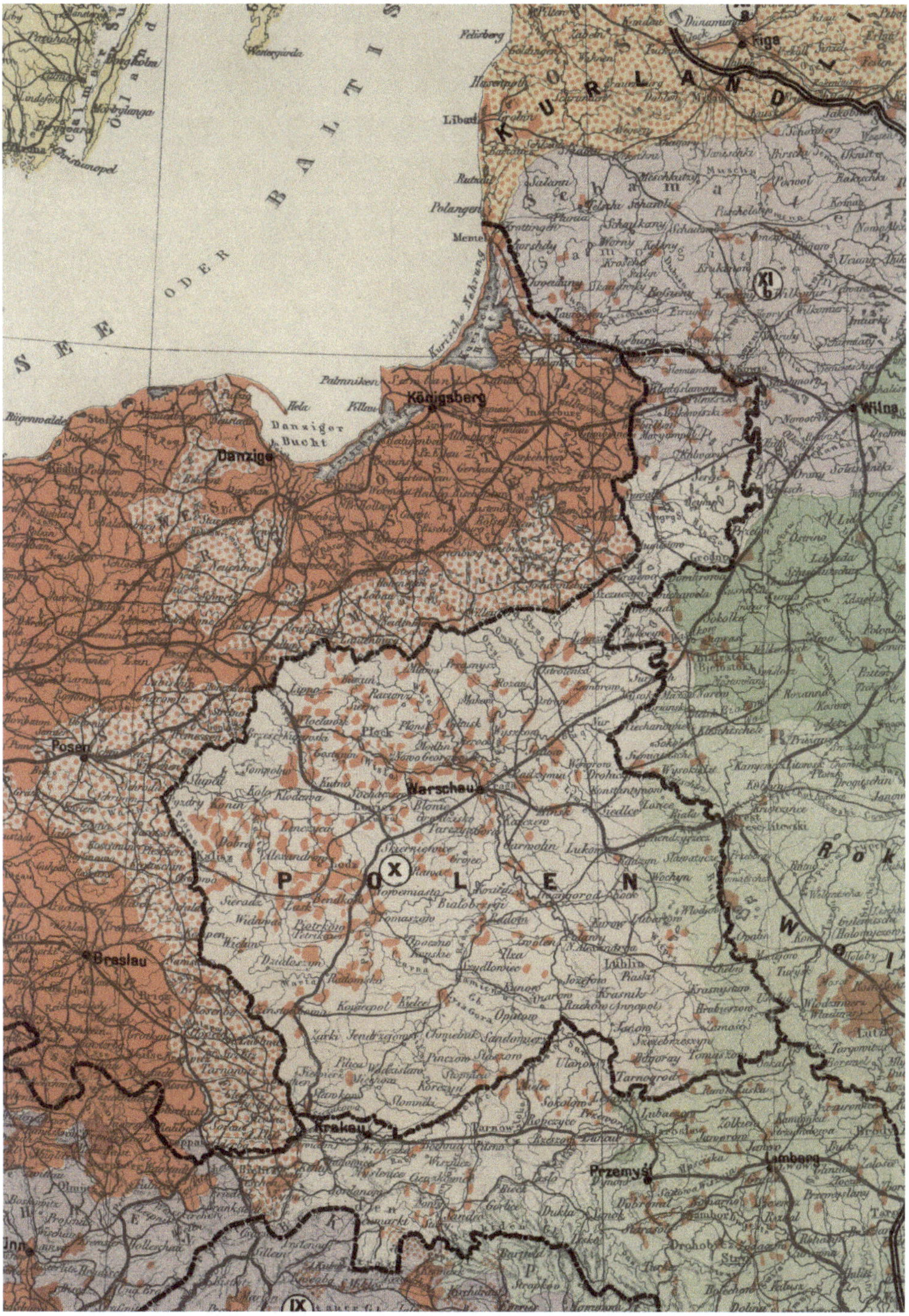

Plate 1. Compare the representation of German minority distribution patterns in the west with that of the Ukrainian minority in the east. The German population is depicted by a distinct sign system that is adjusted to emphasize the German border to Congress Poland, while the Ukrainian minority appears as a vague wash of color that seeps over the border.

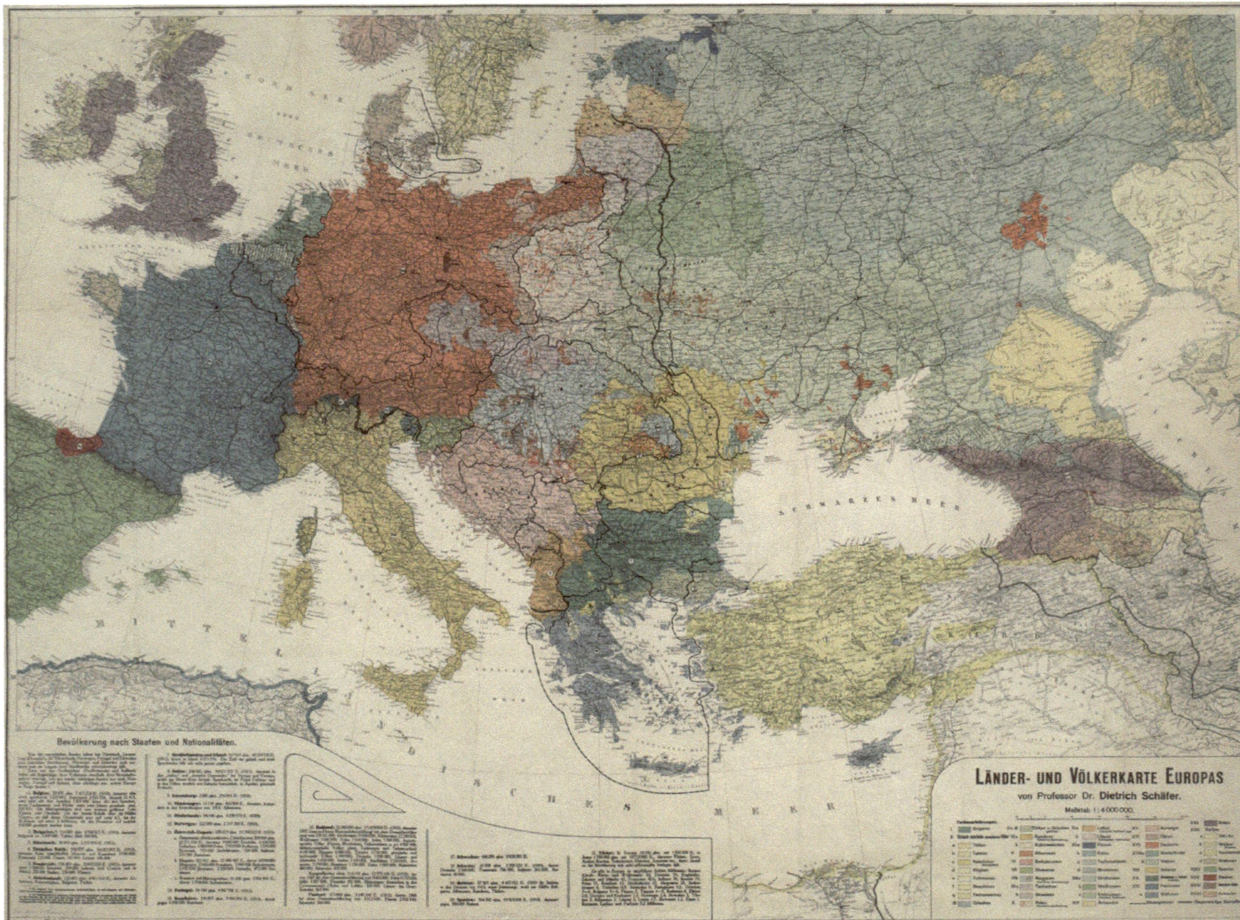

Plate 2. Dietrich Schäfer, "Länder und Völkerkarte Europas (Berlin: Reimer, 1916). Image reproduced courtesy of the Earth Sciences and Map Library, University of California, Berkeley.

Plate 3. The map's legend includes Kalmucks, Mordvins, and "Kutzowalachen" (Aromanians); while Sorbs, Kashubes, and Jews are all missing. Category X is "Poles with German admixture."

Plate 4. In the 1914 edition of the school atlas, the map of ethnic and language distributions in the German-Polish borderlands employ a consistent sign system that indicates Polish majorities in the area that would later become the "Polish Corridor." *Diercke Schulatlas für höhere Lehranstalten: Mittelausgabe* (Braunschweig: Georg Westermann, 1914), 144.

Plate 5. Beginning in the mid-1920s, the sign system used to depict population distributions in the borderlands steadily changed. In this 1928 edition, we see the Polish regional majorities visually erased through the use of a dual sign system that changes at the former German-Polish border. *Diercke Schulatlas für höhere Lehranstalten* (Braunschweig: Georg Westermann, 1928), 144.

map) is the only place on the map where a state border changes the sign system used to denote ethnic distributions. There is a great discrepancy between the cartographic codes used to represent the German minority in Poland's western regions and Poland's Ukrainian minority to the east. In the west, geometrically arranged red dots give way to analogic splotches, while in the east, a light green shade washes indefinitely over the border. Two separate sign systems suggest two separate phenomena. Attempting to attribute meaning to this difference, the viewer can only deduce that the nature of German and Polish intermixing changes once the German border is crossed, and that the German-Polish relationship is essentially different from the Polish-Ukrainian one.

Schäfer depicts a nonrational, inchoate, and irresolute distribution of ethnic groups over geopolitical space in the East. While firm ethnonational borders can be drawn in the West, population distributions in the East are too watered down and intermixed to allow for any such rational demarcation.

> The peoples of the West and of the North have achieved states grounded in national unity as products of their histories. Things are different in the East. . . . [There,] the peoples and population fragments have been so jumbled up by the course of history that it would be impossible to separate them by any continuous borders.[21]

The strategy is analogous to the colonial trope depicting a cartographic terra incognita: although eastern space is neither empty nor uncharted on the map (as was often the case in descriptions of overseas areas), it is nonetheless "empty," and boundless, and devoid of those qualities the map defines as "civilized." By showing the viewer that there is no possible rational congruence of ethnicities and political borders, the map visually undermines the idea of legitimate sovereignty arising in the region. Eastern Europe appears unspatialized, save for the framing function performed by the spread of red symbols marking German eastward settlement.

German settlement exclaves are not depicted with the dots of "admixture" but are regions of solid red; Germans are not "jumbled up," they have, instead, moved eastward to inhabit clearly demarcated spaces. These red patches have their own logic: against the jumbled morass of Eastern European ethnic groups, the Germans have staked a claim.

> The Europe that lies between the North Sea and the Black Sea is forced to collect its peoples into states that are not strictly divided by nationality. And amongst them, the German can demand to assume the position that it

> is his duty to claim due to a thousand-year-long history and his rank among the civilized nations [*Kulturnationen*].[22]

Schäfer has thus presented Germans with a conceptualization of Europe in which their country is located on the edge of demographic chaos. Against the solid ethnic-national blocks he depicts in the West, the washed-out, intermixed groups of the East visually stake no discernible territorial claims. Germans, with their long history and firm (visual) presence, have the right—and perhaps even the duty—to expand into this region. Although Schäfer was unsuccessful in achieving this desired expansion, the cartographic strategies he employed during the war would later come to dominate postwar cartographic depictions of the German-Polish Wild East.

Cartographic Education in the Postwar Period

In 1914, Germany's colonies in Asia and the Pacific fell quickly to the Allied forces, and German contact with its African colonies was almost completely severed for the remainder of the war.[23] Recognizing their compromised position, the German delegation arrived at the peace negotiations in Versailles prepared to negotiate an unfavorable compromise with regard to the colonies. But the territorial dispossessions that were exacted exceeded expectations: Germany was stripped of the entirety of its overseas colonies, which became mandates of the League of Nations, and it was forced to cede significant stretches of state territory on the European continent. Germany lost Alsace-Lorraine to France, Schleswig to Denmark, and Posen and large portions of West Prussia to Poland, which together amounted to approximately 13 percent of Germany's previous European territorial expanse.[24] With this loss of land came the loss of inhabitants—some 6.5 million, including 3.5 million identified as German.

Particularly difficult for Germans were the official explanations for these territorial decisions. The Allies presented the dispossessions as punitive measures undertaken to address wrongs committed prior to the war. Their report cited atrocities perpetrated by the Germans in their colonies, including various forms of forced labor and illegitimate tribal property seizure in addition to the destruction of native populations in the colonial wars of the early twentieth century. Such severe mistreatment of the natives, the Allies argued, proved that Germans were unfit guardians of fledgling populations. In the well-publicized negotiatory letters of the peace deliberations in Versailles, the Allied delegation summarized their position.

> The history of this German dominion, the traditions of the German government, and the ways in which these colonies were used as a base for raids on the agents of world trade make it impossible for the Allies and Associated Forces to give the colonies back to Germany or to entrust the German Reich with the responsibility for the education and upbringing of the people.[25]

In a similar move, the Allies justified the seizure of Germany's land in the East as compensation for the injustice introduced by the Polish Partitions of the late eighteenth century, and by the subsequent waves of Germanization enacted upon the population.[26] Germans were, in effect, being cast out of the European community of civilized nations.

Poland was reinstated after World War I according to terms outlined by President Wilson's Fourteen Points of January 8, 1918. In this document, Wilson officially introduced the "principle of the self-determination of peoples" that would guide ensuing peace negotiations. With the professed goal of creating a basis for lasting peace in Europe, each major ethnic-national group was to be given sovereignty over its own independent territory. The result of these international deliberations was the establishment of several new countries in Eastern Europe. Poles joined other Eastern European and Baltic populations that were sanctioned as legitimate national groups and granted political independence. Reaching from Finland in the north to Yugoslavia in the south, these new states formed a belt including Estonia, Latvia, Lithuania, Poland, Czechoslovakia, and Hungary. Accommodating these new countries involved significant territorial losses for Russia, Germany, Austro-Hungary, Rumania, Serbia, and Montenegro, and resulted in various degrees of border readjustments in every other Eastern European country. In the jigsaw puzzle of the postwar European map, half of the pieces had become unrecognizable due to changes in the outlines of their borders.

The contours of this new Europe were drawn by an interdisciplinary team of advisers assembled by President Wilson and known collectively as the "Inquiry."[27] Although similar commissions were established in other European countries, the Inquiry (as well as its successor, the American Commission at Paris) held a privileged position in the international arena; it was perceived to be more impartial and objective than its European counterparts because the United States had no direct territorial issues at stake in its recommendations.[28] Yet despite the fact that this new map of Europe had been drafted under the sign of scientific objectivity, there was widespread condemnation of its results. The dramatic realignment of national borders had unavoidably created a multitude of new minority populations overnight. Each new state could point to members of its majority ethnic group residing just over the border, and there were prolonged attempts to acquire territory bestowed upon each new country's respective new neighbors. Significant unrest continued throughout the early and mid-1920s, expressing itself in violent border skirmishes, on the one hand, and, on the other, in attempts to persuade the international community that the borders had been faultily drawn. In this postwar battle for hearts, minds, and *land,* maps became the weapon of choice.[29]

During the phase of peace negotiations, it became clear that maps depicting ethnic distributions would form the basis for decisions regarding border demarcations, and that each nation-state would need to articulate its territorial claims—and challenge those of its opponents—within an international arena delineated by conventions of scientific objectivity. German cartographers recognized their role in this process because they had the ability to scrutinize the statistics used by the Poles, and the authority to argue that Polish cartographic practices misled through deceptive representations of available data. Meanwhile, German geographers rushed to produce their own maps of German territory, a project neglected during the war in the drive to legitimize German desires for expansion. Now, the need for maps of German space had become critical, but German cartographers were proving ineffective at producing them. Prioritizing scientific accuracy over effective visual communication (they produced, for example, cumbersome maps charting demographic distributions on a village-by-village scale), they were often very complicated to read; produced as individual maps, they were difficult to circulate; and introduced later than those of their opponents, they ultimately played only a negligible role in the peace proceedings.[30]

A domestic audience was more successfully targeted. Here, there were three main goals: to naturalize the legitimacy of German territorial claims, to encourage public outrage at the loss of the eastern territories, and to maintain the German minority population in Poland as a "fifth column" that would strengthen and agitate for inclusion within the German state. German public resentment—on both sides of the German-Polish border—would be useful to the territorial revisionists because the legitimacy of Wilson's principle of self-determination was based upon its assumed ability to achieve peace in Europe. Insofar as German outrage could be characterized as both justified and threatening to such peace, revisionists hoped it might serve as leverage in international deliberations.[31]

School textbooks were the first domestic target. The Twentieth Convention of German Geographers passed a 1921 resolution requiring the outline of the prewar German border to be included on every map used in school instruction.[32] This decision was in keeping with the Prussian *Kultusministerium,* which had already banned all atlases for school use that didn't present Germany's prewar boundaries.[33] The intention was to naturalize the validity of the prewar German outline through consistent repetition, and to maintain an identification with this particular silhouette among the nation's youth.[34] Accordingly, on its map of contemporary Europe, the *Diercke Schulatlas* inscribes the prewar German border in bright red onto an otherwise pastel-colored map, presenting an image of the bleeding border that refused to heal.[35]

Such repetitive encounters with this border's form would have constructed what Benedict Anderson terms the "map-as-logo."[36] Identified so strongly with a particular shape, the "logo-map" takes on the autonomous character of the piece in a jigsaw puzzle and becomes recognizable even when wholly detached from its geographic context. The form of the silhouette achieves a legitimacy of its own, a perceived fundamental immutability of its shape. Against this normalized image, the new border would appear as an aberration and fail to gain public legitimacy.

To validate the messages presented by their textbooks, schoolchildren were being taught to respect the science behind the cartographic image. An educational film from 1928 entitled *Karte und Atlas* (Map and atlas) seeks to present maps as mimetic reproductions of objective, natural fact.[37] The film follows all stages of cartographic production, from geographic surveying of land to the final color editing of the printing process. After animated film segments review the geometric and geographic principles underlying map production, we see enormous, complex machines deployed in the etching of cartographic plates, carefully watched over by serious men in white lab coats. With all of the equipment involved, it appears as if the maps create themselves as objective products of autonomous technology. The final cartographic print is thus depicted as the rationalized product of the modernmost technologies and as unquestionably scientific. The film ends with a shot of a school atlas lying open on a table, just like the one the students would have found on their own desks.

Once students were educated to accept maps as "mirrors of nature," this apparatus of authority could be mobilized to validate and naturalize the irredentist arguments delivered by their school atlases. A pair of maps taken from two different editions of the popular *Diercke Schulatlas* (Diercke school atlas) illustrate the trajectory of the argument (plates 4 and 5). Both versions of the map, one from 1914, the other from 1928, present distributions of languages and peoples, much like Schäfer's map, but within a reduced frame including only Germany and the lands immediately to its east.[38] Although both maps depict the same geographic space, the cartographic strategy is significantly altered in 1928 to present a very different image of the ethnic identity of this space. In the 1914 version of the *Völker- und Sprachenkarte* (Map of peoples and languages), Germans in the German-Polish borderlands are represented by islands of color that appear to analogically reflect geographical areas inhabited by closed German settlements. Germany's eastern border is indicated, but we can also clearly see that it runs through a geographic area predominantly inhabited by Poles. In the later version of the map, we see a mobilization of the cartographic code introduced by Schäfer, which "Germanizes" the Polish population existing within Germany's (prewar) borders. On the Polish side of this border, the map remains unchanged. The tiny islands of pink marking German presence are distributed in precisely the same locations on both maps, and their morphologies remain unchanged. Inside the prewar German border, however, the sign system changes to resemble Schäfer's map, except that here stripes are used instead of Schäfer's dots.

This new cartographic code allows the map to deliver two arguments: first, it validates the former border as immutable—the map suggests that the former border continues to mark a distinction between two different modes of population distribution, such that land ceded to Poland still expresses a unique form of population mixture characteristic of German, not Polish, space. Second, the map contests the status of the so-called Polish Corridor as legitimately Polish. The ethnic distributions on the 1914 map clearly show a Polish demographic majority in this contested region, while the stripes used in the 1928 version visually erase this problematic fact. By manipulating the shapes of the stripes, the demographic argument made by the map is effectively reversed: now Germans appear to be the majority onto which a rather negligible Polish minority is mapped. The stripes erase the continuous area inhabited by Poles, which are clearly visible on the 1914 map—a visual redistribution that erases the clear Polish path through the "corridor."

This second map was published in the wave of expansionist agitation that followed the 1925 signing of the Treaty of Locarno. In the treaty, Germany agreed to recognize the legitimacy of its new western border (and thereby cede Alsace-Lorraine to France) in exchange for the early withdrawal of Allied occupation troops from the Rhine and the readmission of Germany into foreign diplomatic relations. While the French had initially demanded that Germany also recognize its eastern border with Poland, they had been unable to achieve this concession and had left the issue unresolved.

In this new phase of international relations, the need to articulate territorial claims within the international context of scientific cartography lost its urgency: the primary audience for territorial concerns was no longer located within foreign circles but instead within the domestic German sphere. As a result, new spatial models arose whose arguments for a revision of Germany's eastern border included, but were not limited to, population statistics.

This was useful for irredentists frustrated by their failed attempts to cartographically manipulate census statistics to support their case. Polish-speaking Poles comprised strong majorities in most of the territories in question, and their numbers only grew stronger as the German minority continued to flee the new Polish state. Even reinterpretations of the population statistics that grouped the Kashubes and Jews together with the Germans only potentially granted irredentists a fraction of the space they desired. Therefore, in the post-Locarno period, new conceptual models were introduced that marginalized the question of population statistics altogether in their claims for additional German space.

These new models were created by a new generation of geopoliticians and presented to the public in cartographic form. One of the leading figures in German geopolitics, the geographer Karl Haushofer, led the call for "suggestive maps" that would communicate political messages through strong graphic symbols.[39] The most important figure in the ensuing project was the graphic designer turned völkisch activist, A. Hillen Ziegfeld. In the early 1920s, Ziegfeld had been in Munich working with the anthropologist Leo Frobenius on the latter's *Atlas Africanus* project. Frobenius had been experimenting with ways of depicting dynamic processes on maps but had been dissatisfied with the results. Ziegfeld brought his background in commercial art to the problem and developed a new cartographic genre he referred to as "commercial cartography" (*Kartographik*).[40] He saw himself as a graphic artist hired to render the geopolitical ideas of others into a communicative visual form. To accomplish this, he developed a signature aesthetic for which he became quite well-known: his stark black-and-white images present a minimum of information reduced into bold visual statements. Ziegfeld's maps are not scientific products but instead persuasive texts designed to present spatialized narratives: his maps told stories about German space, its geopolitical and geoeconomic strengths and weaknesses, the threats it faced, and the identity it exuded. Ziegfeld's maps filled the pages of völkisch organs like the journal *Volk und Reich,* were circulated by the press departments of völkisch organizations like the *Deutscher Schutzbund,* were featured in the first published geopolitical atlas (of 1927), and circulated prominently in a wide range of mainstream publications and venues.[41]

In his examination of Ziegfeld's "Kartographik" and the spatial models his maps represent, Guntram H. Herb identifies three key conceptual innovations introduced to delineate "rightful" German space in terms independent of ethnic distributions. Ziegfeld was instrumental in developing the visual strategies used to present each of these, which Herb labels "geo-organic," "negative," and "*Kulturboden*" models of German space.[42] Significantly, the most successfully persuasive of these models was the last, which, as I will address below, depicted Eastern Europe as German colonial space, and which argued for German eastward expansion with a model that was, quite literally, "post–colonial."

Geo-organic maps drew upon völkisch conceptual models depicting the nation as a living organism. Such maps portray German space defined and linked by the infrastructural networks (primarily roads and railway lines) that pervade it. Analogous to biological arteries bringing blood to the body, these networks are understood to facilitate the circulation of vital elements (economic goods and capital) throughout the body of the nation. The geo-organic model asserts that, once a Volk occupies a certain territory, it grows into this space, developing infrastructural networks that extend throughout, but that naturally stop at its borders. Transportation and communication networks, resources, and markets are all developed with respect to this overarching "border consciousness."[43]

Geo-organic maps typically show transportation networks casting a dense, homogeneous, and rationally organized web over the space enclosed by Germany's prewar borders (as is the case in fig. 1). To the east of this former border, in former Congress Poland, one finds only a sparsely developed network, and there are only few points of cross-border intersection. These two spaces thus appear to be fundamentally disconnected. The geo-organic model thus argues for the return of previously held space to reinstate the organic whole. In the contrasting densities of infrastructural development, an additional argument is presented by such geo-organic maps, namely, that Polish space is backward and undeveloped. Because the Poles don't have an organic relationship to the new space they have acquired, their attempts to develop it must certainly fail. Figure 2 thus shows the corridor being "strangled" by Poland's planned railway projects; while German infrastructure networks appear rational and organically harmonious, the Polish plans exude an irrational sense of hysteria and chaos. Now that such regions as Upper Silesia and the so-called Polish Corridor have been ceded to Poland, these highly developed areas have been cut off from their German "heart centers" and, like limbs with restricted blood supply, will wither and die.[44]

In 1924, Karl Haushofer, perhaps the most prominent German geopolitician, wrote an article about "German border consciousness," in which he described national space thus.

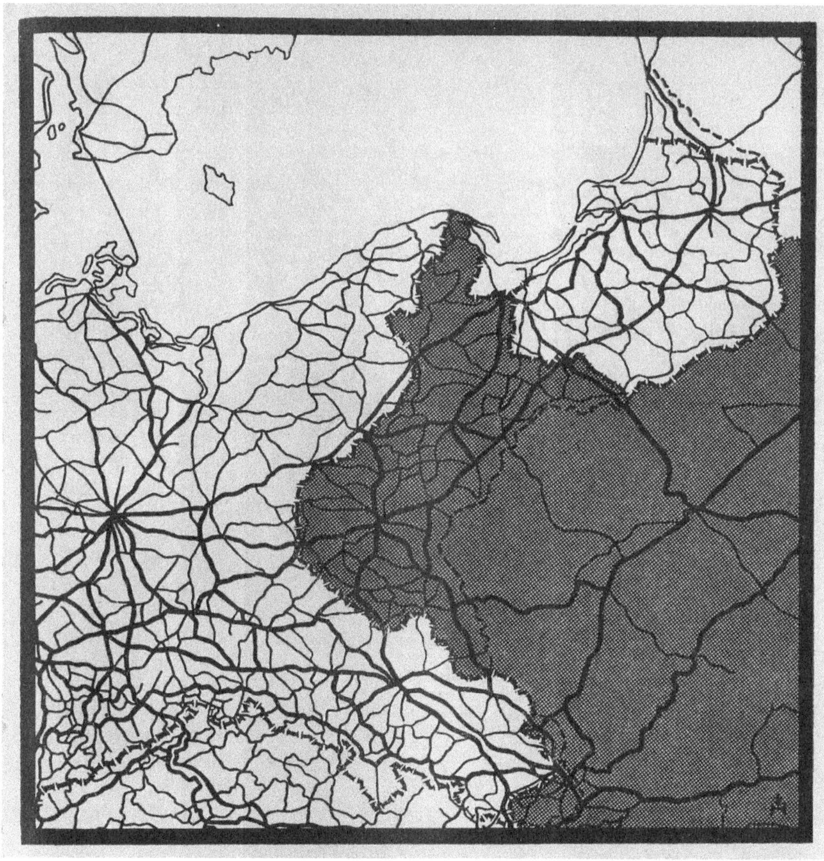

Fig. 1. A. Hillen Ziegfeld's map of the East Prussian railway network exemplifies the "geo-organic" model of German space. "Die Verkehrswege—Die Eisenbahnen," in *Volk und Reich* (1930), 233.

> The whole length of [the German *Volk*'s] border is a gaping wound and it will bleed out on all sides unless iron and fire act upon it, either from within or from without, to close it at least enough to allow its vital organs to function again.[45]

Such depictions of German national space as an organic body resonated with a whole host of terms broadly used in the German press that described the new eastern border as an "open wound," and the territories lost as "amputated limbs." A study of the interwar press identifies prominent references to "a

Fig. 2. "The strangling of Danzig by the Polish railway projects" shows Poland's inability to rationally develop German space. A. Hillen Ziegfeld, "Danzigs Abdrosselung durch die polnischen Bahnprojekte," in *Volk und Reich* (1930), 185.

'bleeding border' or a 'bloody border'; the border was considered to be an 'open wound' or a 'bloody wound'; references were to a 'burning/blazing border,' a 'ripping apart' of transportation routes, a 'gash in the east,'" etc.[46] This language graphically argued for the inviolability of German national space, and therefore for the return of Germany's prewar landholdings. But the geo-organic model also had the unintended consequence of delegitimizing any thought of German expansion beyond the prewar state borders (because this land was not organically linked to Germany) and was therefore rejected after 1933, when expansionists aimed their sights further east.[47]

The second model, which Herb refers to as the "negative model" of German space (fig. 3), was based upon geopolitical principles of border rationalization. This model stressed the negative effects that the changed borders had on Germany's ability to protect itself from future foreign invasion. Geopoliticians stressed the man-made nature of state borders and argued that those drawn up at Versailles were both arbitrary and faulty, and that they needed to be reconfigured (and, in Germany's case, expanded) to fix the problem. The main issues of concern were the ratio of the border's length to the size of the space it enclosed, and the distance from this border to key political, military, and population targets that lay within. Optimally, a nation's borders would be circular, because the circle provides the smallest ratio of border length to volume and thus minimizes the amount of border that must be protected while also allowing for key targets to be located near the center of the enclosed space. The maps drawn according to the negative model show weaknesses in Germany's current borders, most frequently by indicating potential routes of enemy attack. These maps, with aggressive arrows dangerously slicing across Germany's borders, are the ones most commonly associated with the geopolitical cartographic aesthetic. In these images, Germany appears vulnerable, the victimized object of external aggression. After 1933, this model too was quickly phased out, because it depicted Germany as weak and, like the geo-organic model, only justified a limited amount of territorial expansion (fig. 4).[48]

The third main geopolitical model was that of German *Volks- und Kulturboden* (land of the German Volk and land of German culture), which came to be espoused by virtually all völkisch theorists after its introduction in 1925. Due to its flexibility, it continued to circulate in various modified forms well into World War II; the concept of *Kulturboden*—land impregnated with German cultural identity—was useful because it was vague enough to be extended almost indefinitely to the east.

The "Post-Colonial" Model of *Kulturboden*

Directly after the war, publicists had begun asserting Germany's right to the areas ceded to Poland due to the role Germans had played in the development of the region.

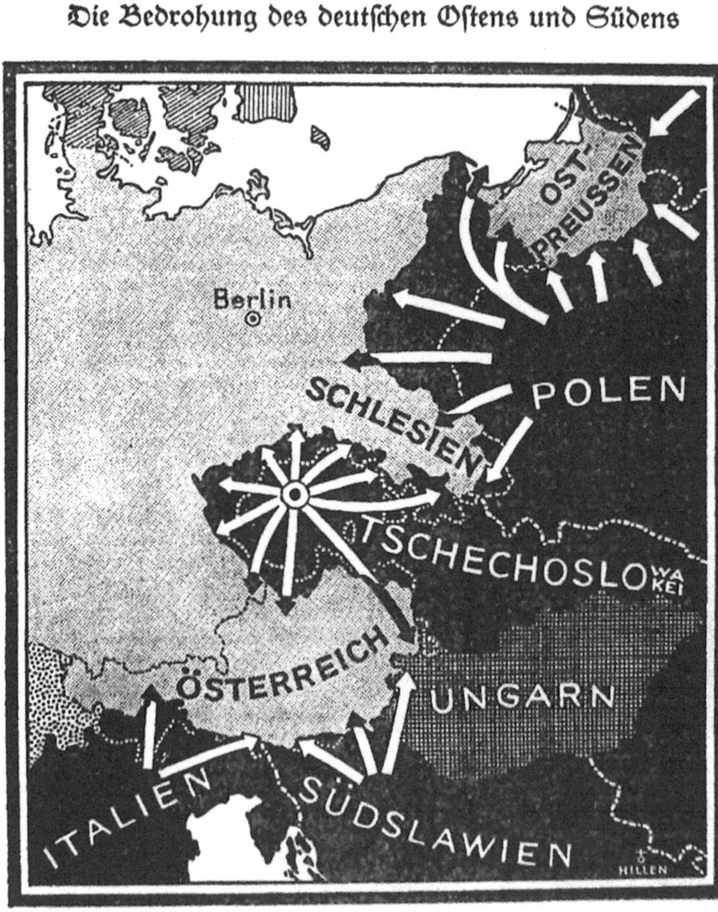

Fig. 3. The "negative" model of German space. A. Hillen Ziegfeld, "Die Bedrohung des deutschen Ostens und Südens," in *Volk und Reich* (1926), 435.

> Most of those goods and values reflecting a provenance in spiritual and economic culture, and everything that Polandom itself has become, was brought about by German order, German industriousness, and German tenacity. Posen is thus a land of unquestionable German culture.[49]

The German Volk, they argued, had invested a great deal of cultural labor (*Kulturarbeit*) in the East, without which the region would never have become as civilized and advanced as it now was. This argument continued the colonial

Die Gefahrlage Schlesiens
auf Grund der derzeitigen Staatsgrenzen

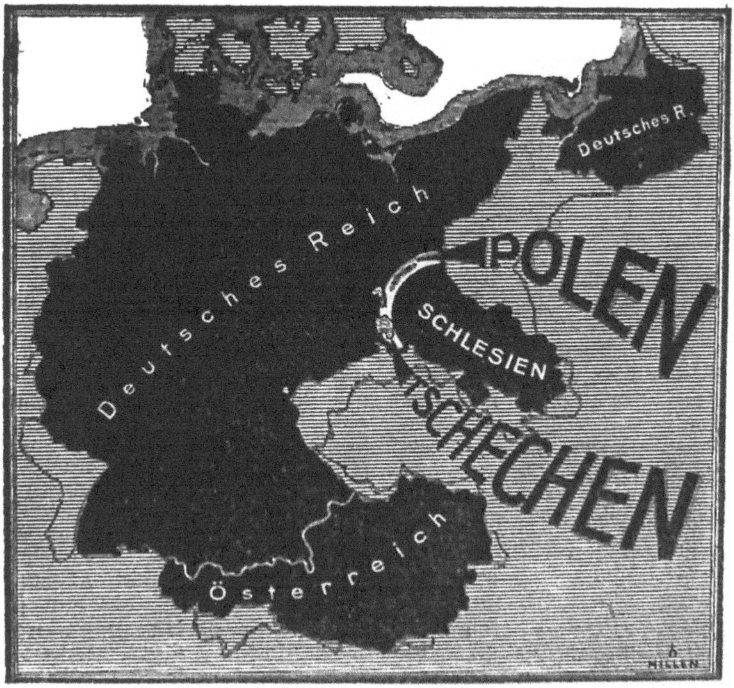

Diese Skizze stellt nicht das deutsche Siedlungsgebiet dar, sondern die Grenzen der deutschen Staaten auf Grund der Pariser Vorortsverträge und ihre Bedrohung durch das Slaventum

Fig. 4. "This sketch doesn't depict the area of German settlement, but instead the borders of the German states . . . and the threat posed to them by Slavdom." A. Hillen Ziegfeld, "Die Gefahrenlage Schlesiens auf Grund der derzeitigen Staatsgrenzen," in *Volk und Reich* (1926), 165.

discourse of the prewar period in claiming that the "primitive, backward Slavs" would not have been able to bring this region into its current state of development on their own. In the absolute and mythic terms in which völkisch discourse was often couched, revisionists listed the German accomplishments achieved.

> West Prussia owes to Germandom everything that the present has derived from the past, and all of the historical memories and treasures that it

> holds; and, as in Posen as well, it was Germandom that brought economic and cultural progress to the province in all times in history.[50]

But such claims of German historical presence and agency in the contested eastern regions did not translate into a functional revisionist argument. Revisionists could accuse Poland of being ungrateful, "despite everything that it owed to Germandom," but such sentiments were ineffective for staking territorial claims.[51] Albrecht Penck's model of German *Volks- und Kulturboden* soon became the dominant paradigm within revisionist discourse because it offered a way of connecting arguments to specific spatial claims.[52]

Albrecht Penck (1858–1945) was an Austrian geologist and geographer initially noted for his scientific research on the glacial period in the Alps.[53] He became a professor in Vienna in 1885 and took the chair of geography in Berlin in 1906. Early in his career, he began seeking ways to combine scholarship with völkisch politics and came to exemplify "the transition from positivism to activism" that characterized many geographers in early twentieth-century Germany.[54] Prior to the war, he had attempted to justify Germany's borders based on natural features; he published a popular-science work on the topic in 1887 and continued to address this question publicly throughout the war.[55] During the subsequent international peace negotiations, Penck turned to cartography to help Germany make its case and led a team of geographers to create a scientific map of demographic distributions in the contested eastern regions, a project that met with little success.[56]

During the postwar period, Penck became active in several prominent völkisch organizations (including the Deutscher Schutzbund für das Grenz- und Auslandsdeutschtum and the Verein für das Deutschtum im Ausland), and, in 1923, he cofounded the institute that would become the Stiftung für deutsche Volks- und Kulturbodenforschung (Foundation for the Study of German Volks- und Kulturboden) in 1926.[57] Here, Penck continued to engage the tools of cartography to challenge the new location of Germany's borders. But, unlike in his earlier work, Penck now shifted from scholarly scientific cartography to popular persuasive mapping. Working together with A. Hillen Ziegfeld, Penck created the "Map of German *Volks- und Kulturboden,*" which was published alongside his essay in Karl Christian von Loesch's 1925 *Volk unter Völkern,* a book designed to present a conceptual tool kit for addressing revisionist concerns in the East (fig. 5).[58]

Penck's essay describes two different kinds of space distinguished by their different relationships with the German Volk: there is the land currently inhabited by the German Volk (*deutscher Volksboden*), and there is the land that has been shaped by past German cultural labor (*deutscher Kulturboden*). Ziegfeld's map presents these two spatial categories through graded shades of areal coloration; upon a recognizable outline of Central Europe's postwar political borders, a solid black region covers an area roughly demarcated by the borders of Germany and Austria; this space is labeled "*Deutscher Volksboden.*" To the east of this region lies a smaller area shaded in gray, labeled "*Kulturboden.*" A third formation approximates Schäfer's islands of settlement colonies extending eastward in strings of "scattered settlement and language islands." They re-create in miniature the pairing of *Volks- und Kulturboden.*

Penck defines the German *Volksboden* as space currently inhabited by Germans.

> German *Volksboden* is where the German Volk is settled; here, one hears the German language and sees the fruits of German labor. Until now, emphasis has been placed upon the former; the German-language region has been equated with the German *Volksboden,* and the size and location of our *Volksboden* has been derived from maps of language distribution.[59]

Although he doesn't refer directly to the Versailles Treaty in his definition, it is clear that, for Penck, the *Volksboden* represents that space which is arguably German according to the criteria attending the principle of self-determination. Penck, however, does not restrict *Volksboden* to regions of population majorities, and even a minority presence seems to be enough to meet his definition. Ziegfeld's map accordingly extends the reach of the *Volksboden* across the political borders of Germany and Austria to claim borderland areas in each of their neighboring countries, including France, Italy, and Denmark. Meanwhile (with only a few, barely perceptible exceptions) the entirety of Germany and Austria is covered by a solid pool of black, which is visually uninterrupted by any presence of script or other markings. According to cartographic convention, such emphatic coloration suggests that the features being mapped are as homogeneously spread and as unquestionably hegemonic as the color itself. The western industrial region of the Ruhr Basin is thereby rendered identical and equal to Alpine Switzerland and the agricultural areas of East Prussia. Recalling that *Volksboden* is defined as an expression of German language and culture, such unquestioned homogeneity is all the more striking. While extending the German *Volksboden* provocatively far to the west of the Rhine, the map presents a strong black-and-white territorial distinction with little ambiguity,

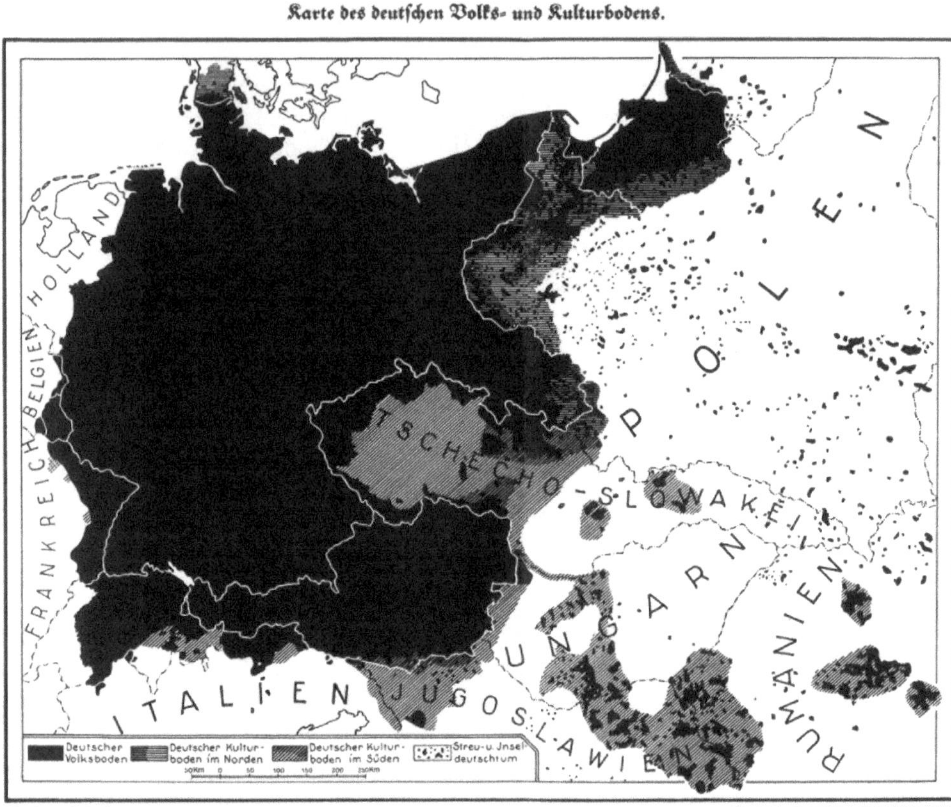

Fig. 5. The map of German *Volks- und Kulturboden* drafted by A. Hillen Ziegfeld for Albrecht Penck. "Karte des deutschen Volks- und Kulturbodens," in *Volk unter Völkern,* ed. Karl C. Loesch (Breslau: Hirt, 1925), 72. Image courtesy of Digital Initiatives at the University of British Columbia Library.

little transitional or overlapping space at the border with French, Belgian, and Dutch space in the west.

The area labeled as German *Volksboden* covers an exaggerated amount of territory—more than had been held by Germany and Austria prior to the war—yet Penck envisions an even greater area of future German control. Therefore, instead of identifying national space based upon current distributions of ethnicity or language, he argues that focus should shift to the consideration of a space's cultural identity, which, according to his model of *Kulturboden,* can be determined by observing the visible signs of various spatialization strategies. Through the cultural labor of its population, German space

> has gained a decisive imprint clearly recognizable everywhere. The German *Volksboden* is accompanied by a unique German *Kulturboden* that differentiates itself from neighboring cultured terrain. It is characterized by an extremely meticulous cultivation that doesn't stop where it becomes difficult.[60]

Penck enacts a shift from a consideration of ethnic distributions in the present to rather mysticized acts of land reclamation in the past; it is therefore important to note that the grammatical subject in this passage is not the German Volk but a specific geographic space: *der Boden* (the land). *Der Boden* becomes the constant onto which the benefits of human labor are conceptually mapped. Penck casts *Kulturarbeit* as the cultural labor able to render natural space into human space (such that the word *Kultur* manifests its dual resonance in *culture* and agri*culture* or *cult*ivation),[61] and he argues that such labor took unmarked and unbounded natural space and provided it with a human, and thus cultural, identity. The landscape itself thus becomes the marker of that which can be referred to as "Germany," and, given the specificities of Penck's model, it remains "Germany" even in the absence of living ethnic Germans: German *Kulturboden* exceeds the boundaries of German *Volksboden* to include space from which the German population has withdrawn but which bears the visible traces of a cultural identity imprinted upon it *in the past.*[62]

Penck's ideas about culturally imprinted space were not entirely new. We saw them in Gustav Freytag's *Soll und Haben,* where Polish space was colonized by Germans who arrived in a landscape depicted as primitive and unbounded, and then enacted German spatialization practices to order it. We saw it too in the *Ostmarkenromane,* where Germans and Poles each created villages, public establishments, and domestic spaces endowed with the progenitive capacity to racially mold anyone who came to inhabit them. Thus, when the geographer Friedrich Ratzel produced his theoretical model of culturally imprinted space at the turn of the century, he was simply providing new language for a conceptual model already in broad social circulation. He describes the *Kulturlandschaft* (cultural landscape) as follows.

> As the Germans increased their numbers and bonded ever closer with their land, an entirely new landscape arose, a *Kulturlandschaft* that is full of the signs of the labor that a Volk invests into land through clearing,

> plowing, and planting it. We see a similar set of small effects achieved by similar means in many different areas; they are signs of the active energy [*wirkende Kraft*] of a laboring and developing Volk.[63]

The development of the *Kulturlandschaft* was, for Ratzel, a dialogical process whereby a Volk, as defined through a set of cultural practices, encountered a landscape that placed restrictions and demands upon these same cultural practices. The ensuing interaction between *Volk und Raum* (a people and its space) was responsible for the unique creation of the *Kulturlandschaft.* Attempting to describe what this landscape actually looked like in the German case, Ratzel introduces a rather banal image: German space is recognizable by "the sharp furrows of the fields, the arrow-straight ditches of the irrigation systems, and even the neat outlines of the haystacks."[64] Penck draws on Ratzel and arrives at a description of *Kulturboden* equally prosaic.

> It is characterized everywhere by the great care with which the land is cultivated; by the coziness and cleanliness of the dwellings, whether they are of straw, bricks, or—as in Australia—covered by corrugated metal; by the easily passable roads . . .[65]

While Penck thus took Ratzel's *Kulturlandschaft* as a starting point, he added a further element that greatly strengthened its value as a political tool. Originally, Ratzel's model had allowed for change and flux between different *Völker* and different landscapes over time. Groups occasionally migrated and, as a consequence, culturally developed through the new demands placed on them by new geographic realities. In the same way, the landscapes themselves changed with each new set of inhabitants. There was a symbiotic relationship between a population and the space it inhabited, but one that was constantly in a state of ebb and flow. Penck's model, in contrast, limited such notions of fluidity by claiming the existence of an *originary act,* a singular historical moment when a particular landscape was brought out of its primordial natural state and into the realm of human culture, an event that was brought about by the cultural labor of a specific population. Penck suggested that, once this event occurred, it could be neither reversed nor altered. This ahistorical permanence was particularly important in the case of the land ceded to Poland, because it allowed Penck to assert its essential German-ness despite the long history of migrations traversing it.

> It is not possible that the land vacated by the Teutonic tribes in the East during the time of the *Völkerwanderung* was an unaltered natural land-

> scape. The Teutons were agricultural, and the significant height reached by their culture has been proven by prehistoric finds. The Slavs who migrated in from the East stumbled upon a Teutonic *Kulturboden,* but its full valuation was first reached when German settlers came again from the West, again took this land under cultivation, and taught the Slavic immigrants to do the same.[66]

The landscape, once it had been lifted into history and imprinted with a cultural identity, thereafter demanded that it be inhabited according to the forms established by this foundational culture. A geographic space had been created that remained immutably *German,* and the Slavs who later came to occupy this land were forced to adapt themselves to the demands made by its "German imprint." When Germans leave this space and return to find it inhabited by Slavs it is the latter, not the German newcomers, who are identified as "immigrants" because the *Kulturboden* model argues that non-Germans will always be foreigners in this space.

Although Penck doesn't discuss the difference between Germans and Slavs, and although he doesn't make use of this vocabulary, a close reading of his text reveals that he is operating within rather conventional colonial models differentiating primitive and civilized peoples (*Natur- und Kulturvölker*). He implicitly divides mankind into two categories, only the first of which is able to produce the space of *Kulturboden.* The Slavs are excluded from this category along with all other colonized peoples of the earth (i.e., Penck would not agree that there was any such thing as a "Slavic *Kulturboden,*" because the Slavs were not a *Kulturvolk* capable of undertaking *Kulturarbeit*). Meanwhile, Penck claims that the Russian Baltic states, the Siebenbürgen region (Transylvania), the Brazilian tropical rim, and the Chilean coast are all areas in which a small number of Germans had been able to transform a large territory into German *Kulturboden,* despite the presence of various native populations. He contrasts these scenarios with the case of North America, where Germans were not successful in this project because they were mixed among members of other *Kulturvölker* (the French, Spanish, English, etc.), such that no clear symbiosis between a specific people and a specific space could occur.[67]

The dichotomy of *Natur- und Kulturvolk* also explains why Germany's border to France is so unambiguous for Penck ("One doesn't only hear evidence of leaving the German language area, one also perceives it in the *Kulturlandschaft*"),[68] for here, one *Kulturvolk* borders upon another. The contested eastern frontier, however, is an entirely different matter. Here, Penck follows Schäfer's argument that the language boundaries have never been clear.

> But German *Kulturboden* prevails as far as the German permeation either extended or extends. It is not difficult to distinguish between the neat German villages and the often rather shabby Polish ones; and the intensive German land cultivation, along with the good roads and streets that accompanied it, reaches all the way to the Russian border. This was the big cultural border that the German soldiers felt only too clearly as they marched to the East. The border is so trenchant that one can even see it from the train. One no longer sees attractive stone houses in the towns. The fields show less care, the forests are visibly less managed. . . . In the Reich, the land is most carefully cultivated, the stones have been gathered from the fields, well-paved roads, neat villages.[69]

German space was thus identifiable and localizable. One could allegedly *see* it—and thus one could map it. Penck's model gained rapid popular currency because it shifted attention from population to space; from the quantitative assessment of German ethnic distribution statistics to the qualitative investigation of the völkisch identity imprinted upon the landscape itself. Now, German space could also be understood to include areas devoid of Germans (regardless of how these were defined) because "Germany" was defined as that set of landscapes bearing indelible marks of past German cultural labor.

The map of German *Volks- und Kulturboden* that accompanied Penck's article soon came to be widely circulated. It was reproduced in various journals, and numerous different versions were adapted for dissemination in outlets ranging from schoolbooks to propaganda posters (figs. 6, 7, 8).

The *Kulturboden* concept became the basis for völkisch territorial revisionism during the interwar period and was quickly adapted to extend the reaches of both German *Volksboden* and *Kulturboden* ever further eastward. The geographer Wilhelm Volz, director of the Stiftung für Volks- und Kulturbodenforschung, was the first to challenge what he held to be the conservative claims of the Penck/Ziegfeld map. Volz argued that the past German colonization efforts in the East had not only transformed the landscape but the primitive peoples (the Kashubes, Poles, etc.) they found there as well. Living in German space, these Slavs had been "Germanized," such that the space they occupied could be added to the area of *Volksboden* claimed by the Penck/Ziegfeld map, and the subsequent reach of *Kulturboden* extended much further east.

> This land has been Teutonic-Germanic *Volksboden* for 3,000 years . . . for, in the tenth century, the re-settlement by the Germans began. The ad-

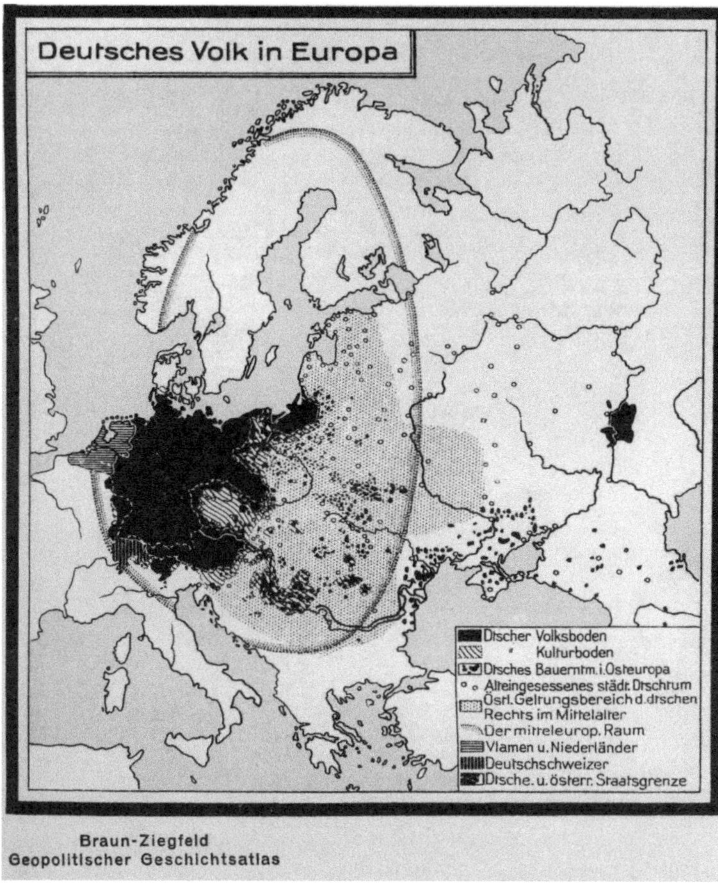

Fig. 6. Ziegfeld's subsequent mappings of German *Volks- und Kulturboden* added various additional categories that extended spatial claims ever further to the east. A. Hillen Ziegfeld, "Deutsches Volk in Europa," in Franz Braun and A. Hillen Ziegfeld, *Geopolitischer Geschichtsatlas* (Dresden: Ehlermann, 1930), 43.

vanced German culture defeated primitive Slavdom, the Germans wrested immense stretches of new settlement land from the primordial forest—of course much Slavic and German blood was shed, but overall, it was a magnificent victory of culture, and most of the small number of Slavs melted into Germandom, steadily over time. . . . The Kashubes and Masurians, the Upper Silesians and the Wends are all of German culture, are

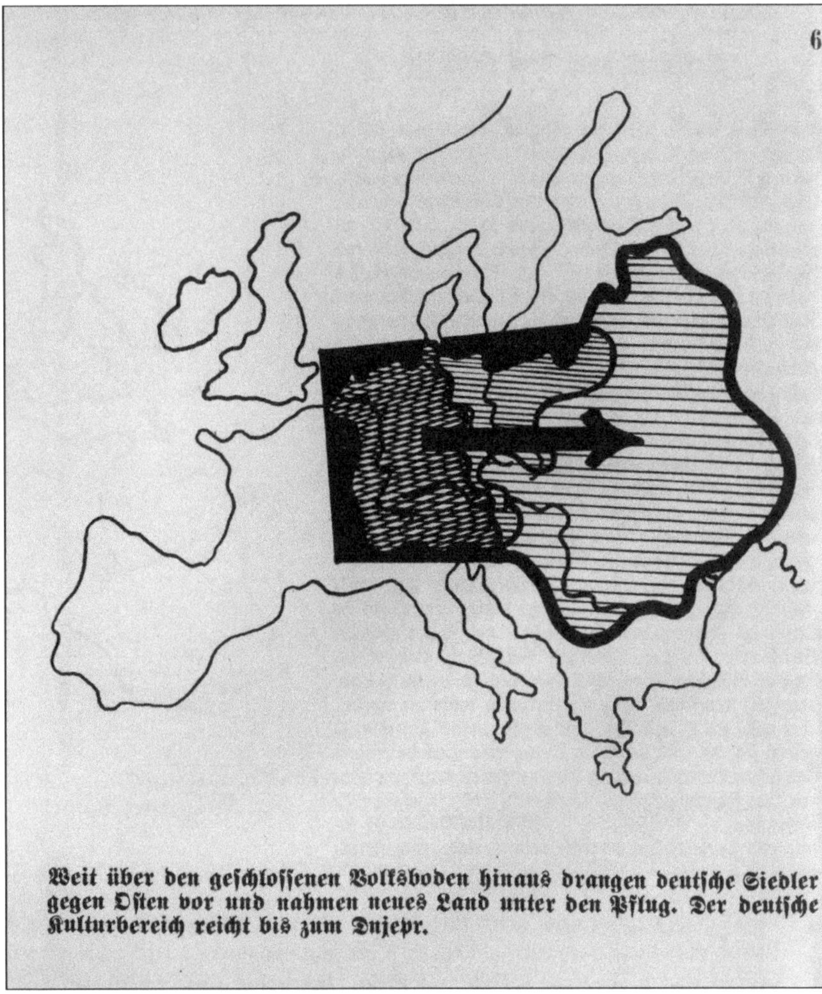

Fig. 7. "German settlers pushed eastward far beyond the enclosed space of the *Volksboden* and subjected new land to the plow. The realm of German culture reaches all the way to the Dneiper." Karl Springenschmid, "Das Ergebnis der Ostwanderung," in *Deutschland und seine Nachbarn: Geopolitische Bildreihe* (Leipzig: Ernst Wunderlich, 1935) 6.

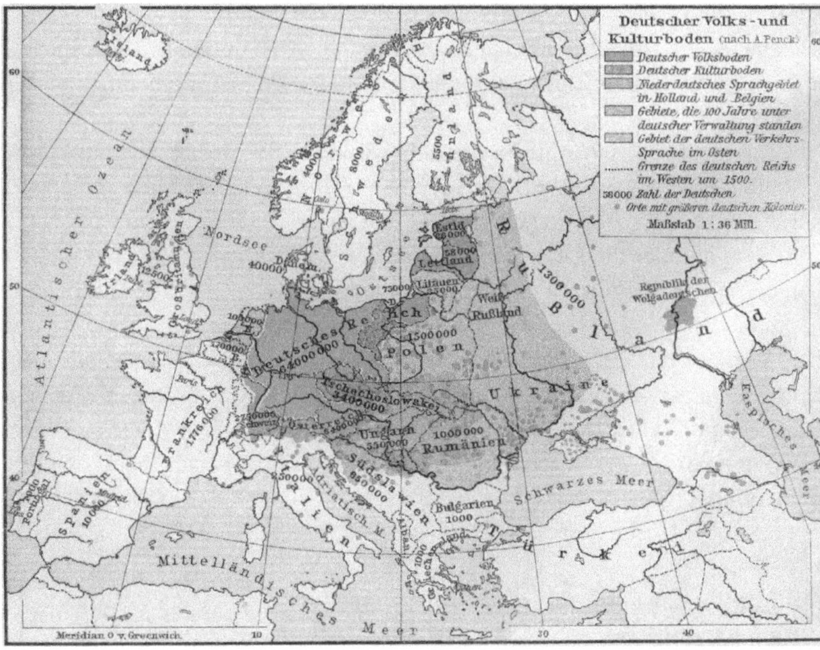

Fig. 8. The map of "Deutscher Volks- und Kulturboden" was included in one of the most prominent school atlases, which credits "A. Penck" in its legend. Max Pehle and Hans Silberborth, eds., *F. W. Putzgers Historischer Schul-Atlas. Große Ausgabe* (Bielefeld: Velhagen und Klasing, 1931), 134.

> members of the German Volk, Germans. . . . Their collective will [*Volkswille*] and their collective consciousness [*Volksbewußtsein*] is German. Race doesn't determine collective identity [*Volkstum*]—is the Wend physically different than the Saxonian? the Upper Silesian who speaks *Wasserpolnisch* from the one who speaks German?—but instead *Volkswille* and *Volksbewußtsein* determine *Volkstum*. . . . The language border is not the *Volks*-border! The eastern *Volksboden* encompasses the peripheral mixed populations [*Mischvölker*] of the German *Volkstum*.[70]

Volz's model revisits prewar discussions questioning the ability of colonization to assimilate Slavs into the German collectivity (or to "Germanize" them). He agrees with those who claimed that such assimilation would be possible if Polish spaces of (degenerate) racial reproduction were replaced by German racialized space. For Volz, the German *Kulturarbeit* enacted upon the landscape had been successful in fundamentally changing the nature of the population that resided upon it.

But most völkisch thinkers were not willing to follow Volz's assimilationist model, and they also seemed reluctant to follow Penck in his complete denial of any Slavic ability to generate cultural space. Yet they continued to work within the logic of the *Kulturboden* paradigm, either seeking evidence of Germanic/Teutonic *Kulturarbeit* in contested landscapes, by seeking "proof" that Germanic peoples had been the first to settle in a given location, or by arguing that Germans had been the first to introduce various technological advancements into a particular region. Such claims of autochthony became the embattled turf upon which revisionist battles were fought, a development that resulted in an explosion in scholarly interest in the Middle Ages that took place in the interwar years.

The Implications of *Kulturboden* for Overseas Colonial Ambitions

In 1920, the Head Office for Colonial Affairs was established in the Ministry for Reconstruction. Although tasked with overseeing overseas colonial affairs, the official slogans of this agency—"Don't forget, but instead always remember" and "That which was German must become German again"[71]—also resonated with the rhetoric of territorial revisionism in the East. In this period of postwar loss, the project of reclaiming lost colonies overseas became entwined with that of regaining land lost to Poland, because their lines of argumentation became mutually interdependent. The narrative of *Kulturarbeit* in the East not only provided a conceptual model for eastward expansion but also came to strengthen the narrative of a German national colonial identity. As we saw above in the case of Langhans's *Kolonial-Atlas,* a long history of *Ostkolonisation* (fig. 9) had been evoked in the decades prior to the war to claim that the Germans were a people predestined to colonize, and that they should pursue additional overseas possessions. Now, völkisch activists pursued a similar strategy to address the accusations of colonial misconduct *(die koloniale Schuldlüge)* proclaimed by the Allies to justify stripping Germany of its overseas colonies. A narrative of peaceful, yet glorious German medieval colonization intended to counteract the Allies' concentration on more recent events. In their version of the tale, the Germans had peacefully migrated, bringing welcomed diffusions of culture and technology. Their interactions with the native populations had been so beneficial that they were even invited by Polish leaders to bring order and development to their lands. The ensuing colonization took place without the intensity of bloodshed characterizing the early colonial ventures of other European nations, who had no such successful history to present and were thus illegitimate judges of Germany's colonial endeavors.

Two popular books on German colonial history published in 1938 and 1943 illustrate the extent to which Penck's *Kulturboden* model came to frame this colonial revisionist tack during the National Socialist period. A. Hillen Ziegfeld usually created suggestive maps to illustrate the ideas and publications of others, but he also penned a few monographs of his own, including *1000 Jahre deutsche Kolonisation und Siedlung: Rückblick und Vorschau zu neuem Aufbruch* (1000 years of German colonization and settlement: a review of the past and a look forward to a new dawn), published in 1943. While the main body of the text treats the acquisition and loss of Germany's overseas colonies, this content is framed by long introductory and concluding sections on Germany's earliest colonial experiences—and future colonial mission—in Eastern Europe. The book opens with two maps, both depicting the "resettlement" of the East, the first during the 900s under Heinrich I, and the second titled "*Die größte Kolonialleistung in der Geschichte: Die deutsche Wiederbesiedlung des Ostens im 12.–14. Jahrhundert*" (The greatest colonial achievement in history: The German resettlement of the east in the 12th–14th centuries). Both maps strongly echo the map of German *Volks- und Kulturboden* that Ziegfeld crafted for Penck, by presenting clearly defined, black regions in the west paired with nebulous, gray shadow regions in the east. This silhouette was readily recognizable but works here to project the relationship between *Volksboden* and *Kulturboden* into two different periods of the past. The map's title indicates that we are to read the arrows as symbols of eastward migration during the twelfth through fourteenth centuries, and the key labels the gray (*Kulturboden*) space as "resettled" land, which would indicate that the migrants were heading into land that had been settled, evacuated, and then resettled in the past—all prior to the arrival of the medieval migrant. The map thus depicts a German relationship with the East that was always already a "return" to German space.

This strategy is also present in Paul Kuntze's *Volksbuch unsrer Kolonien* (The Volk's book of our colonies), a much more ambitious völkisch history of

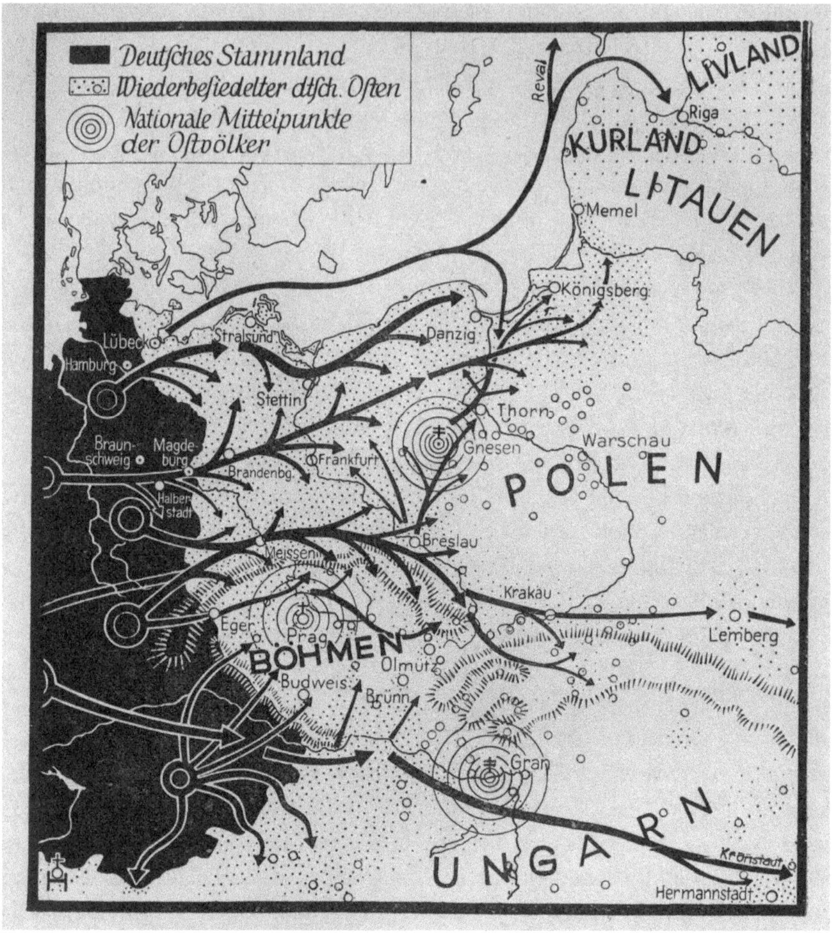

Fig. 9. A. Hillen Ziegfeld opens his history of German settlement and colonization with a map of German *Ostkolonisation.* "Die größte Kolonisationsleistung in der Geschichte: die deutsche Wiederbesiedlung des Ostens im 12.–14. Jahrhundert," in *1000 Jahre deutsche Kolonisation und Siedlung: Rückblick und Vorschau zu neuem Aufbruch* (Berlin: Edwin Runge, 1943), 15.

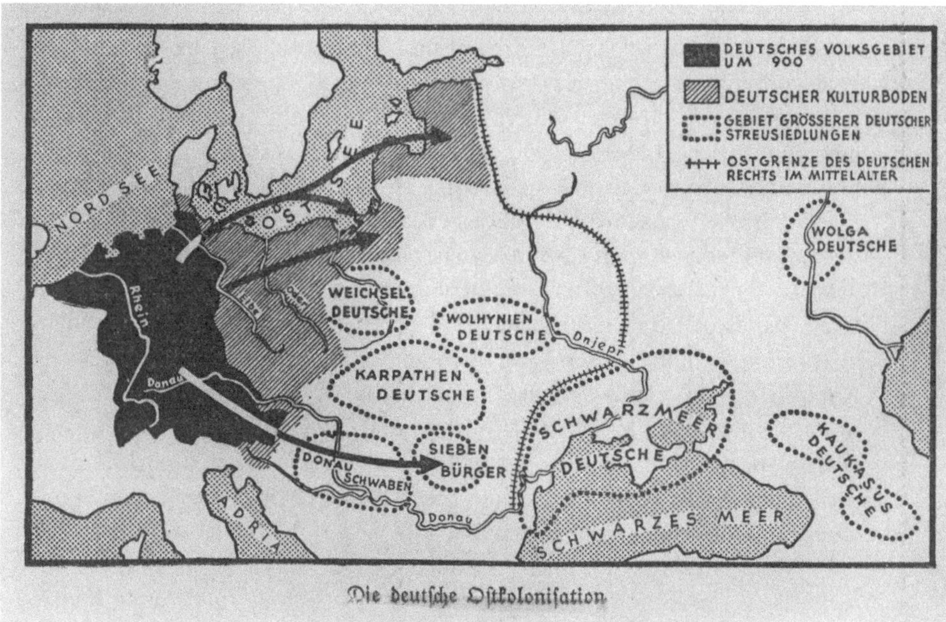

Fig. 10. Paul H. Kuntze pursues the same strategy in his volume on German colonial history. Paul H. Kuntze, "Die deutsche Ostkolonisation," in *Das Volksbuch unserer Kolonien* (Leipzig: Georg Dollheimer, 1938), 10.

German colonization first published in 1938, with a second, reedited version appearing four years later (fig. 10).[72] Kuntze's book is quite spectacular; in addition to dozens of maps, the text features photographs, sketches, paintings, photomontage compositions, graphs, charts, and diagrams—all frequently structured by cartographic elements.

Like Ziegfeld's book, the *Volksbuch* opens with a lengthy section on medieval *Ostkolonisation,* which Kuntze introduces to locate German overseas activity at the end of a long historical trajectory. Kuntze's book also opens with a map that refers—both in its visual structure and in its terminology—to the Penck/Ziegfeld map.[73] It even makes use of the terms *Volksboden* and *Kulturboden,* a set of geopolitical concepts with which, because they are not defined anywhere in the surrounding text, we can assume Kuntze expected his readers to be familiar.

While the black region in the west is identified in the map's legend as *"Volksgebiet um 900"* (the territory of the Volk around 900), the large region labeled *"Deutscher Kulturboden"* remains undated. Recalling that Penck introduced this term to refer to land currently displaying signs of *past* German cultural influence, but *no longer* controlled by a German majority presence, its presence on this map is quite perplexing. Is this land that was already left behind by the Germans in 900 but already bearing their cultural identity? Or land that would become marked by German culture after 900? A third territorial category exacerbates this temporal ambiguity. Directly reproducing the scattered islands of German settlement on the Penck/Ziegfeld maps, large encircled areas east of the *Kulturboden* represent "scattered German settlement" on Kuntze's map. But are we to understand that the Volga Germans were already in Russia in 900? Even the interwar history of *Ostkolonisation* written by Rudolf Kötzschke—one of the most well-known historians supporting German land claims in the East—hesitates to speak of any German settlements in this area prior to the mid-sixteenth century.[74]

While other maps worked to extend German *Kulturboden* further eastward, these maps project it further back in time in order to create a mythic image of the Germans perpetually colonizing eastward. These maps manipulate the temporal cartographic code to depict several centuries in one image suspended in a simultaneity that never historically existed. The text surrounding Kuntze's map discursively reproduces this temporal conflation.

> Certainly the most important colonization, even if it didn't go overseas, was the colonization to the north- and southeast that took place in the early middle ages. Here, the Germans reclaimed the eastern regions they had evacuated during the *Völkerwanderung,* and reacquired the ancient Teutonic seacoast. In this eastern space arose what would later become the great states of Austria and Prussia, the forces behind German history in the modern era. Without this colonization, without the fresh energies that coalesced here, the growth of Germany into its current greatness, unity, and culture would not have been possible. Let us also think to the future![75]

In this text, land colonized in the east becomes a perpetually progenitive resource for an organically conceived German nation: each of the final sentences of this passage discursively reproduces the temporal conflation visually depicted on the map. Actions that began in various moments of the past are repeatedly drawn into the text's present (the colonization of the past flows directly into the German state of the present), which constructs not only a sense of uninterrupted continuity but, more suggestively, of a flattened temporal *simultaneity.* The moralistic imperative "Let us also think to the future!" similarly projects onto Germans of the past an intentionality that links them directly to the present.

CHAPTER 5

Architectural Doppelgänger and "Post-Colonial" Spatial Claims in Fritz Lang's *Nibelungen*

"Post-Colonial" Colonialism and the Lost Eastern Territories

In this final chapter, I'd like to highlight the ways in which the geopolitical *Kulturboden* model featured in the narrative form. Whether texts directly depicted the creation of *Kulturboden* or, like Fritz Lang's 1924 *Nibelungen* film, presented a world in which this history was silently assumed, the *Kulturboden* ideology pervaded German representations of the East.

The argument underlying this geopolitical model claimed that Germans had a right to land in the East—at a minimum, to the territory that they had been forced to cede to Poland after the war but perhaps to even much greater stretches of land—because this space was German in its very essence. As a *Naturvolk,* the Slavs had been incapable of bringing land out of a primordial, natural state during the early periods of civilizational development and incapable of developing it into culturally cohesive landscapes in later periods. This inherent inability to engage in spatializing practices had left a developmental void on the continent that Germans had felt called to fill. The ensuing ancient and medieval *Ostkolonisation* had resulted in the steady introduction of German cultural innovations and cultivating labor into a space that would have otherwise remained "empty." Through these centuries of diffusion, an indelible German identity had been imposed on this Eastern space: to the extent that it was now inhabitable, spatially organized into recognizable village and town structures, and blessed with productive fields and sturdy dwellings, it was due to the innate capacity of the Germans to undertake such acts of spatial cultivation and to the ethical drive to industriousness that motivated them to steadily attack this long-term project over such vast stretches of time.

As a result, the argument continued, the signs of past German *Kulturarbeit* were still present in the contested landscapes today, rendering them "legible" as German space. In this regard, the *Kulturboden* argument was "postcolonial" in the literal sense of the word: its proponents claimed territorial rights in the present based upon colonial efforts undertaken in the past.[1]

As we saw in the previous chapter, cartographic texts mobilized public consensus around the *Kulturboden* argument through the broad circulation of key visual images. Taken as a whole, these maps depicted arrows tracing paths of eastward diffusion into an expanding frontier steadily encompassing ever more territory in the East. This spatial diagram became the conceptual frame into which narrative content could be infused. As popular historical accounts, fictional novels, and press reports came to engage the theme of German *Ostkolonisation* in ever greater numbers, the "truth" of the visual image was further validated.

Just as Germans responded to the loss of their overseas colonies with a rise in the production and consumption of colonial novels, so too did the loss of territory in the East unleash a new wave of *Ostmarkenliteratur* after World War I.[2] Significantly, while overseas colonial literature was largely cast in the present or near-distant past, the authors of interwar *Ostmarkenliteratur* frequently turned to the medieval period for the settings and historical material on which their texts were based. This choice may have been driven by the rather lackluster results of prewar inner colonization that made it difficult to cull heroic tales from this history, but we should also keep in mind that over the course of the nineteenth century, the medieval period had already been recast as the stage for epic migrations of German settlers, a conquering of the land by the valiant Teutonic Knights, and the undaunted reclamation of previously uninhabitable space. Triumphant narratives of medieval *Ostkolonisation* could thus subsume contemporary territorial setbacks under a much longer history of a German mission, drive, and entitlement to the East.

Karl Hampe's popular 1921 history of German eastward settlement set the tone: *Der Zug nach dem Osten: die kolonisatorische Großtat des deutschen Volkes im Mittelalter* (The drive to the East: the German Volk's great colonial achievement in the Middle Ages) delivered a proud narrative of collective German endeavor and generated a mental map of the East overlaid with the trajectories of German cultural and technological diffusion.[3] With this text and the historical discourse that followed in its wake, the history of *Ostkolonisation* was effectively rewritten as a modern chapter of European colonial history set in the past. That which other Europeans were now attempting to accomplish overseas, Hampe's text showed, Germans had already achieved in the East: the mastery of space and its resources and the subjugation of the native population to serve the interests of progress.

Popular literature followed suit: from Curt Kühns's 1920 *Marienburg* to Wilhelm Kotzde's 1925 *Die Burg im Osten* (The castle in the East) to Hans Venatier's 1939 *Vogt Bartold,* texts of the interwar period told stories of medieval Germans in the East that emphasized the ways in which they shaped the spaces they inhabited.[4] Ubiquitous themes were the clearing of previously uncultivated land, the relandscaping and rationalization of crop fields, and the introduction of the iron plow, all developments that were depicted increasing the productivity of the land and fundamentally changing the image of the landscape. Even more prominent was the trope of the house or castle made of stone. While German migrants might initially have built temporary structures out of wood, these novels showed them establishing permanent structures made of brick or stone as soon as this option became possible. Slavs, in contrast, were either too lazy or too primitive to take on such a laborious and complicated task.[5] They therefore often lived in wooden dwellings that were typically depicted in various stages of decay: their roofs leaked and wind blew through the walls, and, ultimately, these dwellings disintegrated. The distinction between wood and stone was thus rendered in both moral and temporal terms: their superior work ethic and level of technological achievement allowed the Germans to alter the landscape in their own image, and they did so in ways that would stand the test of time. Significant in this regard were narratives of the Teutonic Knights building and reinforcing the Marienburg castle. Founded by the Teutonic Order in 1274, and later the seat of the Grand Master of the Teutonic Knights, the fortress was (and continues to be) the largest brick structure in Europe. Located southeast of Danzig, it remained in German hands following World War I but was located in East Prussia near the border of the territory ceded to Poland (hence near the eastern border of the "Polish Corridor"). The reconstruction and renovation of the structure that had begun in the nineteenth century gained new importance in the interwar years and was continued until the beginning of World War II.

The Marienburg became an icon of German longevity in the region; erected during the period of *Ostkolonisation,* the castle represented a continuous German architectural presence. The word *Marienburg* therefore sold books, and in the years between 1920 and 1933, dozens of fictional works appeared that included it in their title. They told tales of the building and renovation of the castle, and, more important, of its protection against adversaries, particularly in the period directly following the Order's 1410 defeat at the Battle of Tannenberg, when, despite the enormous losses suffered by the

Knights in the hands of the allied Polish and Lithuanian forces on the battlefield, Heinrich von Plauen had managed to maintain control over the castle.[6] This victorious episode gained new meaning following the second Battle of Tannenberg, which took place in 1914, where the Germans dealt the Russians a decisive blow. *Tannenberg* and *Marienburg* thus became associated with narratives of victory following great bloodshed.

In the context of German postwar territorial revisionism, the popular media were increasingly called upon to "educate" the German public about the nation's territorial dispossessions.[7] Revisionists hoped that a consistent narrative encounter with the lost overseas colonies and the lost eastern territories would strengthen German identification with these geographic spaces. Film, radio, and popular fiction all had a role to play in maintaining public outrage over the results of Versailles and in supporting demands for the reversal of its mandates. Educational films were particularly useful for this project because they could combine cartographic images into their narratives—even animating maps into depictions of spatial change over time.[8] Schoolchildren in the early Weimar years were introduced to the African territories previously under Germany's control through such titles as *Auf deutschen Farmen in Deutsch-Südwestafrika* (On German farms in German Southwest Africa, undated), *Deutsch-Ostafrika 1914–1916* (German East Africa, 1914–1916, undated), and *Die Weltgeschichte als Kolonialgeschichte* (World history as colonial history, 1926).[9] While all of these films present maps to geographically orient their viewers, the last title also includes a prominent animated map sequence that depicts colonial diffusion in cartographic terms. Initially, a white Europe is set against a global geographic periphery colored completely black. The movement of Europeans is depicted by white arrows traveling over black oceans and landmasses, turning the latter white as these spaces are symbolically brought out of a primordial darkness by the mere arrival of the Europeans.[10]

Educational films depicting Germany's former eastern territories presented similar diffusionist arguments. *Pommern* (Pomerania, undated), for example, opens with an animated map depicting a version of Hampe's aggressive and historically successful *"Ostdeutsche Kolonisation,"* while *Schlesien* (Silesia, 1926) presents this same model in narrative form: "The sparsely settled land and the lowly culture of the Slavs led the Silesian Piast rulers to call German settlers into the land."[11] Both films begin by introducing eastern spaces as landscapes produced by German *Kulturarbeit* during the process of *Ostkolonisation,* and then lament their transition into Polish hands. Now that these areas have been ceded to the Pole and are thus no longer being maintained by the

Germans, the films argue, they are falling into disrepair and abuse in the hands of their new, Slavic inhabitants who are not culturally (or perhaps even racially) developed enough to properly maintain what they have acquired.

In addition to educational films, colonial themes were also taken up by full-length feature films. The German overseas colonial films most well-known today were all released after the National Socialist rise to power: *Die Reiter von Deutsch-Ostafrika* (The Riders of German East Africa; Herbert Selpin, 1934), *Ohm Krüger* (Hans Steinhoff, 1941), *Carl Peters* (Herbert Selpin, 1941), and *Germanin—Die Geschichte einer kolonialen Tat* (Germanin—The history of a colonial deed; Max W. Kimmich, 1943).[12] While this type of directly revisionist colonial film had been rare during the Weimar years, Tobias Nagl has shown that feature films of the period were nonetheless quite heavily invested in issues derived from a colonial idiom.[13] Adventure films such as Joe May's 1919 eight-part series *Die Herrin der Welt* (The mistress of the world) were extremely popular, and although they did not overtly engage the question of Germany's past colonial endeavors, Nagl finds that they were engaged in the practice of reestablishing a German colonial identity for the nation. These films may not have directly featured the colonies, but they were nonetheless working through colonial loss. In their treatments of such issues as race and the global relationship between center and periphery, these films were "only articulable and understandable as contestations of foreign policy."[14]

A similar case can be argued for the filmic depictions of the lost territory in the East. There was a relative paucity of films directly arguing for the return of the lost eastern territory, but this list would include the following: *Brennendes Land* (Burning land; Heinz Herald, 1921) and *Der Kampf um die Heimat* (The battle for the homeland; James Bauer, 1921), which both addressed the contemporary issue of the plebiscite vote in Silesia (which would determine which country this region would join, and which unleashed a flurry of propaganda on both the German and Polish sides). *Brennende Grenze* (Burning border; Erich Waschneck, 1926) and *Land unterm Kreuz: Ein Film aus Oberschlesiens schwerster Zeit* (Land under the cross: A film of Upper Silesia's hardest times; Ulrich Kayser, 1927) depicted Germans suffering in the regions ceded to Poland and thus argued for their return. In addition, a handful of films were based upon literary texts set in the German-Polish borderlands: *Soll und Haben* (Carl Wilhelm, 1924), *Der Katzensteg* (Betrayal; Gerhard Lamprecht, 1927), *Der Bettelstudent* (The Beggar Student; Jakob and Luise Fleck, 1927), and *Polnische Wirtschaft* (E. W. Emo, 1928).[15]

Fritz Lang's *Nibelungen* is not a film that directly depicts Polish space as such. Instead, in the broad strokes of the epic form, it paints a picture of the medieval world divided into two vastly different realms—East and West—in such a way as to allow these conceptual categories to be mapped onto the spaces of concern to contemporary viewers. As the German national epic, the *Nibelungenlied* is of the most revisited and reworked narratives in German cultural history, and there is a precedent for rewriting it as the tale of German-Polish borderland dispute. Lang's film thus served as a screen onto which viewers could project their own anxieties regarding Germany's relationship with its eastern neighbors in ways that exceeded the exigencies of the present to position the threat arising from the East in epic timelessness.

Filmed in two parts (*Siegfried* and *Kriemhild's Revenge,* both released in 1924), Lang's *Nibelungen* retells the well-known medieval German epic: in part I, Kriemhild marries the hero Siegfried, who is subsequently murdered in a plot supported by her brother, the king of the Burgundian kingdom at Worms. In part II, Kriemhild marries Etzel, king of the Huns, in order to best position herself to exact revenge.[16] After the birth of her first child, Kriemhild invites her brothers and their entourage to visit her. In both the original epic and Lang's film, this visit ends in a battle between the Huns and the Burgundians in which almost all participants die in a violent bloodbath.

Given the lengthy scenes of warfare and mass death with which part II ends, Anton Kaes reads Lang's *Nibelungen* as a prime example of "shell shock cinema," or films that "found a way to restage the shock of war and defeat" in ways desired by a public struggling to come to terms with the trauma of wartime experience.[17] I would like to follow in the line of such a symptomatic reading but recontextualize the film in a way that shifts our understanding of the nature of the trauma Lang's *Nibelungen* brings into representation. For, next to the ways in which the film engages the traumatic memory of warfare, the *Nibelungen* also reflects the collective sense of crisis unleashed by the loss of state territory after the war and by the ensuing period of spatial instability. Germans sensed a lack of secure state borders and an inability to protect their national space from external violation, an anxiety we can see reflected across the canon of early Weimar cinema. From Robert Wiene's 1920 tale of the pain suffered in a small German town when the traveling showman Caligari unleashes his murderous somnambulist upon the population, to Paul Wegener's 1920 *Golem,* in which the eponymous monster breaks out of the walls of the Jewish ghetto in which he had been created and runs amok, to Murnau's 1922 retelling of Bram Stoker's *Dracula* as the arrival of a Transylvanian monster bringing rats and the plague to infect German space—Weimar cinema could be rewritten as a cinema of reverse-diffusional anxiety in which German spaces are repeatedly invaded by primitive elements against which the military and the police are incapable of fighting.

As such, Lang's *Nibelungen* becomes a film about space, and, more specifically, a film about the differences between the wild and unspatialized East and the civilized, deeply structured West. The dream of boundaries, order, and control in the Burgundian lands is contrasted with the nightmare of the fluidity, boundlessness, and impermanence in the land of the Huns.

The Shift to Spatial Narration in Lang's *Nibelungen*

In the various forms of advertisement used to announce the *Nibelungen* films (posters, pamphlets, catalogs, etc.) two images predominate. While the first of these depicts one of the best-known events of the epic, and perhaps the most famous scene of the film: the dramatic murder of Siegfried (fig. 11), the second evokes a rather obscure moment: Siegfried's arrival at the border to Worms (fig. 12). Not a central plot point, but the moment of an impending border-crossing, the prevalence of this image is indicative of a larger shift the epic undergoes in Lang's hands: the shift to emphasize space and spatial practice.

The murder of Siegfried by Hagen marks the narrative climax of the first half of the *Nibelungen.* Having tricked Kriemhild into revealing the one place where her beloved husband's skin is vulnerable, Hagen has driven a spear through this spot on Siegfried's back, and the first advertising poster depicts the dramatic result: Siegfried collapses to his knees and grasps the spearhead jutting out from his naked breast; his face is contorted into a wild expression of rage and disbelief. The figure depicted in this sketch resembles the actor, Paul Richter, who played Siegfried in the film, but the poster otherwise differs significantly from the actual filmic rendition of the scene. While Siegfried had been fully clothed in a tunic (onto which Kriemhild had stitched the cross marking his site of vulnerability) and had been slain in a fairy-tale field of flowers alongside a mountain spring, the rough chalk sketch of the poster strips Siegfried of both his clothing and his locational setting. The image is removed from the particularized narrative context of the film and relocated to a mythic state of timeless abstraction.

In his work on the history of *Nibelungen* reception, Joachim Heinzle explains the function of such decontextualization. Over the course of time, the complex and internally conflicting contents of the epic have been reduced to a small set of semantically condensed visual icons. Especially for purposes of

Fig. 11. Film poster depicting the murder of Siegfried. In *Das UFA-Plakat: Filmpremieren 1918–1943*, ed. Peter Mänz and Christian Maryška (Heidelberg: Umschau Braus, 1998), 49.

Fig. 12. Film poster depicting Siegfried's entrance to Worms advertises both halves of the film, although Siegfried is killed at the end of part I. In *Das UFA-Plakat: Filmpremieren 1918–1943*, ed. Peter Mänz and Christian Maryška (Heidelberg: Umschau Braus, 1998), 51.

political propagandizing, the main approach to the national epic has been to isolate particular narrative moments and construct meanings for them that can be manipulated outside of the larger textual logic.[18]

The image of Siegfried present on advertising posters and billboards is an example of such a visual icon. In the immediate postwar period, as Kaes has shown, the function played by the Nibelungen myth was largely a negotiation of the meaning associated with this very image. For Siegfried was the victim of a tragic betrayal—he had literally been "stabbed in the back." In many reproductions of his death, Siegfried comes to represent Germany, in the claim that it too had been betrayed and that the nation's defeat in the war could only have been the result of traitorous oppositional forces on the home front.[19] In this political and historical context, the discourse of Germany's *Dolchstoß* (stab in the back) was mapped onto the murdered Siegfried—in spite of his death by spear and not by dagger.[20] This poster might therefore have suggested an enticing plot or cinematic spectacle, and the targeted audience may also have seen in this image the promise of a filmic enactment of the *Dolchstoßlegende*—one commensurate with the prevailing sentiments surrounding this image.

The second of the two poster images, in contrast, would seem to lack such strong semantic force. While this moment of Siegfried's arrival and entrance into the Burgundian realm marks a progression along the plot's narrative trajectory, this scene had not previously been included in the popular iconography derived from the epic. It does not appear in the long history of German artwork as one of the scenes commonly reproduced from the *Nibelungen,*[21] nor did it enter the German vernacular in the form of a popular set phrase (as did, for example, the term *Hagentreue,* "the loyalty of Hagen").[22] Unlike the well-known dramatic scenes of Siegfried slaying the dragon, Kriemhild accusing Hagen, or the Danube mermaids prophesying Hagen's doom, Siegfried's entrance into Worms would not have been able to draw upon preexisting emotional attachments to the Nibelungen epic. An explanation for this image's frequent appearance in *Nibelungen* film advertising is thus not to be found in expectations of immediate audience recognition.

Indeed, the attraction of this image seems to be divorced from its role as a plot point: the scene of Siegfried's arrival at the gates of the Burgundian kingdom at Worms not only was used to promote part I of the *Nibelungen* but also appeared on posters advertising part II—despite the fact that Siegfried is murdered at the end of the first film, and thus not even present in the second. And, confronted with this advertising poster, it is questionable whether the intended viewer would have been able to identify which border is being traversed. So, why was this particular image expected to resonate with the German public in advertising for the film? Paradoxically, it may be the very turn from a focus on the plot to a focus on the construction of space (here in the form of a mythically inviolable border) that Lang enacted in his filmic rendition of the epic. In Lang's hands, the *Nibelungen* became a film about the relationship of a Volk to its space, and about the nature of the borders that divide these symbiotic units.

In his early negative assessment of the *Nibelungenlied's* potential to become Germany's national epic, Hegel famously wrote:

> In the *Nibelungenlied* . . . we are geographically on native soil, but the Burgundians and King Etzel are so far removed from all of the conditions of our contemporary culture [*Bildung*] and national interests that we can feel much more at home in Homer's verse, even if we aren't highly educated.[23]

In the effort to address Hegel's criticism and to locate "contemporary culture" and "national interests" in the text so that the newly rediscovered *Nibelungenlied* could be elevated to the status of national epic, nineteenth-century German authors set about reinterpreting it. They either isolated various scenes of the legend to reinscribe them with national meaning or rewrote the text in its entirety. In these reinventions of the narrative, the geography of the text—the German "native soil"—frequently gained emphasis, particularly with regard to national conflict in both the East and West.[24]

Arguing in 1825 that the *Nibelungenlied* could become the German *Iliad* ("*die teutsche Ilias*") Johannes von Müller identified the original development of the Nibelungen material as having been driven by Germany's position on the eastern border of Europe and their concern with this spatial location. He claimed that the epic poem was revised in southern Germany in the late tenth century, when Germans were threatened on the eastern border of the Holy Roman Empire by the pressure of the Slavs. Seeing this threat reflected in the role played by the Huns during the period of the great tribal migrations, they reinvented and reembraced the *Nibelungenlied*.[25]

Such geopolitical concerns returned during the interwar period, when the *Nibelungenlied* was reinterpreted in the context of the German-Polish and German-French border contestations. In 1934, Karl Busch claimed the epic to be "the great song of German borderland struggles," in which the idealistic notion of the border (the "*Grenzgedanke*") itself played a role in the origins of the epic. As "the Huns, rushing back in defeat, slaughtered vengefully into the

Volk of Cologne . . . , the borderland mission of the Franconians [their "*Grenzlandaufgabe*"] became clear to them."[26]

But Hans Salzwedel had already taken the border analogy much further in his *Der schwarze Lupno* (The black Lupno, 1926), in which he rewrote the entire epic as a modern-day *Ostmarkenroman.* In his version, the Lupno is a river that marks the border between the German estate of the von Falk family and that of the Polish Sadnitzkis. Etzel is recast as the Polish landowner who has driven the Sadnitzki estate into ruin through his gambling and *polnische Wirtschaft.* When it is discovered that he has been systematically swindling his guests during gambling evenings, his house is brought into shame, and he becomes insane and decides to burn down the castle with all of his family and servants trapped inside. In this tale, the order of the epic is reversed, for it is following this great catastrophic event that the Siegfried character (the son of the von Falks) appears. He purchases the ruined estate and, through his hard labor, turns it into a model for the surrounding German colonial community.[27]

In the various lectures and articles in which Lang discussed his own *Nibelungen* project, he stressed that he had wanted his film to shift the focus of the epic from a heavily Teutonic Wagnerian aesthetic and onto a detailed portrayal of the four starkly different worlds he found in it, starting with Worms.

> The world of Worms, which is the world of an already over refined culture, in which every gesture, every garment, every greeting is of an almost weary but nonetheless noble artlessness. Here, it was important to make believable that people lived and found their fates in these almost bare, and inexpressibly severe spaces. That meant that the style of the structures built around the people couldn't suffocate them, but had to remain a frame that allowed them to come to the fore.[28]

And, similarly, he showed the mystical forest of Siegfried's youth, the cold world of Brunhild, "in which the people appear to be captured in glass," and the world of the Huns and Etzel, "the Asian, the Lord of the Earth."[29]

In his investigation of these four diverse worlds, Lang devotes long stretches of his film to depicting acts of border crossing—Siegfried's entrance into the mystical forest, the Burgundians forging a path through the flames surrounding Brunhild's kingdom, Siegfried's arrival at Worms, Kriemhild's departure from Worms, her arrival at Etzel's kingdom, etc.—border crossings that Kaes reads in military terms as "warlike deployments and excursions into foreign territories."[30] The abilities of the various borders to delineate spaces and to control the conditions under which they can be crossed communicate much about the identities of the respective peoples. A comparison of Siegfried's entrance into Worms and Kriemhild's arrival at Etzel's realm reveals the extent to which border crossings are used to convey the differences between "Europe" and "Asia"—between West and East.

The isolated film still of Siegfried's arrival at Worms presents the striking image of a drawbridge created by Lang's set designer, Otto Hunte (fig. 13). But it is unable to capture the impact generated by the dimension of time. Whereas the average shot length was only five to seven seconds long in the films of the early 1920s, the camera focuses on this particular image for a full twelve seconds.[31] The sheer length of this shot communicates a gravity that is exacerbated by the fact that the scene it captures is almost completely static.

This set was one of the engineering feats of the film, and this long take allowed the audience to indulge in the filmic spectacle. But these twelve seconds also communicate meaning by monumentalizing Siegfried's act of *waiting* at a border that has the power to control his movements. When Siegfried arrives at Worms, he and his entourage are held up at the border while their desire to enter the kingdom is announced and considered at court. While a short situating shot would have sufficed to indicate the mere fact of Siegfried's location at the border, the length of the take renders visible the passive act of waiting that is imposed upon him. The lingering of the camera upon the static constellation formed by Siegfried and his men upon the drawbridge stresses the immobility and lack of threat carried by these potential visitors prior to being granted access to the kingdom.

Thus understood, we can begin to see how this image came to stand as an icon for the film from the very beginning. For each time that the border into Worms is crossed, its status as a stable agent of regulation and control is reinscribed. Access to the kingdom is only possible via this drawbridge, and it is incontestably under the control of the castle's inhabitants.

The Trauma of Border Violations

To understand the weight of this image, we must resituate it in the geopolitical context of Germany in the early 1920s. In this immediate postwar period, the nation's own borders were the site of territorial vulnerability and state crisis. In addition to the territory France annexed or occupied on Germany's western flank, Germany had also lost territory in the East that it was forced to cede to

Fig. 13. Siegfried waits at the border to Worms.

the newly reinstated state of Poland. Given the history of German colonial endeavor in the East, the resulting sense of loss came to be expressed in the terms of a post–colonial anxiety of reverse diffusion: the Slavic flood was again threatening from the East, this time in the form of a Polish nation that was encroaching upon German space and pressuring the Germans westward. The floodwaters were amassing much closer to home, and there was no reliable national border to stave off their flow.

After World War I, Germany's vast territorial losses (amounting to approximately 13 percent of its prewar continental expanse) were accompanied by dramatic changes in the nation's border. Not only were the contours of the state's periphery altered (in some areas quite drastically), but the perceived nature of this border itself changed. It could no longer serve as a symbolic representation of Germany's strength and sovereignty, because the Allied nations repeatedly proved that Germany's border was no longer under Germany's control.

The armistice commission had failed to draw a "permanent" line of demarcation separating Germany and Poland until February 1919. Prior to this, armed rogue militias were formed on both sides of the provisional border, and armed conflict continued. The Posnanian War broke out between Germany and Poland on December 27, 1918, and was only settled by the Treaty of Versailles several months later.[32] The Silesian War, on the other hand, was not brought to an end by the signing of this document nor by the official act of demarcation in 1919. Repeated outbursts of violence at the border (the longest lasting for two months in the spring of 1921) only ended in 1922 with the signing of the Silesian Convention.[33] The historian Martin Broszat characterizes this early period of German-Polish relations as "border skirmishes accompanied by aspects reminiscent of civil war: the reciprocal harassment and denunciation, the taking of hostages and a canon of hate and propaganda."[34]

Germany's sense of its postwar border crisis is perhaps best introduced by the systematic typology of "border violations" developed by the geopolitician Ernst Tiessen in his 1924 article on the relationship between the Peace Treaty of Versailles and political geography.[35] He begins with a definition of the state.

> In geographical terms, the state is a section of the earth's surface with solidly fixed borders and its entire contents. Here, the emphasis is placed on the characteristic of solidly fixed borders . . . precisely because solidly fixed borders are never drawn by nature, but only ever by man.[36]

Understanding the state as the symbiotic product of a land region with its border—and indeed prioritizing the role assumed by the latter—Tiessen can argue that a territory lacking firm borders cannot be considered a "state." In his article, he will attempt to prove that the provisions of the Treaty of Versailles indeed intend to strip Germany of its statehood and thus its identity as a member of the European center.

Tiessen first describes various features of Germany's new contours that have weakened the ability of this border to carry out its principal function—that of providing defense against military attack. Appealing to the "negative" geopolitical model of the state, he stresses that the new arbitrarily meandering shape of the border had resulted in a disadvantageous extension of its length, making it harder to protect, especially given his claim that the borders are more easily penetrable in their new location. Then, mobilizing the "geo-organic" model, he claims that the new borders cut the nation off from its previous sources of raw materials and that its reduced coastline restricted its doorway of contact with the rest of the world. The imposition of these new borders, he argues, had greatly compromised Germany's viability as a state. But vastly more injurious than the myriad flaws in the contours of the nation's periphery were the seemingly endless violations inflicted upon it by the Allies.

> That which has been inflicted upon the German Reich—in the excision [*Beschneidung*] of its territory and in the new borders drawn up in the Versailles Peace Treaty—only amounts to a fraction of the damage incurred by the methodically undertaken violations over the border and into the body of the state.[37]

Where the state is understood as a body (*Staatskörper*), the language of border violation becomes one of symbolic castration followed by symbolic rape: an appeal to tropes of sexual violation as the attempt to give expression to a very real sense of border vulnerability.

Tiessen draws out a typology of border violations to describe the practices through which the Allied powers defied the sanctity of the postwar German state. First was the lack of finality regarding the placement of Germany's borders. The territories subject to popular plebiscite (*Volksabstimmungsgebiete*) were German border regions of ethnically mixed populations that had been given the opportunity to vote for the country to which they wished to belong. These plebiscites were motivated by the principle of national self-determination, a principle that U.S. president Wilson had established as necessary for creating a lasting peace in Central-Eastern Europe. For Germany, this meant that southern East Prussia, Upper Silesia, Schleswig, and Alsace-Lorraine were all regions of uncertain fate in the immediate postwar period. Whether these areas would fall within Germany's new borders or those of its neighbors was an issue of enormous political and economic import. The size of Germany's territory and population was at stake, as were—particularly in the cases of Alsace-Lorraine and Upper Silesia—the state's coal deposits and industrial centers.

In this situation of utmost gravity, the international demarcation commission, which was in charge of resolving territorial contestations throughout Eastern Europe, was widely held to be ineffective and inconsistent. Their decisions were frequently challenged by all parties involved.[38] Perhaps most deleterious was the commission's inability to reach timely decisions, for the process of organizing the plebiscites often took months, if not years. This delay resulted in a lasting sense of instability and lack of finality. The Treaty of Versailles was signed on June 28, 1919, and yet two years later, in 1921, the case of Upper Silesia had still not been decided. There could be no process of "coming to terms" with the new shape of the nation while Germans were still uncertain about what this would actually be. Individual questions of staying or leaving, investing or divesting, continuing to fight or resigning oneself to a new set of circumstances—all such decisions were kept in limbo as the international decision-making process dragged on. Meanwhile, border warfare continued, with independent militias on each side attempting to gain as much territory as possible before final border decisions were rendered.

Tiessen also decries the foreign occupation of the Rhineland area (which others referred to as the "enslavement of the Rhine").[39] Under the provisions of the Treaty of Versailles, this region was to be occupied for fifteen years. The sense of humiliation suffered by the Germans was exacerbated by several measures undertaken by the French that echoed German inner colonial policies in the former Eastern Territories. Where Germans had attempted to eliminate Polish in the official public sphere through increasingly restrictive language laws, the French now mandated that the French language was to be used in all schools, allegedly in order to facilitate communication between them and German civilians.[40] The perception that Germans were now positioned as colonial subjects was reinforced by French constructions of the situation as such. The message underlying their claims of "educational opportunities that the French were offering to their backwards neighbors"[41] was clear: Germany no longer belonged to that Europe understood to be the source of world culture and civilization but was instead the recipient of diffusions imported by the French.

Most loudly protested was the French deployment of black soldiers (enlisted from the French colonies in Africa) in their occupation of German territory. For not only had Germany been stripped of all of its own colonies, but now Germans perceived themselves to be placed (at least symbolically) under the domination of foreign colonial subjects. The French occupational soldiers became the object of reverse-diffusional anxiety and aggression. Widespread allegations of the rape of white German women by black soldiers served to reinforce the discourse of the (sexually) violated body of the nation.[42]

It is in the context of this traumatic reverse-diffusional perception that we must understand Tiessen's summarizing condemnation of the Treaty of Versailles.

> A treaty that doesn't create firm borders but instead nullifies them thereby nullifies the state identity of one of the signing parties and therewith the very nature of a state treaty. As long as the Versailles Peace Treaty persists, the German Reich is not a "state" according to the political-geographic definition of the term.[43]

The deconstruction of Germany's sovereign control over its borders threatened its very identity as a legitimate, viable state.

Fritz Lang's *Nibelungen* films were conceptualized and created in this socio-historical context of border crisis. The filming of part I began in 1922, following a wave of violent border skirmishes on Germany's border with Poland (at a time when such destabilizing warfare seemed to permeate Eastern Europe). In the following year, the French invaded and occupied the Ruhr Valley for some nine months. The premiers of the two *Nibelungen* films followed in February and April 1924.

The *Nibelungen* project reveals its fascination with the status of territorial borders in such scenes as that represented by the second advertising poster. Returning to this image, we see that it is highly symbolic: a drawbridge is suspended over a seemingly bottomless divide. Siegfried, dressed in white and mounted upon his white horse, is followed by his twelve vassals. The drawbridge divides the image into two realms. In the upper realm, Siegfried and his men face unwaveringly toward the massive bulwark of the barbican, which rises up on the right. Below the bridge exists a cavernous gorge. The vertical framing on the right extends the limits of the border beyond visual range at both extremes of the filmic frame. Neither the upper extent of the bulwark nor the bottom reach of the chasm are ever revealed in any of the film's multiple scenes involving this border. The viewer is thus hindered in creating any specific particularity for it. This is not an artificial, man-made boundary; it is not a rerouted river, nor is it a trench with a moat. It is instead a mythical instantiation of the very notion of "border" itself.[44]

As such, it is evocative of wartime dreams of the permanent, inviolable national border, such as that envisioned by the politician and publicist Friedrich Naumann. His model of *Mitteleuropa* advocated the digging of huge, unsurpassable trenches that would extend from north to south on either side of Germany. Naumann had delineated this plan in his wartime call for a united federation of *Mitteleuropa* under German leadership. His 300-page *Mitteleuropa,* first published in 1915, had been immensely popular and was reprinted in the following year in two different editions, including an expanded *Volksausgabe* published in an affordable paperback format. Here, Naumann set forth his vision for the postwar German landscape thus.

> According to the experience we have gained during this war, one must rely on trenches when one has no allies. For this is the first and most im-

> portant war-technical conclusion: that in the future, all fighting will take place along long lines, and that the *trench will be the fundamental form of homeland defense.* The politics of the trench will result in each state calculating which of its borders it can convert into trenches. . . . After the war, trench barricades will be erected everywhere where there is the possibility of future warfare. New Roman ramparts will be created, new Chinese walls of earth and barbed wire. . . . Europe will gain two long ramparts running from the north to the south. The first will somehow run from the lower Rhine to the Alps, and the other from the Courland to either right or left of Rumania.[45]

Naumann's trench model thus envisioned a territory under German control, and radically severed from its surroundings. The trench had come to define the war imagery of World War I, and Naumann's model envisioned its perfected execution.

The border into Worms presents the viewer with an idealized rendition of Naumann's trans-European trench, the strong, easily defendable border Germany so strongly desired. Under the bridge, in the focused center of the shot and framed heavily on all three sides, lies a triangular wedge marked by nothing but absence. There is no indication of the surrounding landscape, which, apart from rendering this border geographically abstract, also suggests that the chasm is so vast that it is no longer visible. This is an unquestionably inviolable border seemingly cut deep into the landscape. While the man-made drawbridge allows the border to be crossed, it remains completely under the control of the guards at Worms—once removed, this chasm becomes impassable.

The ensuing entrance ceremony undergone by Siegfried and his entourage reinscribes the power of the border to regulate and control human movement. Siegfried and his men, organized in a tight geometric alignment, traverse two thresholds: the first on horseback into the kingdom of Worms, and the second on foot into the king's throne room in the castle. Trumpeters announce the arrival of Siegfried and his application for passage, and King Gunther and the members of his court don ceremonial garments. Siegfried's entourage first rides into the kingdom in solemn parade fashion, and later enters Gunther's throne room in a highly ordered formation. They are overseen by structured rows of onlookers who geometrically line the balconies and aisles of the reception hall and watch Siegfried and Gunther exchange ritualized gestures of greeting (figs. 14–17).

Many readings of Lang's *Nibelungen* focus on the heavy, monumentalized aesthetic found in the Burgundian kingdom. In Worms, strong geometric shapes and patterns dominate throughout: they are painted onto walls and ceilings, laid into the stonework on the floors, woven into the fabrics of clothing and curtains, and even reproduced in the arrangements of human bodies in space. These geometric forms and the heavy lines of the architecture and textiles create multiple layers of visual frames, visually interpolating the individual, subsuming him according to the dictates of the surrounding aesthetic.

In many ways, these images recall the filmic mass ornament that Siegfried Kracauer so famously identified as a defining component of Weimar popular culture; and indeed, he too discusses the ornamental aesthetics of Lang's film. In the kingdom of Worms, ornament visually communicates the "overculturedness" in which Lang envisioned this realm.

> Often, the actors form themselves into ornaments. One scene in Gunther's hall shows the king and his men sitting like statues in symmetrically ordered niches. The camera misses no opportunity to capture such arrangements. When Siegfried pays his first visit to Gunther, his entrance into the hall is recorded from a high angle in order to reveal the ornamental nature of the ceremony.[46]

But, although these groups of bodies organize themselves into ornamental patterns, such ornaments were not "ends in themselves" but meaningful depictions of space.[47] This rigorously orchestrated ceremony functioned to reaffirm the power and sanctity of the border as an ordering social structure. Within this ceremony, the assemblage of human bodies into disciplined, patterned constellations is explicitly meaningful. The ordered column of twelve knights accompanying Siegfried into the reception hall signifies his social power. According to medieval courtly tradition, these are knights that Siegfried has conquered in battle, and who now serve him. The bird's-eye camera shot interpolates this constellation of men into the bold geometric patterns established by the floor tiles and carpets (fig. 16). The ornamentation attributed to Siegfried thereby becomes integrated within that of the space of Worms. This easy aesthetic fusion indicates that Siegfried and the Burgundians share a common cultural register (every other border crossing is governed by radical aesthetic incompatibility, especially, as I will show below, in the case of the Burgundian arrival in Etzel's kingdom).

Participation in this performance of ritual order signifies Siegfried's respect for the legitimacy of this border-crossing ceremony, and thereby communicates his membership within the community for which it holds. This reciprocal submission to a ceremony of order will be contrasted with chaos and

Fig. 14. Siegfried enters the gates to Worms.

disorder in parallel scenes of border crossings into territory coded as non-Germanic.

Siegfried's entrance into Worms is disturbed by momentary conflict when Hagen violates the chivalric code (proposing that Siegfried serve as Gunther's vassal in exchange for Kriemhild's hand). The discord even reaches the level of threatened physical violence, and weapons are drawn. As Siegfried's men lower their spears and Hagen's men rejoin, the camera again adopts the bird's-eye view in order to observe that even this act maintains the strict geometry and precise synchronicity of the entrance ceremony itself (fig. 18). A circle is formed and weapons are raised, all in metric time. The disturbance is only momentary and the violence remains contained within the orchestrated performance.

In the second of the two *Nibelungen* films, Siegfried has been murdered, and Kriemhild is his vengeful widow. She agrees to marry Etzel, the king of the Huns, because she believes that this liaison will best allow her to exact revenge upon Hagen and those members of her family who protect him. After the birth

Fig. 15. Siegfried enters the palace at Worms.

of her first and only child with Etzel, Kriemhild will invite her brothers and their entourage to visit her. Once they have arrived, she will orchestrate an attack on them by the Huns, which will ultimately lead to the death of almost all involved in a lengthy battle sequence with which the film ends.

This violence is foreshadowed at the moment of Kriemhild's departure from Worms. The geometric rigidity that had dominated the depiction of the Burgundian kingdom breaks down in the moment when Kriemhild prepares for her journey. As the members of her entourage mount their horses, visual chaos replaces previously disciplined symmetry. Crowds of people traverse the scene, and the horses appear panicked, their riders struggling to direct them toward the gate of exit. Beyond the palace gate waits a throng of crippled beggars whose mass of rags, canes, and crutches adds to the confusion of the scene. Significantly, this visual chaos is framed by an architectural structure featured only in this scene, a huge recess in the castle's facade shaped like a World War I military helmet (*Stahlhelm*). Kriemhild will depart Worms under this unmistakable sign of death and violence (fig. 19).

As she leaves Worms, the location of the narration shifts to Etzel's eastern

Fig. 16. Geometric ornament

kingdom, where the film's fascination with borders continues—for here, they will be of a much different nature than was observed in Worms.

In his reading of the role he set out to play as King Etzel, Rudolf Klein-Rogge shows that he understood the Huns to represent a threat amassing in the East, and that this threat was related to the lack of borders and other spatialization practices in Etzel's world.

> Where does he come from? From the land of boundlessness, from the land of the mountains with peaks that one cannot see, from the land of unfathomable plains, from the land of the iciest cold and of searing heat, from a land in which the oldest creative culture often existed right next to chaotic dimwittedness. This Asia, which finds its mythic expression in King Etzel, Attila, the scourge of God, has lain next to Europe like an immense threat for thousands of years. From time to time, it is set in motion. The Great Migrations, Etzel with his Huns, Genghis Khan—these are the

Fig. 17. Scripted rituals of greeting

> signs of such movement that have remained in our collective consciousness. He rolls over Europe, Etzel at the head of his yellow swarms of riders. . . . He has both possibilities that only the Asian unites with such perfection: the absolute concentration upon the self and the limitless expansion of the self into the world.[48]

The lack of borders defines Etzel both physically and psychologically: he lacks the physical, territorial borders necessary for the development of a bond between a people and its space, and this lack of an external spatial form is reflected in a boundless internal sense of self, a self with no firm contours of identity. Etzel becomes the embodiment of that which knows no boundaries, of that which flows across borders without regard for their sovereignty.

Etzel's kingdom is located on the wide, expansive steppes of Eastern Europe. From his throne, he can look through an open portal and enjoy an unrestricted view over this vast plain. The camera frequently adopts his point of view to meander over the landscape. The extent to which Etzel's gaze is un-

Fig. 18. Geometric containment of conflict

bounded seems to reflect his limitless power, but it also reveals the vulnerability of his kingdom, which lacks firm borders.

When Kriemhild arrives at the land of the Huns, there are two "borders" she must cross, which are analogous to Siegfried's two-phased border crossing into Worms. The first is the threshold to Etzel's realm, the exact location of which is impossible to determine. Is it located somewhere in the center of the expansive plain, its contours invisible to the uninitiated eye? Here, scouts crouch hidden in a tree and drop from their perch in a race to report the impending arrival of their new queen.[49] We follow the lead scout as he heads back to announce the sighting of Kriemhild (and collect his bag of gold as a reward for this service). A low-angle shot captures the heroic action as the leading Hun charges through a river on horseback, and a surveying high-angle shot follows his deft navigations through the mounds of earth that mark the underground hovels of the Huns that surround the palace.

This border to Etzel's realm might also be marked by the dilapidated and sagging waist-high picket fence that surrounds Etzel's palace. A break in the

Fig. 19. Leaving Worms under the sign of the *Stahlhelm*

enclosure is flanked by two billowing torches but is ignored by the incoming scout, who instead springs over the fence, his horse kicking it over in the process, as if to accentuate its flimsiness. The scout races on and, without breaking pace, gallops straight up the steps and through the gate of the palace, rearing his horse directly at the foot of Etzel's throne (fig. 20). While the king's enthusiastic reception of the scout reveals no sign that he objects to the presence of a horse in his chambers, this image shocks the viewer. The threshold between internal and external space that had been so ritualistically protected in Worms has been rendered completely fluid in the kingdom of the Huns.

The lack of a functional territorial border is reflected in the lack of an entrance ceremony upon Kriemhild's arrival. The chaos that began in the moments of her departure from Worms is amplified in her approach to Etzel's palace. The notes of Harbou's screenplay call for "men, women, and children who run towards Kriemhild and look as if they had just crawled out of underground burrows."[50] The film far exceeds Harbou's directives, as the crowd of taunting, half-naked Huns is joined by their tussling children and panicking

Fig. 20. The fluid borders between internal and external space in Etzel's kingdom are revealed as a sentry's horse gallops straight from the field into Etzel's throne room without breaking pace.

livestock in an unsettlingly tumultuous scene. Kriemhild will ultimately make her way to the palace door and enter the reception hall alone and, save for the presence of Rüdiger, who stands off to one side, unescorted (figs. 21 and 22).

The structuring oppositions of a mythically encompassing border versus the complete absence of one, of a bottomless cavern versus an open stretch of plain, of impassability versus fluid traversal, and of ritual ceremony versus ominous chaos participate in the construction of a radical dichotomy of civilization and primitivity by highlighting the different relationships the Burgundians and the Huns have to the spaces they inhabit. In introducing such geographical and geopolitical elements, the film seems to draw on the theories of the state and its border that had been developed by Friedrich Ratzel at the end of the nineteenth century and thereafter popularized in his schoolbook on German *Heimatkunde* (study of German local history and geography), and by the continuing work of his students (most particularly that of Karl Haushofer, whose 1926 volume *Grenzen* [Borders] is largely a reworking of Ratzel's model).[51]

Fig. 21. Kriemhild's arrival at Etzel's palace lacks an entrance ceremony

Written in the period of German imperial growth and conquest, Ratzel's work imagines the state as a biological entity undergoing natural organic cycles of birth, growth, and death. In this early geo-organic model, a state's border was likened to the external membrane of a body, and the maintenance of its "health" was of utmost importance. A healthy border was elastic and allowed for the robust growth of the organism. Where the state's border encountered those of other vigorous states, the border underwent a change from an expansive "border zone" (*Grenzsaum*) to a more rigorously defined "border line" (*Grenzlinie*), the site at which "border dispute" (*Grenzstreit*) led to the most firmly constructed and maintained borders.

> In the development of a state, the earliest stages are characterized by an openness of the land and the vagueness of its borders. The longer a Volk settles and works on its land, and the more intimately it grows together with it, the more distinctly and permanently it defines its borders.[52]

Fig. 22. Depicting spatial degeneracy: slop buckets lie overturned, and scattered straw can't hide the puddles of liquid covering the floor of Etzel's throne room.

Ratzel delivers a model of center and periphery separated by geopolitical categories: The world's *Kulturvölker* have borders that are well-maintained and that steadily expand into the periphery. Primitive *Naturvölker* lack strong identifications with territorial borders, which eases the process of diffusion into these spaces, thus allowing *Kulturvölker* to expand their borders into the spaces inhabited by the *Naturvölker,* who are thus destined to be overrun and eliminated in the Darwinian struggle for the survival of the fittest.

In the late nineteenth century, Ratzel's model had relegated the German state to a most advantageous position. For while it had firm and rigorously maintained borders in the West with France, the East was imagined as offering an endless potential for growth. The Germans were a *Kulturvolk* in a healthy stage of development. The Poles, meanwhile, were a Volk without a state (hence without a border) and were thus destined to dissolve into the states that had expanded into their territory. After World War I, the assurance of this conviction, of course, turned back upon itself. For now, Germany was a shrinking state, lacking firm borders, while its Polish neighbor appeared to demand ever more territory.

In the envisioned landscape of the *Nibelungen* film, the Ratzelian model of the state and its border adds a clear geopolitical dimension to the *Kulturvolk/Naturvolk* dichotomy that is so rigidly maintained. In its boundlessness, Etzel's kingdom is marked by a geography of barbarism.

Architectural Doppelgänger

Etzel's palace is a veritable embodiment of chaos. He sits at the head of his throne room, and below him, his hall teems with disorder, filth, and brutish behavior. Etzel looks out over the brawling Huns with an expression of forlorn resignation, and the camera follows his gaze as it passes first over women sloppily ladling stew out of a large vat and the childlike grabbing of the hungry that sends it sloshing to the ground. On the other side of the hall, Etzel's gaze lingers over men playing darts against the palace wall; they beat and pounce on one another like scuffling animals (fig. 23).

This portrayal of the Huns was not infrequently criticized. Such a lowly, bestial Volk was not held to be an honorable match for the Burgundians and thus was not worthy of the ultimate sacrifice of their mass bloodshed.

> Lang only really misses the mark once—in the case of the Huns. King Etzel's palace looks like a pigsty. And his Huns behave themselves in his great hall like devils at their grandmothers'. Here, Lang likely wanted to stress the distinction between barbarism and the refined style of the court at Worms, but he forgets that even though Etzel was a Hun, he amassed such vast riches on his campaigns, that it is hardly possible that his wife Kriemhild would have had to sleep on a simple wooden frame covered merely with a bear skin.[53]

This reviewer presents two observations without further interpretation: that Etzel's hall resembles a "pigsty," and that his Huns' behavior is not appropriate within such a space. These two observations must be brought into connection with a third: namely, that Etzel's palace is obviously a Germanic, not a Hunnic building. Not only is this huge stone structure a complete anomaly among the various primitive and organic structures otherwise inhabited by the Huns, but

Fig. 23. Spatial chaos and destruction in Etzel's throne room

Etzel's palace is also an almost exact duplicate of the Burgundian palace at Worms. The behavior of the Huns is incongruous with this space because on a cultural level, this space was not theirs to begin with.

Underneath the layers of filth and the external signs of deterioration, Etzel's palace reveals a solid building able to withstand the harsh treatment afforded to it by the Huns. The thick, sturdy walls are organized along stark, geometric lines, and, as was seen at Worms, a balcony runs along the sides and against the back of the room. The two reception halls are roughly the same size, and their interior spaces are both similarly arranged. Etzel, when seated upon his throne at the back of the hall, looks straight ahead to a half flight of stairs that broadly stretches across the expanse of the opposing wall. At the top of these steps, a massive arched portal marks the threshold to the kingdom lying beyond. While Gunther's view from his throne overlooks a different geographic landscape beyond this entrance, he nonetheless sees the same architectural forms within the confines of the hall's walls. This includes, for example, the massive, arched wooden doors that close off this entrance (see fig. 22).

The similarity of these two palaces is further reinforced in their compara-

Fig. 24. Brunhild's throne room in the "Northland"

tive contrast to the film's third castle, located in Brunhild's Iceland. Her throne room is much smaller, and much differently designed. Seated upon her throne, the wall to Brunhild's right is divided by huge windows reaching from the ceiling to the floor (there are no windows in the throne rooms at Etzel's or in Worms). Instead of the grand flight of steps leading to an arched portal, Brunhild's gaze rests upon a low and narrow doorway leading into a long, dark hallway (figs. 24 and 25). The aesthetics of this Icelandic space differentiate it from the Germanic halls of Etzel and Gunther, which emphasizes the underlying similarities of this latter pair.

Similarly, within his own kingdom, Etzel's palace is a complete architectural anomaly that cannot be structurally compared to the earthen hovels, animal-hide tents, or cliff-dwellings of the Huns (figs. 26–28). The stone walls of the palace are not reproduced in any of these other Hunnic structures, which all appear much more organic in form, and much less solid and permanent than the palace. Against the primitivity of the Hunnic spaces, the similarities between Etzel's and Gunther's castles become even more readily apparent.

Etzel's palace in the middle of the Eastern European Steppes thus exists

Fig. 25. The portal to Brunhild's throne room

as an architectural Doppelgänger in Lang's film, a displaced copy of an almost identical structure found in Worms. The duplication of the palace hall, however, forces the viewer to construct meaning from the antagonism between two vastly different visual idioms (figs. 29 and 30).

That Etzel's building is somewhat older than its duplicate in Worms can be seen in the building's ornamentation. Along the balcony that runs across the back of the hall stands a series of structural pillars. While the artwork of the Huns shown in the film otherwise consists of primitive representational renderings of recognizable (usually animal) forms, the building's pillars are decorated with abstract shapes in bold patterns. Although this ornamentation does not yet attain the strong geometric regularity of the forms found at Worms, it does appear to be prototypical, the product of an earlier period.

But the two palaces differ most obviously in their states of repair. For not only is Etzel's hall filthy, it is also being steadily destroyed by the Huns. The walls are scorched, the balcony timbers are damaged, and the stone steps are

Fig. 26. Etzel's tent

cracked and crumbling. Etzel is allowing the hall to fall into ruin. Meanwhile, one of the connotative effects of constructing the Huns as such a primitive *Naturvolk* is the understanding that this building will not be reconstructed once it has been burned down and destroyed at the end of the film. The eastern barbarians presented by the Huns have not yet reached the level of human development from which such a refined cultural product might derive.

Iconographies of Barbarism

In his review of the second part of Lang's *Nibelungen,* Weimar film and theater critic Herbert Jhering rejects the film *in toto.* He finds the acting horrible and stiff, the direction weak, and the whole film "sterile," plagued by its "motionlessness."[54] He deems Margarete Schön "impossible as Kriemhild," her minimalist acting ridiculous ("She stands with arms crossed, and sometimes she

Fig. 27. The Huns' cliff dwellings

stretches them out vengefully, only to bring them back into the crossed position.").[55] Jhering is also extremely critical of the depiction of Etzel (played by Rudolf Klein-Rogge) and the Huns, who have been reduced to

> ethnological rarities. The world of the Huns must also have its greatness—a barbaric, Asiatic, yet heroic greatness. Otherwise, the downfall of the Nibelungen will be diminished by its opponent. Klein-Rogge as Etzel has little more than glued-on facial features. He doesn't carry a foreign world in himself; he hails from the ethnographic museum.[56]

Etzel was indeed quite literally a product of the ethnographic museum, specifically that of the well-known Umlauff family, a fact with which the film was often advertised.[57] Heinrich Umlauff had collaborated with Fritz Lang on his earlier film projects, *Harakiri* (1919) and *Die Spinnen* (The Spiders, 1919/20). For the *Nibelungen* project, the "Umlauff-enthusiast" Fritz Lang arranged for his costume designer, Änne Willkom, to work with this eccentric collector in

Fig. 28. The Huns' underground mud huts

drafting costumes for the Huns. Together, they would use African and Asian artifacts in the creation of "the Hun." The children and even some of the adults were to appear more or less naked, save for various primitive ornamentation—animal bones, bird feathers, and strings of beads. Others were clad in scraps of animal fur that appear to be extensions of their own wild and unkempt hair, while they brandished crude weapons.

Fritz Lang's biographer Lotte Eisner would later defend the filmmaker's primitive portrayal of the Huns and refute the claim that it was based on a concept of racial difference. She claimed it was the attempt to distinguish the film's four different worlds that demanded such a contrasting aesthetic.[58] Yet given the cultural and geopolitical context of the early 1920s, it is important to show that the effect was otherwise.

In Decla's film catalog, the *Nibelungen* is introduced by an article in which each of the main actors is celebrated in their various castings. George John performed three roles, all of which are described in terms of the physical anomalies each exhibits.

Fig. 29. Siegfried's entrance into the throne room at Worms

> Georg John plays no fewer than three roles in the "Nibelungen": the brothers Mime and Alberich; the sword-smith—a cripple, Alberich—a dwarf; and Blaodel, Etzel's brother, a half-animal Hun [*ein hunnisches Halbtier*], doltish, evil, and loyal.[59]

While Alberich and Mime arguably represent much more important roles for John, only Blaodel is described with detailed reference to character traits. To indicate only that he was a "Hun" would not have been sufficient to convey the intended connotations of this figure, for this referent was one with which the Germans might have intuitively identified. One thinks here of Kaiser Wilhelm II's famous "Hun speech" of 1900. As his troops were heading to China to exact revenge for the assassination of the German envoy to China during the Boxer Rebellion, he sent them off with this message.

> As the Huns a thousand years ago under King Etzel made a name for themselves that has lasted mightily in memory, so may the name "Germany" be known in China, such that no Chinese will ever again even dare to look askance at a German.[60]

Fig. 30. The portal to Etzel's throne room closely resembles that at Worms.

Of course this speech later came back to haunt the Germans, who were referred to pejoratively by their enemies as "Huns" during World War I in reference to their purported savagery. Given this set of associations, Lang's Huns had to be brought into semantic alignment through the additional terms *doltish, evil, loyal*—and, most important, *half-animal.*

In her screenplay for the film, Thea von Harbou makes frequent use of animal referents in her stage directions for the Huns. The portrayer of a Hunnic scout is instructed to crouch in a tree like "a glaring vulture" before climbing "down from the tree like an ape."[61] At Etzel's palace, the king chases away his subjects who scamper in all directions, "disappearing like a horde of beaten dogs."[62] The Huns are thus understood as not only culturally but moreover biologically primitive. The Hun as a "half-animal" is evinced not only in the animal-hide clothing of this eastern race but also in their body posture and movements, for they do not walk upright but bound about in hunched positions, strongly resembling the primate movements of apes. Even King Etzel stands dwarfed next to Kriemhild as a result of the stooped posture he adopts (fig. 31).

Fig. 31. Etzel's consistently stooped posture lets him appear less than human.

Alongside exaggerated visual references to animalistic and childlike behaviors, the film deploys an additional, unmistakable iconography in its construction of the Huns—an appeal to the stereotype of the "Indians" of the American Wild West. For example, Hunnic scouts squat perched in a tree, overlooking the surrounding plain, as they keep watch for Kriemhild's approaching caravan (fig. 32). The lead scout has long black hair decorated with feathers and bones, and the silhouette of his horsewhip resembles that of a bow and arrow in a quiver. Dropping from the tree to mount his galloping horse and charging in a band across the steppes adds to the set of iconographic referents.

Lutz Koepnick's reading of Lang's film also notes this connection: "At first sight, one wonders why Lang, in order to picture the savagery that prevails in the heart of central-European darkness, transports his German spectator of the 1920s to the Far West."[63] In answering this question, Koepnick points to the enduring popularity of the American Western genre: when a foreign embargo limited the importation of American-made films after World War I, Germans responded by filming their own Westerns.

Fig. 32. The Huns pose in the role of Apaches in a clichéd vignette of "cowboys and Indians."

Arthur Wellin's 1920 *Der letzte Mohikaner* (The Last of the Mohicans) starring Bela Lugosi is one of many films made in this early period. In chapter 1, I showed that the hero of Gustav Freytag's *Soll und Haben,* Anton Wohlfart, read Cooper's 1826 novel *The Last of the Mohicans* and that it served to construct his imaginative expectations for his future encounters with *Poles* in Krakow. Now Wellin's film adaptation functioned in a similar fashion, solidifying an iconography that was also reappropriated in the imagination of a "Wild East."

However, this depiction of the Huns in a Western idiom is always only partial. Elements of the Wild West are fused together with images of eastern barbarism, racial underdevelopment, and spatial boundlessness in the creation of something new—the "Wild East." Or, indeed, perhaps this is not new at all. For, as I have detailed in the preceding chapters, the practice of mapping elements of "Wild West" adventure onto the Eastern Territories was a common strategy in constructing this region as German colonial territory.

On this level then, the architectural Doppelgänger narrates a historical development: King Etzel, "the Lord of the Earth" swept in from the East, occupying territory previously inhabited by the Germanic tribes. He and his Huns are living on land they invaded and conquered, and inhabiting a castle that they did not build. The resonance with the contemporary westward expansion of the Slavs allows the Huns' mistreatment and destruction of this building to be conceptually linked with the fear concerning the fate of German property that has fallen under Polish domain. The strong visual connection between Etzel's "pigsty" and the iconography of *polnische Wirtschaft* cannot be overlooked in this context. Seen through the lens of 1920s German revisionism, the land in the East should be returned to German control, because the new occupants were not responsible for culturally developing this territory, nor were they able to take care of it properly.

In this respect, the film's depiction of the East easily falls under the aegis of the *Kulturboden* ideology. However, we can also read in this Doppelgänger a more ominous expression of the anxiety of borderlessness—two versions of the same space but positioned in two different possible worlds: one well-protected by a mythical border, the other completely unprotected and vulnerable; one the site of advanced culture and ritually contained violence, the other a primitive amassing of unrestrained violence and mass slaughter. The Burgundians inhabit—and seek to defend—this space twice: first, in the reception of Siegfried at Worms, and, second, in the battle against the Huns. In the first instance, the Burgundians are easily able to defend their space: it is only reachable by a drawbridge that spans an otherwise impermeable border. In the second space, coded by a stateless boundlessness, the Burgundians are overwhelmed by primitive forces and unable to defend their space. For here too, the Burgundians seek to defend themselves within this same hall, only now it is vulnerably located in a radically different geopolitical context.

In this nightmare vision of border violation and massive bloodshed, wartime slaughter is imagined to be located in this other, unprotected eastern landscape. The earthen hovels of the Huns suddenly transform into a memory of the trenches of World War I combat, as wildly contorted dead bodies fall into heavy piles at their bases.

For such readings of Etzel as the impending threat of eastern invasion, it becomes irrelevant that in both the Nibelungen epic as well as the film, it is the Burgundians who travel so far east to engage in their battle with the Huns. In Lang's film, the castle being defended—a modern-day evocation of the Marienburg—is Germanic territory, and the inability of the Burgundians to defend it is perhaps the most uncamouflaged depiction of the anxiety of reverse diffusion in the Weimar-era invasion narratives. The primitives—a conflation of the Asiatic hordes of the earliest periods of human history with the *polnische Wirtschaft* of contemporary post–colonial Slavs—are encroaching from the East. The viewing public is presented with two opposing constructions of the nation: Etzel's kingdom, which reenacts the current crisis at the nation's borders, and Worms, which depicts the healed nation, the nation which has closed the "open wound" of the violated border.

Conclusion

Over the course of the century preceding the National Socialist rise to power, a complex discourse developed representing past and present German engagement in Poland and further stretches of the East in colonial terms. Depictions of German colonial endeavor and its purported impact circulated in novels and atlases, political speeches and press publications, feature films and history textbooks, printed scholarship and classroom lessons. These visual and narrative representations arose out of specific political contexts but ultimately came to define the nation's collective sense of its colonial identity.

The prevalence of this discourse challenges conventional understandings of colonialism's object. While the European colonization of Africa, Asia, Australia, the Americas, and the Pacific have dominated scholarship in colonial and postcolonial studies, the evidence presented here indicates that the exclusion of the Slavic East (and the European periphery more generally) has led to an incomplete understanding of colonial discourse and its attendant geographic imagination of global order. The European colonial imagination (or at least our perception of it) may have been grossly structured by Manichean categories of difference mapped over spaces separated by expansive oceanic divides. But, quite aside from our current postcolonial insights into all of the ways in which these categories were morally, scientifically, and ideologically flawed from the outset, such radical lines of demarcation had always been impossible to draw on the Eurasian continent (or across the Mediterranean expanse, for that matter). There was no saltwater barrier separating continental Europeans from the East—the choice to access the Asian regions of the continent by sea may have temporarily bracketed off the intervening space and allowed for a punctuated experience of Otherness, but it didn't erase the expectation of the continuities that would have been encountered along land routes. The difference between self and Other therefore had to be conceived and addressed in gradational terms.

Although this model of difference is more complex, it is nonetheless consonant with an overarching diffusionist worldview. Diffusionism was the unstated premise upon which both adjacent and overseas colonialisms were based, but it held greater resonance in those areas where adjacent lands had histories of sustained contact. My investigation of the colonial construction of such proximal space allows us to see that the mental map of global diffusion patterns could accommodate even lands just beyond the gates of "the West."

The texts I analyze reveal a basic set of diffusionist premises: that German/European civilization occupied a certain geographic expanse; that this space was created and defined by a population endowed with the capacity for innovation, development, and historical progress; and that non-Western space existed as an unbounded and ahistorical frontier, a space often depicted as "empty" even in the presence of native inhabitants. These spaces in the global "Outside" were slowly being developed and filled, each at a rate directly proportional to its proximity to the German/European spring-well of diffusion.

The specificity of the German colonial experience can thus be found in its unique combination of colonial belatedness and proximity to the adjacent "Outside." Both of these factors led Germans to develop more nuanced language to describe colonial relationships not imagined in Manichean but in proximal, gradational terms. There were, as I've shown, attempts to depict Poland and the Poles as radically Other—as racially different and spatially distant—but these constructions proved difficult to uphold in the context of adjacency. Germans thus turned much more frequently than their western rivals to notions of gradients extending eastward over the Eurasian continent and over the globe as a whole. The familiar notion of an east-west cultural gradient *(Kulturgefälle)* thus came to be depicted and theorized as the positive result of German diffusion into space otherwise devoid of the means to achieve historical progress.

In addition to a mental map marked by a cultural or civilizational decline extending eastward from the German center, two additional derivations of diffusionist thought specify the German case. First is the notion of *Kulturboden* as a spatial repository of diffusion over time. While Germans certainly joined their European rivals in claiming that they had developed the overseas lands they colonized and settled, the discourse of *Kulturboden* in the East was different. It went beyond any mere discussions of technological or agricultural improvements to stake metaphysical claims about the immutable völkisch identity of the space itself. This land was created by Germans and it would remain in an unbreakable symbiotic union with Germans, rejecting or forming antagonistic relationships with any non-Germans who would attempt to inhabit it. German *Kulturboden* extends eastward and shapes the contours of the diffusional gradient. There were no factors impeding its spread because the peoples to the East were thought to lack the ability to create *Kulturboden* in their own image.

The second derivative of diffusionist thought was the imagined threat of reverse diffusion. Invasion narratives were a wider European phenomenon in the late imperial period; they brought into representation fears that the imperial power was in a state of decline marked by physical weakness and impotence at both the individual and collective levels. In its weakened state, the metropolis was no longer able to prevent its space from being infiltrated and attacked by atavistic elements arising out of the global periphery and diffusing backward into imperial space. These invasions threatened to bring about the destruction of the imperial power with a counterdiffusion of anticivilizing forces that would reach its very heart center.

In the German context, the proximity to the adjacent Slavic periphery exacerbated the unease out of which such invasion narratives were born. In German texts, we see this anxiety expressed at both the individual and collective levels. Individually, infiltrations took the form of sexual seductions that threatened to destroy the German domestic sphere through racial contagion—in the fluid German-Polish borderlands, how could the lines between self and Other be guarded against those who would mask their true identities to cross these very lines? For some, the only solution lay in the physical removal or containment of the Polish population. On a collective level, this reverse-diffusional threat was imagined as a Polish or Slavic flood that would wash over the German nation. It would not only have the power to sweep away the visible (although not metaphysical) signs of German *Kulturboden,* but, perhaps more insidiously, it would erase all of the rational signs of civilized spatialization, leaving an irrational chaos of boundless space in its wake.

These representations of colonial diffusion, *Kulturboden,* and reverse-diffusional anxiety arose in response to specific historical, political, and social contexts, and they changed over time in dialogue with the changing circumstances. Significant phases of this development are marked by Germany's ascension to the status of imperial power in the 1890s and by its loss of this status after World War I.

Between the 1840s and the 1870s, many Germans had envisioned a future, state-driven overseas colonial project; in its absence, they increasingly turned to the Slavic East as the source of compensatory narratives of past and present colonial endeavor. As a space under German control but inhabited by a largely non-German population, Polish Prussia played a specific role in these colonial narratives. In Freytag's *Soll und Haben,* this Polish East becomes the testing ground for German class antagonisms. Legitimacy for national leadership is derived from a class's ability to successfully expand German space into the colonial periphery, and Freytag fashions the history of the Polish East as the history of German mercantile (i.e., bourgeois and protobourgeois) diffusions past and present.

In the mid-1880s, Germany simultaneously pursued overseas colonial acquisitions and an adjacent continental inner colonial campaign. While these two projects were undertaken in pursuit of different goals, they were discursively linked: the goal of overseas expansion was justified with references to a long, successful history of *Ostkolonisation,* while proponents of various forms of inner colonization presented their arguments in terms adapted from an overseas idiom. In the context of the colonial and territorial dispossessions that followed Germany's defeat in World War I, these two discourses only became more tightly linked as narratives of medieval *Ostkolonisation* were used to legitimize Germany's desire for the return of the territory it had been forced to cede in the East as well as overseas.

Over the course of the interwar period, an ever-increasing number of scholars, politicians, and publicists argued that the land lost to Poland owed its current state of cultivation and civilization to past German colonial labor; that this space was historically, practically, and perhaps even in its very essence *German;* and that it therefore rightly belonged back in German hands. Within this logic of an essentialized *Kulturboden,* the presence of Slavs was merely incidental: they may have occupied this territory during various historical periods, but, given their inherent inability to bring about progress or innovation on their own, their relationship to the space was represented as arbitrary and transient; Slavs might temporarily occupy a region and benefit from the agricultural and architectural infrastructure left behind by Germans, but they would be unable to maintain or expand upon this infrastructure themselves. Instead, through abuse and neglect, they would reduce the space to ruins. The Slavs were now occupying land previously inhabited by Germans, but they had not created it, could not lay any claim to it, and threatened it with their very presence.

The *Kulturboden* model was steadily extended to encompass territory far to the east of the former German border as historians and publicists found "evidence" that it too had been cultivated and civilized by German colonization in previous eras. German irredentists—their numbers drawn largely from the ranks of völkisch activists—orchestrated propaganda campaigns to promote this model of German history in the east. Their ideas fell on receptive terrain, and the discourse gained strong footing during the interwar period. By the end of the 1930s, even those Germans who didn't support the renewed eastward extension of Germany's political borders (such as the Communists and left-wing Social Democrats) nonetheless affirmed the underlying assumption that diffusion had created Eastern space.

This conviction became so widespread that Hitler could reference it in the introduction to his infamous declaration of war to the Reichstag on September 1, 1939.

> Representatives! Men of the German Reichstag!
>
> For months we have all been suffering the agony of a problem bestowed upon us by the dictate of Versailles that—in its deterioration and degeneration—had finally become intolerable.
>
> Danzig was and is a German city! The Corridor was and is German!
>
> All of these territories owe their cultural development exclusively to the German people, without whom the deepest barbarism [*die tiefste Barbarei*] would prevail in these eastern territories.[1]

With these lines, Hitler opens a speech intended to mobilize the German masses behind his war plans. Their rhetorical function, therefore, is to establish an initial point of consensus, to unite his audience in a shared conviction from which he can then derive his decision to go to war. The colonial narrative provided this point of consensus, while also delegitimizing the Poles as equal partners in negotiations from the outset: if the Poles are only capable of barbaric behavior when left to their own devices, then they can not be expected to act as rational human subjects and will best understand messages delivered with brute force.

The speech sets the stage for the atrocities that would be committed in Polish space once Germany invaded and occupied the country. The nucleus of Nazi genocide was established in Poland: most of the death camps were built here, and most of the Jews killed had lived in Poland prior to the war. It was as if the barbarism Hitler ascribed to the Slavs actually inhered in the space they occupied, or as if the diffusions he imagined radiating from Germany's center into the Polish periphery had ceased to represent the transfer of progress, humanity, and development, and had become instead the excretion of civilization's most abject by-products across the border into adjacent space.

This geography of the Holocaust links the "Final Plan" with a second, but overlapping agenda, the *Generalplan Ost.*[2] In it, the Nazis undertook a spatial engineering project (*Raumplanung*) to colonize the Eastern European frontier, beginning with the territory located just over the German border. The goal was the establishment of a racially cleansed Lebensraum in the East, where German farmers would be set up to exploit the region's agricultural resources, which could then be used to sustain the industrialized population in the western Reich.

In its relationship to the categories of space and race, the *Generalplan Ost* was clearly derived from colonial precedents. The occupied East was divided into several administrative units, each intended to play a different role within the overarching plan. The *Warthegau* was located in the province of Posen, space acquired in the Polish Partitions and ceded to Poland after World War I. It was annexed into the German Reich in 1939, and its non-German inhabitants were expelled into the neighboring *Generalgouvernement,* a much larger territory located to the east of the *Wartheland,* and comprising the districts of Warsaw, Lublin, Radom, Krakow, and Lemberg. Hundreds of thousands of Jews and Poles were dispossessed of their property and forcefully expelled—albeit to face different fates once reaching the *Generalgouvernement.* Their former homes and belongings were requisitioned by offices of the German government that brought in ethnic Germans—specifically those who had been brought *Heim ins Reich* (home to the Reich) from the Baltic states—to settle the region.

This forced resettlement was the first part of the larger, undisclosed *Generalplan Ost,* which envisioned a period of spatial reorganization following the war and lasting for some twenty-five to thirty years; at this point, the Jewish population would already have been eliminated from the eastern space in question, and the Slavic population would then face a similar fate: those not exterminated would either be dispersed and expelled far into Siberia (where they would no longer be in a position to organize themselves politically, economically, or militarily), or they would be reintroduced into the colonized areas as dependent or slave laborers to work the fields.[3]

To the extent that the German public was made aware of various aspects of this colonization project, it was presented to them as a continuation of medieval *Ostkolonisation* and celebrated in the language of continuity, legacy, and colonial grandeur. It was the "colonial skills" held by the ancestors of the *Ostkolonisation* that would now make the development of the Wartheland possible, as one propaganda poster claims (fig. 33). The map features arrows representing the mass movement of populations into and out of the Wartheland and proclaims this project to be the "most grand-scale resettlement campaign in world history." The language Karl Hampe had introduced to construct the medieval past in colonial terms was now reintroduced to describe the colonial plans of the present.

Fig. 33. "After the 18-day military campaign began the most grand-scale resettlement campaign in world history. All members of the Volk who had fulfilled their missions abroad were called back home to the Heimat of their fathers by the Führer. They are now helping to develop and consolidate the Greater German Reich. Their colonizing skills will be particularly useful in the development of the Warthegau." German Federal Archives, Image R 49 Bild-0705. Reproduced with permission.

In the European East, we find evidence of colonization as a set of material practices, both carried out and envisioned, that were justified through appeal to colonial categories of spatial and racial difference. Although various aspects of this adjacent colonial discourse and practice differed from their overseas analogues, they were nonetheless derived from an overarching diffusionist worldview that encompassed both experiences within its explanatory framework.

My hope is that an understanding of colonial diffusionism and its specific German idiom will help to further identify and interrogate the ways in which these conceptual models were operative in the past. But I also hope that it will sharpen our critical gaze in the present, where diffusionist models continue to underlie a subset of representations of German-Eastern European relations.

To take two recent examples: First, the past decade has seen a rise in histories of Germans in Eastern Europe. To a significant degree, these studies are being undertaken by a new generation of scholars exploring the questions raised by the new post–Cold War landscape or attempting to bring closure to the traumatic narratives of flight, expulsion, and loss of property in the East following World War II. But riding this new wave of scholarship are also works that discuss German-Eastern relations in decidedly diffusionist terms. In these modern versions, the concept of *Kulturboden* is operative but has been reworked and is now referenced as the "German East," which is also a portmanteau term of sorts. On the one side, the "German East" may simply refer to a specific history of German presence in the East prior to World War II. But on the other side, this term stakes a claim about the essential Germanness of the space in question. Seemingly innocuous discussions of German architecture, village structures, and cultural achievements in the East present themselves as objective history but steadily communicate the diffusionist claim that the Germans developed this space and can therefore rightly speak of a "German East."[4]

Hans Henning Hahn and Eva Hahn have offered a provocative rejoinder by comparing the statistics of German presence in these regions with those of nonnaturalized immigrants in Germany today. After showing that these numbers are quite comparable, they ask if, by way of analogy, it would be legitimate to refer to contemporary Germany as the "Turkish West." This latter term is meant to make the unstated claims of the term *German East* more readily apparent, for it erases Slavic presence and agency in the space in question by suggesting that this Eastern space only gained identity under German stewardship.

A similar meaning is communicated by a second case. When Erika Steinbach, president of the Federation of Expellees (Bund der Vertriebenen), opened the 2006 exhibit "Erzwungene Wege" (Paths unchosen) treating the question of "flight and expulsion in twentieth-century Europe," it was met with criticism in Germany, Poland, and abroad for its revisionist account. A rich body of scholarship had investigated the political implications of the new wave of German victimization narratives that appeared around the turn of the twentieth century, and critics were thus able to analyze the exhibit and address both its overt message and its unstated politics. Steinbach's 2009 "Die Gerufenen" (Called), in contrast, met with much less critical scrutiny. Perhaps this relative silence can be explained by Steinbach's seemingly innocuous shift in focus from victimized Germans to the question of their cultural achievements in the East. "Die Gerufenen" portrayed the history of Germans in Eastern Europe that had been "called" by Slavic leaders to settle and develop their lands. Although the text of the exhibit opened with a statement about the multiethnic communities in which Germans in the East had resided, these other groups easily disappeared from the exhibit's historical stage on which only Germans appeared as agents of progress and development. Maps of the East showed the location of German settlements, while the corresponding displays featured the technological, agricultural, and social improvements that Germans had introduced into these spaces. Where Eastern Europeans were mentioned, it was either as the passive recipients of these diffusions or as the active agents of the expulsions that removed the German element from their space. They did not, however, feature in their own capacity as developers of this space but only in the destruction of the German communities. Now that the Germans were gone, the exhibit explicitly argues, their material legacy is threatened by neglect and deterioration.[5]

The exhibit then concludes with an awkward assertion: that ethnic Germans left an "impressive legacy of towns and villages, buildings and works of art" in the East, and that the "responsibility of caring for it in a united Europe falls equally on the shoulders of the Germans and those who live in these countries today."[6] Perhaps this statement means to assert a right to claim ownership—if only symbolically expressed through the "care" of Germany's "legacy in the East"—or perhaps it is meant as an admonition to those Germans who are not as invested in claiming this legacy.

Either way, the diffusionist rhetoric of "Called" was countered by a much larger and more elaborate exhibit housed just across the street at the German Historical Museum. Here, an international team including both German and Polish historians had collaborated to produce a joint depiction of German-Polish history in which both Germans and Poles featured as historical agents. While the exhibit did not refrain from addressing the most painful episodes of this shared history, it also included rich descriptions of the ways in which Germans and Poles had each introduced innovations within their own and each other's communities. The mental map of German diffusion into the unbounded frontier of the "Wild East" was displaced by one of a shared European identity.

Notes

Introduction

1. Paul Langhans, *Deutscher Kolonial-Atlas,* 2nd ed. (Gotha: Justus Perthes, 1897). All subsequent citations refer to this edition.

2. Thus, while *Brockhaus' Konversationslexikon* of 1894–96 describes a "colony" as an area of closed ethnic settlement in foreign territory, it proceeds to identify "real colonies" (*eigentliche Kolonien*) as "overseas provinces of a European state that are completely under its control." *Brockhaus' Konversations-Lexikon,* 14th ed. (Leipzig: F. A. Brockhaus, 1894–96), s.v. "Kolonie."

3. Langhans, *Deutscher Kolonial-Atlas,* first page of introduction (unpaginated).

4. *Das Digitale Wörterbuch der deutschen Sprache des 20. Jh.* s.v. "Kolonie," accessed Feb. 25, 2010, http://www.dwds.de/?kompakt=1&sh=1&qu=kolonie.

5. The diversity of colonial experience also applies to colonies administered by the same nation. See George Steinmetz, *The Devil's Handwriting: Precoloniality and the German Colonial State in Qingdao, Samoa, and Southwest Africa* (Chicago: University of Chicago Press, 2007), for an analysis of the divergent colonial policies found in these three German colonies.

6. Jürgen Osterhammel, *Kolonialismus: Geschichte, Formen, Folgen* (Munich: C. H. Beck, 1997), 20.

7. Susanne Zantop, *Colonial Fantasies: Conquest, Family, and Nation in Precolonial Germany, 1770–1870* (Durham: Duke University Press, 1997), 28–29.

8. See Larry Wolff, *Inventing Eastern Europe: The Map of Civilization on the Mind of the Enlightenment* (Palo Alto: Stanford University Press, 1994). While Wolff does not read the shifting discourse in colonial terms, the patterns he identifies can be brought into alignment with the categories of my discursive colonization model.

9. See Wolfgang Wippermann, "Die Ostsiedlung in der deutschen Historiographie und Publizistik. Probleme, Methoden und Grundlagen der Entwicklung bis hin zum Ersten Weltkrieg," *Germania Slavica* (1980); Jan M. Piskorski, "The Medieval Colonization of Central Europe as a Problem of World History and Historiography," *German History* 22, no. 3 (2004).

10. I place Poland in scare quotes to reflect the fact that Germans referred to "Poland" even during the long period of this state's absence. It was a floating term with a vague referent, referring interchangeably to Russian-controlled "Congress Poland," the entirety of space populated by Polish ethnic majorities, the space of the pre-partition state, or simply "Germany's eastern frontier."

11. Edward Said, *Orientalism* (New York: Vintage, 1979), 3.

12. J. M. Blaut, *The Colonizer's Model of the World: Geographic Diffusionism and Eurocentric History* (New York: Guilford, 1993), 1.

13. Said, *Orientalism,* 31–35.

14. See Martin W. Lewis and Kären E. Wigen, "The Spatial Constructs of Orient and Occident, East and West," in *The Myth of Continents: A Critique of Metageography* (Berkeley: University of California Press, 1997), 47–72.

15. David Blackbourn, *The Conquest of Nature: Water, Landscape, and the Making of Modern Germany* (New York: Norton, 2007), 256; Elisabeth A. Drummond, "'Einen kräftigen Damm gegen die polnische Hochflut zu errichten': Natur und Kultur im deutschen Ostmarkendiskurs, 1886–1914," in *Die nationale Identität der Deutschen: Philosophische Imaginationen und historische Realität deutscher Mentalität,* ed. Wolfgang Bialas (Frankfurt am Main: Peter Lang, 2002), 99–114.

16. Vejas Gabriel Liulevicius, *The German Myth of the East: 1800 to the Present* (Oxford: Oxford University Press, 2009), 3–5.

17. See Thomas Serrier, "'Deutsche Kulturarbeit in der Ostmark.' Der Mythos vom deutschen Vorrang und die Grenzproblematik in der Provinz Posen (1871–1914)," in *Die Nationalisierung von Grenzen: Zur Konstruktion nationaler Identität in sprachlich gemischten Grenzregionen,* ed. Michael G. Müller and Rolf Petri (Marburg: Herder-Institut, 2002), 13–33. Serrier describes an anxiety of diffusionist impotence.

18. Gustav Frenssen, *Peter Moors Fahrt nach Südwest* (Berlin: G. Grote, 1906), 68 (my translation). See John Noyes's treatment of this passage, in "National Identity, Nomadism, and Narration in Gustav Frenssen's Peter Moor's Journey to Southwest Africa," in *The Imperialist Imagination: German Colonialism and Its Legacy,* ed. Sara Friedrichsmeyer et al. (Ann Arbor: University of Michigan Press, 1998), 95–96.

19. Gustav Freytag, *Soll und Haben,* vol. I, 58th ed. (Leipzig: S. Hirzel, 1902), 382–83. All subsequent citations refer to this edition. All translations mine.

20. The nineteenth century saw the creation of a variety of different "states" within the territory of former Poland, but as Norman Davies argues, none of these were more than nominal entities, which were all immediately dismantled as soon as they attempted to exert any degree of autonomy. Norman Davies, *God's Playground: A History of Poland,* vol. 2, *1795 to the Present* (New York: Columbia University Press, 1982), 6.

21. Wolff, *Inventing Eastern Europe,* 18.

22. Robert F. Arnold, *Geschichte der Deutschen Polenlitteratur [sic] von den Anfängen bis 1800* (Halle: Max Niemeyer, 1900), 72–73.

23. Hubert Orłowski, *"Polnische Wirtschaft": zum deutschen Polendiskurs der Neuzeit* (Wiesbaden: Harrassowitz, 1996), 53–67; Wolff, *Inventing Eastern Europe,* 337–38.

24. Werner Rieck, "Das Polenthema in der deutschen Literatur zur Zeit des Konstitutionsreichstags und des Kosciuszko-Aufstandes," *Weimarer Beiträge* 6 (1980): 5–27.

25. Several anthologies of *Polenlieder* have been published, most notably Gerard Koziełek, *Polenlieder: eine Anthologie* (Stuttgart: P. Reclam, 1982). Prior to 1989, this chapter of German-Polish history received much positive attention in East German and Polish scholarship; most significant in this regard is Helmut Bleiber and Jan Kosim, eds., *Dokumente zur Geschichte der deutsch-polnischen Freundschaft, 1830–1832* (Berlin: Akademie-Verlag, 1982); the renegotiation of German-Polish relations following Poland's 2004 ascension into the European Union has led to an additional wave of

interest; see Julia Franke, *Solidarność; 1830: Niemcy i Polacy po Powstaniu Listopadowym = Polenbegeisterung: Deutsche und Polen nach dem Novemberaufstand 1830* (Warsaw: Zamek Królewski, 2005).

26. Brian E. Vick, *Defining Germany: The 1848 Frankfurt Parliament and National Identity* (Cambridge: Harvard University Press, 2002), 141.

27. Hans Rothfels, "Das erste Scheitern des Nationalstaats in Ost-Mittel-Europa 1848/49," in *Deutscher Osten und Slawischer Westen,* ed. Hans Rothfels and Werner Markert (Tübingen: J. C. B. Mohr [Paul Siebeck], 1955), 9.

28. Hinrich C. Seeba, "'So weit die deutsche Zunge klingt': The Role of Language in German Identity Formation," in *Searching for Common Ground: Diskurse zur deutschen Identität, 1750–1871,* ed. Nicholas Vazsonyi (Cologne: Böhlau, 2000), 49.

29. Ernst Moritz Arndt, "Des Deutschen Vaterland," in *Gedichte. Vollständige Sammlung,* 2nd ed. (Berlin: Weidmann, 1865), 233–35. Cited in Seeba, "'So weit die deutsche Zunge klingt,'" 49–50.

30. Heinrich Meisner and Robert Geerds, eds., *Ernst Moritz Arndts ausgewählte Werke in sechzehn Bänden,* vol. 15, *Kleine Schriften III* (Leipzig: Max Hesses Verlag, 1908), 49–66.

31. Michael G. Müller, Bernd Schönemann, and Maria Wawrykowa, eds., *Die "Polen-Debatte" in der Frankfurter Paulskirche: Darstellung, Lernziele, Materialien* (Frankfurt am Main: Georg-Eckert-Institut für Internationale Schulbuchforschung, 1995), 9.

32. The "Poland Debate" took place from July 24 to July 27, 1848.

33. Franz Wigard, ed., *Stenographischer Bericht über die Verhandlungen der deutschen constituirenden Nationalversammlung zu Frankfurt am Main* (Frankfurt am Main: J. D. Sauerländer, 1849), 1184.

34. Ibid., 1143.

35. Ibid., 1146.

36. Jordan uses the term *colonization* not merely as a synonym for settlement but also for territorial conquest: lands in the east "were gradually taken into possession by German colonists, and these conquests were secured through armed conflict." Wigard, *Stenographischer Bericht,* 1146.

37. Wigard, *Stenographischer Bericht,* 1145–46.

38. See Hans Fenske, "Ungeduldige Zuschauer: Die Deutschen und die europäische Expansion 1815–1880," in *Imperialistische Kontinuität und nationale Ungeduld im 19. Jahrhundert,* ed. Wolfgang Reinhard (Frankfurt am Main: Fischer Taschenbuch Verlag, 1991): 87–123; and Hans Fenske, "Imperialistische Tendenzen in Deutschland vor 1866. Auswanderung, überseeische Bestrebungen, Weltmachtträume," *Historisches Jahrbuch* 97–98 (1978): 336–83.

39. Matthew P. Fitzpatrick, *Liberal Imperialism in Germany: Expansionism and Nationalism, 1848–1884* (New York: Berghahn, 2008).

40. Friedrich List, *Das nationale System der Politischen Oekonomie. Neudruck nach der Ausgabe letzter Hand, eingeleitet von Professor Dr. Heinrich Waentig,* 5th ed. (Jena: G. Fischer, 1928), 270, quoted in Mihran Dabag, "National-koloniale Konstruktionen in politischen Entwürfen des Deutschen Reichs um 1900," in *Kolonialismus: Kolonialdiskurs und Genozid,* ed. Mihran Dabag, Horst Gründer, and Uwe-K. Ketelsen (Munich: Wilhelm Fink Verlag, 2004), 29.

41. Ute Ritzenhofen, "'Amerikas Italien.' Texas in der Auswanderungs- und Rei-

seliteratur der 1840er Jahre," in *Reisen im Diskurs: Modelle der literarischen Fremderfahrung von den Pilgerberichten bis zur Postmoderne,* ed. Anne Fuchs and Theo Harden (Heidelberg: Universitätsverlag C. Winter, 1995), 171–87.

42. See List's 1842 essay in which he outlines his proposed settlement colonization in Eastern Europe. Friedrich List, "Die Ackerverfassung, die Zwergwirtschaft und die Auswanderung," in *Friedlich List. Aufsätze und Abhandlungen aus den Jahren 1831–1844,* ed. Edgar Salin, Artur Sommer, and Otto Stühler (Berlin: Reimar Hobbing, 1928), 418–548, esp. 499ff. More dramatic in tone: A. [pseud.], "Auswanderung und Colonisation im Inland," *Grenzboten* 2, no. 15 (1849): 52.

43. A. [pseud.], "Auswanderung und Colonisation," 53.

44. Anon., "Die deutschen Auswanderungen," *Grenzboten* 1 (1846): 580–81. The provinces in question are East and West Prussia.

45. Wigard, *Stenographischer Bericht,* 1175.

46. Izabela Surynt, *Das "ferne," "unheimliche" Land: Gustav Freytags Polen* (Dresden: Thelem, 2004), 24, footnote 51.

47. William Rogers [pseud.], "Beobachtungen auf einer Geschäftsreise in das Großherzogthum Posen," *Grenzboten* 3, no. 27 (1848): 39.

48. See Surynt, *Gustav Freytags Polen,* 186; Eva Hahn and Hans Henning Hahn, "Nationale Stereotypen. Plädoyer für eine historische Stereotypenforschung," in *Stereotyp, Identität und Geschichte: die Funktion von Stereotypen in gesellschaftlichen Diskursen,* ed. Hans Henning Hahn (Frankfurt am Main: Peter Lang, 2002), 29–31.

49. On the historiographical debates regarding the motivation and effects of the Kulturkampf, see Lech Trzeciakowski, *The Kulturkampf in Prussian Poland* (New York: Columbia University Press, 1990).

50. Martin Broszat refers to a shift from the "language struggle and Kulturkampf" of the 1870s to the "politics of population and land control" after 1885: Martin Broszat, *Zweihundert Jahre deutsche Polenpolitik* (Frankfurt am Main: Suhrkamp, 1972), 6. Others refer to the measures taken after 1885 as a politics of "extirpation." Trzeciakowski, *Kulturkampf,* 5.

51. Helmut Neubach, *Ausweisungen von Polen und Juden aus Preussen 1885/86: ein Beitrag zu Bismarcks Polenpolitik und zur Geschichte des deutsch-polnischen Verhältnisses* (Wiesbaden: Harrassowitz, 1967).

52. One now detects a growing tendency within German colonial studies to examine inner colonization as part of a larger German imperial project. See Sebastian Conrad, *Deutsche Kolonialgeschichte* (Munich: C. H. Beck, 2008), and Dirk van Laak, *Über alles in der Welt: Deutscher Imperialismus im 19. und 20. Jahrhundert* (Munich: C. H. Beck, 2005).

53. Ernst von der Brüggen, "Auswanderung, Kolonisation und Zweikindersystem," *Preußische Jahrbücher* 49 (1882): 295.

54. Ernst von der Brüggen, *Russia To-day,* trans. M. Sandwith (London: Digby, Long, 1904), 225.

55. Karl Lamprecht, "Die Lehren der Kolonisation Ostdeutschlands für die Politik der Gegenwart," *Die Ostmark* 3, no. 7 (July 1898): 78.

56. Ibid., 92.

57. Ernst Tiessen, "Der Friedensvertrag von Versailles und die politische Geographie," *Zeitschrift für Geopolitik* 4 (April 1924): 205.

58. Guntram Henrik Herb, *Under the Map of Germany: Nationalism and Propaganda, 1918–1945* (London: Routledge, 1997), 31.

59. Karl Hampe, *Der Zug nach dem Osten: die kolonisatorische Großtat des deutschen Volkes im Mittelalter* (Leipzig: Teubner, 1921). The exact nature of the historical development Hampe describes remains the object of controversy; scholars continue to debate whether such a migration was specifically German, or if Germans merely took part in a larger European settlement process; whether this specific migration was violent or peaceful; and to what degree Poles themselves participated in the settlement and development of what was then Polish space. See Jan M. Piskorski, ed., *Historiographical Approaches to Medieval Colonization of East Central Europe: A Comparative Analysis against the Background of Other European Inter-ethnic Colonization Processes in the Middle Ages* (New York: Columbia University Press, 2002).

60. Wippermann, "Die Ostsiedlung"; Wolfgang Wippermann, *Der "deutsche Drang nach Osten:" Ideologie und Wirklichkeit eines politischen Schlagwortes* (Darmstadt: Wissenschaftliche Buchgesellschaft, 1981); Wolfgang Wippermann, "'Gen Ostland wollen wir reiten!' Ordensstaat und Ostsiedlung in der historischen Belletristik Deutschlands," in *Germania Slavica,* ed. W. H. Fritze (Berlin: Duncker und Humblot, 1980), 187–235.

61. Hampe, *Zug nach dem Osten,* 10.

62. Ibid., 50–51.

63. Ibid., 74.

64. Ibid., 75.

CHAPTER 1

1. Jean Améry, "Schlecht klingt das Lied vom braven Mann," *Neue Rundschau* 1 (1978): 84.

2. I have published ideas presented in this chapter in previous articles, and thank each of the publishers for the permission to reprint them here. "'Ich stehe jetzt hier als einer von den Eroberern': *Soll und Haben* als Kolonialroman," in *150 Jahre* Soll und Haben: *Studien zu Gustav Freytags kontroversem Roman,* ed. Florian Krobb, 225–37 (Würzburg: Koenigshausen und Neumann, 2005); "Gustav Freytags *Soll und Haben* als imperiales Kartenwerk," in *Geopoetiken. Geographische Entwürfe in den mittel- und osteuropäischen Literaturen,* ed. Magdalena Marszałek and Sylvia Sasse (Berlin: Kulturverlag Kadmos, 2010) , 133–58; and "Reinventing Poland as German Colonial Territory in the Nineteenth Century: Gustav Freytag's *Soll und Haben* as Colonial Novel," in *Germans, Poland, and Colonial Expansion to the East: 1850 Through the Present,* ed. Robert L. Nelson (New York: Palgrave Macmillan, 2009), 11–37, reproduced with permission of Palgrave Macmillan.

3. Fenske, "Ungeduldige Zuschauer"; Fenske, "Imperialistische Tendenzen"; and Matthew Fitzpatrick, "Narrating Empire: *Die Gartenlaube* and Germany's Nineteenth-Century Liberal Expansionism," *German Studies Review* 30, no. 1 (2007): 97–120.

4. *Soll und Haben* was the best-selling German novel of the nineteenth century, selling over 100,000 copies by 1900, and its sales figures increased dramatically over the first half of the twentieth century, particularly in the decades of social instability

immediately following each of the two world wars. Its publication figures reached 500,000 by 1925, and one million just prior to 1960. See Sabina Becker, "Erziehung zur Bürgerlichkeit: Eine kulturgeschichtliche Lektüre von Gustav Freytags *Soll und Haben* im Kontext des Bürgerlichen Realismus," in *150 Jahre* Soll und Haben, ed. Florian Krobb (Würzburg: Königshausen und Neumann, 2005), 29; Hartmut Steinecke, "Gustav Freytag: *Soll und Haben* (1855): Weltbild und Wirkung eines deutschen Bestsellers," in *Romane und Erzählungen des Bürgerlichen Realismus,* ed. Horst Denkler (Stuttgart: Philipp Reclam, 1980), 138, 145. For a detailed account of publication statistics, see T. E. Carter, "Freytag's *Soll und Haben*: A Liberal Manifesto as a Best-Seller," *German Life and Letters* 21, no. 4 (July 1968): 320–29.

5. Theodor Fontane, "Gustav Freytag: *Soll und Haben,*" *Literaturblatt des deutschen Kunstblattes* (July 26, 1855). Reprinted in Kurt Schreinert, ed., *Theodor Fontane: Sämtliche Werke,* vol. 11, book 1 (Munich: Nymphenburger, 1963), 214–30.

6. Todd Kontje's reading of the novel shows that this sense of distance is exacerbated through projecting "Oriental" attributes onto Polish space. Kontje, *German Orientalisms,* 200–201.

7. Freytag, *Soll und Haben,* II:44.

8. Surynt, *Gustav Freytags Polen,* 280.

9. Ibid., 286.

10. Ludwig Stockinger, "Polen als 'grüne Stelle'? Ästhetische und politische Implikationen des Polenbildes bei Gustav Freytag," *Convivium: Germanistisches Jahrbuch Polen* (2001), 99–127; and Niels Werber, *Die Geopolitik der Literatur: Eine Vermessung der medialen Weltraumordnung* (Munich: Hanser, 2007), 137–64.

11. Freytag, *Soll und Haben,* I:274.

12. Ibid., I:68–69.

13. Ibid., I:40.

14. Although the event remains both undated and unnamed, the reference is most likely to the Krakower Revolution and peasant unrest of February 1846. Hendrik Feindt, "Dreißig, sechsundvierzig, achtundvierzig, dreiundsechzig. Polnische Aufstände in drei Romanen von Freytag, Raabe und Schweichel," in *Studien zur Kulturgeschichte des deutschen Polenbildes 1848–1939,* ed. Hendrik Feindt, 15–40 (Wiesbaden: Harrassowitz, 1995).

15. As cited in Feindt, "Polnische Aufstände," 21 (my translation).

16. The image of the scythe-bearers dates back to the 1794 Polish uprising, when Tadeusz Kościuszko led a storm of peasants provisionally armed with mounted scythe-blades against their Russian opponents at the Battle of Racławice.

17. As irregular troops of peasants armed with premodern tools of labor attacking armies outfitted with modern weaponry, it was just as easy to see the scythe-bearers as evidence of Polish underdevelopment and disorganization as it was to champion them as heroic. For this reason, they became a popular caricature in such satirical papers as *Kladderadatsch* and *Der kleine Reaktionär.* See Orłowski, *"Polnische Wirtschaft,"* Appendix 11–12; and Eugeniusz Cezary Król, *Polska i Polacy w propagandzie narodowego socjalizmu w Niemczech 1919–1945* (Warsaw: Collegium Civitas Press, 2006), 660.

18. Surynt, *Gustav Freytags Polen,* 186, 269–75.

19. See Colin G. Calloway, Gerd Gemünden, and Susanne Zantop, eds., *Germans*

and Indians: Fantasies, Encounters, Projections (Lincoln: University of Nebraska Press, 2002).

20. Freytag, *Soll und Haben,* I:71.

21. Ibid., I:163.

22. Feindt, "Polnische Aufstände," 19. Feindt offers an in-depth analysis of Anton's reading practices upon which I base my argumentation.

23. Freytag, *Soll und Haben,* II:56.

24. Ibid., I:163.

25. Ibid., I:388, 413.

26. Ibid., I:420.

27. Ibid., I:491.

28. Ibid., I:492.

29. Ibid., I:550.

30. Ibid., I:5.

31. Ibid., I:382–83.

32. *Deutsches Worterbuch,* ed. Wilhelm and Jacob Grimm (Leipzig: S. Hirzel, 1893), s.v. "Rasse." For an in-depth examination of the racial discourse vis-à-vis the Poles in *Soll und Haben,* see Christine Achinger, *Gespaltene Moderne: Gustav Freytags* Soll und Haben: *Nation, Geschlecht und Judenbild* (Würzburg: Königshausen und Neumann, 2007), 141–63.

33. Freytag, *Soll und Haben,* II:155–56.

34. Ibid., II:156.

35. Ibid., II:109.

36. Ibid., II:110.

37. Ibid., II:155.

38. On the popularity of colonial novels and overseas adventure tales in nineteenth-century Germany, see Hans Plischke, *Von Cooper bis Karl May: Eine Geschichte des völkerkundlichen Reise- und Abenteuerromans* (Düsseldorf: Droste-Verlag, 1951), and Zantop, *Colonial Fantasies.*

39. Freytag, *Soll und Haben,* 1:20.

40. Ibid., I:57.

41. Ibid., I:58 (emphasis added).

42. Ibid., I:496.

43. Ibid., I:63–64.

44. Ibid., I:89.

45. Ibid., I:254.

46. Florian Krobb refers to this phenomenon as an ethnic German's *Mittelstandsfähigkeit* (middle-class capacity), Krobb, "Einleitung: *Soll und Haben* nach 150 Jahren," in *150 Jahre* Soll und Haben, ed. Florian Krobb (Würzburg: Königshausen und Neumann, 2005), 12.

47. Freytag, *Soll und Haben,* I:114.

48. Ibid., I:314.

49. Ibid., I:383.

50. Ibid., II:314.

51. Ibid., II:315.

52. Ibid., I:461.
53. Ibid., I:326.
54. Ibid., I:1.
55. The term *polnische Wirtschaft* and the variant *Polackenwirtschaft* appear frequently in the text: Freytag, *Soll und Haben,* I:246, I:375, II:17, II:215. For a history of the discourse of this term, see Orłowski, *"Polnische Wirtschaft."*
56. Freytag, *Soll und Haben,* II:13–14.
57. Ibid., II:14.
58. Ibid., II:19–20.
59. Ibid., II:65–66.
60. Anne McClintock, *Imperial Leather: Race, Gender, and Sexuality in the Colonial Contest* (New York: Routledge, 1995), 5. See also Johannes Fabian, *Time and the Other: How Anthropology Makes Its Object* (New York: Columbia University Press, 1983), 27.
61. Homi K. Bhabha, "Of Mimicry and Man: The Ambivalence of Colonial Discourse," *October* 28 (Spring 1984): 130.
62. Freytag, *Soll und Haben,* II:68.
63. Ibid., II:306.
64. Ibid., I:561.
65. See the claim made explicit in the title of Jürgen Liesekounig's article "'Branntweintrinkende Wilde': Beyond Civilisation and Outside History; The Depiction of the Poles in Gustav Freytag's *Soll und Haben,*" *Yearbook of European Studies* 13 (1999): 133–47.
66. McClintock, *Imperial Leather,* 62.
67. Freytag, *Soll und Haben,* II:174–75.
68. Ibid., II:388.
69. Ibid., II:398.
70. Ibid., I:314.

CHAPTER 2

1. Some of the material in this chapter is adapted from my article "Constructing Racial Difference in Colonial Poland," in *Germany's Colonial Pasts,* ed. Eric Ames, Marcia Klotz, and Lora Wildenthal, 76–96 (Lincoln: University of Nebraska Press, 2005).
2. Clara Viebig, *Das schlafende Heer* (Berlin: E. Fleischel, 1904), 1.
3. David Spurr, *The Rhetoric of Empire: Colonial Discourse in Journalism, Travel Writing, and Imperial Administration* (Durham: Duke University Press, 1993), 93–97.
4. Viebig, *Das schlafende Heer,* 2–3.
5. Ibid., 12.
6. Abdul R. JanMohamed, "The Economy of Manichean Allegory: The Function of Racial Difference in Colonialist Literature," in *"Race," Writing, and Difference,* ed. Henry Louis Gates Jr. (Chicago: University of Chicago Press, 1985), 82.
7. Ibid.

8. The term *Ostmarkenroman* is not well known but is the conventional title for this genre. "Ostmarkenromane und ostmärkische Geschichten" is the title of chapter 4 of Edyta Połczyńska, *Im polnischen Wind: Beiträge zum deutschen Zeitungswesen, Theaterleben und zur deutschen Literatur im Grossherzogtum Posen, 1815–1918* (Poznań: Wydawnictwo Naukowe Uniwersytetu im. Adama Mickiewicza, 1988). The English translation "Eastern Marches novel" is similarly used by Richard Wonser Tims in *Germanizing Prussian Poland: The H-K-T Society and the Struggle for the Eastern Marches in the German Empire, 1894–1919* (New York: AMS Press, 1966).

9. Michael Wegener, "Die Heimat und die Dichtkunst," in *Trivialliteratur: Aufsätze,* ed. Gerhard Schmidt-Henkel (Berlin: Literarisches Colloquium, 1964), 53–65; and Karlheinz Rossbacher, *Heimatkunstbewegung und Heimatroman: Zu einer Literatursoziologie der Jahrhundertwende* (Stuttgart: Klett, 1975).

10. Kay Dohnke, "Völkische Literatur und Heimatliteratur 1870–1918," in *Handbuch zur "völkischen Bewegung" 1871–1918,* ed. Uwe Puschner (Munich: Sauer, 1996), 651.

11. Edyta Połczyńska and Maria Wojtczak, who have undertaken the most extensive research on the Eastern Marches texts, place this notion of "struggle" at the center of their definition of the genre: Eastern Marches literature "thematizes the Prussian *Polenpolitik* in the Eastern Marches and depicts the German-Polish national struggle in the space of Greater Poland." Edyta Połczyńska and Maria Wojtczak, "Die Provinz Posen in der deutschen Literatur um die Jahrhundertwende," *Convivium: Germanistisches Jahrbuch* (1996): 94.

12. Viebig, *Das schlafende Heer,* 9, 36.

13. John Noyes, "Imperialist Man, Civilizing Woman, and the European Male Masochist," *Acta Germanica: Jahrbuch des Südafrikanischen Germanistenverbandes* (1996): 41–65.

14. Viebig, *Das schlafende Heer,* 506–7.

15. The fascination also characterizes the Polish episodes of Gustav Freytag's *Soll und Haben,* a novel that is often considered an early forerunner of the Eastern Marches genre. See Połczyńska, *Im polnischen Wind,* 226, 243, 314.

16. Ernst Below's assimilationist text, *Ostmark und Krummstab* (Berlin: Janke, 1897), is introduced by a three-page foreword in which he praises the *Kulturkampf's* fight against ultramontanism; in Albert Liepe's *Die Spinne* (Berlin: F. Zillessen, 1902), lengthy passages recount stridently anti-Polish speeches delivered by the protagonist at a meeting of the Eastern Marches Society; Elisabeth Grabowski's *Der weiße Adler* (Kattowitz: Phönix-Verlag, 1909), ends with a narratorial commentary on the success of German cultural labor in the east and the duty of Germans in the region to "follow the German Emperor's command to hold their positions in the distant regions of the empire like sentries on watch."

17. Hans-Ulrich Wehler, *Krisenherde des Kaiserreichs 1871–1918: Studien zur deutschen Sozial- und Verfassungsgeschichte* (Göttingen: Vandenhoeck und Ruprecht, 1970), 182.

18. Werner Conze, "Nationsbildung durch Trennung. Deutsche und Polen im preußischen Osten," in *Innenpolitische Probleme des Bismarck-Reiches,* ed. Otto Pflanze (Munich: R. Oldenbourg, 1983), 96. Conze explains that Poles argued they had no logical place in "a nationally based collective held together by shared German bonds

that is supposed to represent, protect, maintain, and develop collective German interests and pursue collective German goals."

19. Broszat, *Polenpolitik,* 134–42; Trzeciakowski, *Kulturkampf,* 115–40.

20. Broszat, *Polenpolitik,* 135.

21. Arthur Pachnicke, *Auf Posten im Osten: Erzählung aus der Ostmark und Kleinstadt* (Berlin: Curt Wigand, 1908), 145.

22. Ibid.

23. Ania Loomba, *Colonialism/Postcolonialism* (London: Routledge, 1998), 173.

24. JanMohamed, "Function of Racial Difference," 81.

25. Traugott Pilf, *Geschichten aus der Ostmark* (Lissa i. P.: Oskar Eulitz, 1908), 106.

26. Trzeciakowski, *Kulturkampf,* 141–83.

27. For detailed discussions of Polish seasonal labor and its ties to global imperialism, see Sebastian Conrad, "Zwischen den Polen: Mobilität und Nation in Deutschlands 'eigentlicher Kolonie,'" chap. 3 in *Globalsierung und Nation im Deutschen Kaiserreich* (Munich: Beck, 2006), 124–67; and Andrew Zimmerman, *Alabama in Africa: Booker T. Washington, the German Empire, and the Globalization of the New South* (Princeton: Princeton University Press, 2010), 80–100.

28. Martin Broszat cites tens of thousands, and others place the numbers much higher, in the hundreds of thousands: Broszat, *Polenpolitik,* 143; Edward Pietraszek, "Zwischen Geldverdienen und Aufstieg: Polnische Arbeitsmigranten in Deutschland von 1871 bis 1939," in *Vom Wandergesellen zum "Green-Card"-Spezialisten: interkulturelle Aspekte der Arbeitsmigration im östlichen Mitteleuropa,* ed. Klaus Roth (Münster: Waxmann, 2003), 110–12.

29. See William W. Hagen, *Germans, Poles, and Jews: The Nationality Conflict in the Prussian East, 1772–1914* (Chicago: University of Chicago Press, 1980), 132, who emphasizes the lack of precedent for such a measure in nineteenth-century Europe. See also Neubach, *Ausweisungen.*

30. Neubach, *Ausweisungen.*

31. Davies, *God's Playground,* 127.

32. References to a Slavic flood appear as early as Joseph von Eichendorff's 1830 drama, *Der letzte Held von Marienburg* (Königsberg: Bornträger, 1830). See Wippermann "'Gen Ostland,'" 205–6. See also Wolfgang Wippermann, *Die Deutschen und der Osten: Feindbild und Traumland* (Darmstadt: Primus, 2007).

33. Uwe Mai, *"Rasse und Raum": Agrarpolitik, Sozial- und Raumplanung im NS-Staat* (Paderborn: Schöningh, 2002), 21.

34. On the *Gesetz betreffend die Beförderung deutscher Ansiedlung in den Provinzen Westpreußen und Posen* see Broszat, *Polenpolitik,* 148.

35. For an exceptional treatment of inner colonization in the context of global colonization practices, see Zimmerman, *Alabama in Africa,* 66–111.

36. Ferdinand Tönnies, "Innere Kolonisation in Preußen: Insbesondere in den ehemaligen Provinzen Posen und Westpreußen," in *Ferdinand Tönnies: Gesamtausgabe,* vol. 15, *1923–1925,* ed. Dieter Haselbach (Berlin: de Gruyter, 2000), 8, footnote 3.

37. The resulting land competition drove up prices, which led to the unintended

consequence that German farmers decided to sell their land. The Settlement Commission soon found itself forced into the position of buying land from Germans in order to prevent it from falling into Polish hands.

38. "The Struggle for the Soil" is the title of chapter 5 in Tims, *Germanizing Prussian Poland.*

39. Wehler, *Krisenherde,* 181–99.

40. Wolfgang Hofmann, "Das Ansiedlungsgesetz von 1904 und die Preußische Polenpolitik," *Jahrbuch für die Geschichte Mittel- und Ostdeutschlands* 38 (1989): 251–85.

41. Alfred Kruck, *Geschichte des Alldeutschen Verbandes, 1890–1939* (Wiesbaden: Steiner, 1954), 38.

42. On the *Alldeutscher Verband* and the *Ostmarkenverein,* see Geoff Eley, *Reshaping the German Right: Radical Nationalism and Political Change after Bismarck* (New Haven: Yale University Press, 1980), 48–67.

43. Hagen, *Germans, Poles, and Jews,* 175. See also Adam Galos, Felix-Heinrich Gentzen, and Witold Jakóbczyk, *Dzieje Hakaty* (Poznań: Instytut Zachodni, 1966), 69–70, 102–3. These accounts differ from that given by Richard Wonser Tims, who claims that the rank and file of the organization was filled by German settlers. However, he concurs with Hagen's claim that large farm owners were not well represented in the organization. Tims, *Germanizing Prussian Poland,* 216–36.

44. Hagen, *Germans, Poles, and Jews,* 175.

45. Połczyńska, *Im polnischen Wind,* 183–84. Połczyńska shows that *Die Ostmark* enjoyed significant circulation, expanding its initial edition of 6,000 copies to 22,000 in 1901 and 50,000 in 1914.

46. Połczyńska, *Im polnischen Wind,* 184.

47. For example, Oskar Eulitz's publishing house in Lissa i. P. (in Posen), which published M. von Witten's (Margaret von Gottschall) *Nach Ostland wollen wir reiten* (1909), Otto Knoop's *Ostmärkische Sagen, Märchen und Erzählungen* (1909), and a small handful of other Ostmarken texts. See Thomas Serrier, *Provinz Posen, Ostmark, Wielkopolska: Eine Grenzregion zwischen Deutschen und Polen, 1848–1914* (Marburg: Herder-Institut, 2005), 170.

48. In 1897, the Eastern Marches Society donated 30,000 books to 35 libraries; in 1903, this number had risen to 108,000 books for 490 libraries. The peak of donations was reached in 1913, with 248,000 books donated to 760 libraries. See Maria Wojtczak, "Hinter den Kulissen des Ostmarkenvereins: Zur Entstehungsgeschichte der 'Ostmarkenromane,'" *Studia Germanica Posnaniensia* 22 (1995): 65–76.

49. Tims, *Germanizing Prussian Poland,* 256; see also Serrier, *Provinz Posen,* 170; Wojtczak, "Hinter den Kulissen," 71–72.

50. In the most comprehensive archival study of the Ostmarkenroman to date, Maria Wojtczak provides listings of the Ostmarkenromane she was able to identify. Of these, the majority were published between 1896 and 1910, their numbers steeply dropping after this date. Maria Wojtczak, *Literatur der Ostmark: Posener Heimatliteratur, 1890–1918* (Poznań: Wydawnictwo Naukowe Uniwersytetu im. Adama Mickiewicza, 1998).

51. Wojtczak, *Literatur der Ostmark;* and Połczyńska, *Im polnischen Wind.*

52. See the typologies of Połczyńska, *Im polnischen Wind;* Wojtczak, *Literatur der Ostmark;* and Helga B. Whiton, *Der Wandel des Polenbildes in der deutschen Literatur des 19. Jahrhunderts* (Bern: Peter Lang, 1981).

53. Witten, *Nach Ostland.*

54. B. Renz [Hugo Behrens], *Die polnische Gefahr und andere Novellen* (Berlin: Hermann Hillger, 1905). See Połczyńska, *Im polnischen Wind,* 210–24, for a treatment of these texts.

55. Representative examples of the first category would include Below, *Ostmark und Krummstab;* Max Berg, *Am alten Markt zu Posen: Polenroman aus der deutschen Ostmark* (Lissa i. P.: F. Ebbecke, 1907); Carl Busse, *Das Gymnasium zu Lengowo: Ein Schulroman aus der Ostmark* (Stuttgart: Engelhorn, 1907); Erich Fließ, *Die drei Erinnyen* (Berlin: R. Eckstein,1896); Grabowski, *Der weiße Adler;* Pilf, *Geschichten aus der Ostmark.*

56. Busse, *Gymnasium zu Lengowo,* 39–40.

57. Pilf, *Geschichten aus der Ostmark,* 5.

58. Similarly the messenger Kossubek in Robert Kurpiun's 1913 *Die Schwarzweißen* (Dresden: Lehmann, 1920), 82.

59. Ivan Hannaford, *Race: The History of an Idea in the West* (Washington, DC: Woodrow Wilson Center Press, 1996), 231.

60. Johann Gottfried Herder, *Reflections on the Philosophy of the History of Mankind,* ed. Frank E. Manuel (Chicago: University of Chicago Press, 1968), vol. 7, book 1, 7. Cited in Hannaford, *Race,* 232.

61. Similar is Max Berg's *Am alten Markt zu Posen,* where the physical features of Poles are frequently brought into comparison with those of Germans and held to be similar.

62. Busse, *Gymnasium zu Lengowo,* 12.

63. Annie Bock, *Der Zug nach dem Osten* (Berlin: Vita, 1898); Paul Oskar Höcker, *Polnische Wirthschaft* (Berlin: Bong, 1896); Pachnicke, *Auf Posten im Osten;* Viebig, *Das schlafende Heer.*

64. Uwe-K. Ketelsen, "Der koloniale Diskurs und die Öffnung des europäischen Ostens im deutschen Roman," in *Kolonialismus: Kolonialdiskurs und Genozid,* ed. Mihran Dabag, Horst Gründer, and Uwe-K. Ketelsen (Munich: Wilhelm Fink, 2004), 92.

65. Ketelsen refers broadly to German literature set in the East, but his examples are taken exclusively from texts with inner colonial themes. Uwe-K. Ketelsen, "Der koloniale Diskurs," 67–94.

66. Robert Young, *Colonial Desire: Hybridity in Theory, Culture, and Race* (London: Routledge, 1995), 91.

67. Hannaford, *Race,* 205–8.

68. Anon., "Entwicklung und Fortschritt, Zivilisation und Kultur," *Grenzboten* 59, no. 18 (May 3, 1900): 239.

69. Viebig, *Das schlafende Heer,* 67.

70. Ibid., 15.

71. Ibid., 16.

72. Bock, *Zug nach dem Osten,* 25.

73. Ibid., 220. See also 11, 183, 220, 256, 278.

74. Ibid., 88–89.
75. Ibid., 18.
76. Viebig, *Das schlafende Heer,* 19.
77. Ibid., 18.
78. Ibid., 28, 336.
79. Bock, *Zug nach dem Osten,* 187.
80. Ibid., 292, 512.
81. Viebig, *Das schlafende Heer,* 389.
82. See Jakob Katz, *Die Hep-Hep-Verfolgungen des Jahres 1819* (Berlin: Metropol-Verlag, 1994).
83. Viebig, *Das schlafende Heer,* 394–96.
84. Ketelsen, "Der koloniale Diskurs," 91.
85. Joachim Warmbold, *Germania in Africa: Germany's Colonial Literature (*New York: Peter Lang, 1988), 247.
86. Hans Grimm, *Südafrikanische Novellen* (Lippoldsberg/Weser: Klosterhaus-Verlag, 1913); Frieda von Bülow, *Deutsch-Ostafrikanische Novellen* (Berlin: Fontane, 1892).
87. *Deutsches Kolonial-Lexikon,* ed. Heinrich Schnee (Leipzig: Quelle und Meyer, 1920), s.v. "Verkafferung."
88. Nancy Reagin, "The Imagined Hausfrau: National Identity, Domesticity, and Colonialism in Imperial Germany," *Journal of Modern History* 73 (2001): 54–86.
89. Liepe, *Die Spinne,* 16.
90. Fließ's *Die drei Erinnyen* is the exception: here, we find a Polish widower with his three daughters, one who is "black" and takes after her father, one who is "white" and takes after her deceased German mother, and one who is "brown" and of ambivalent identity.
91. Heinrich von Treitschke, *Politik: Vorlesungen gehalten an der Universität zu Berlin* (Leipzig: Hirzel, 1922), 1:287. Cited in Orłowski, "*Polnische Wirtschaft,*" 222. Thomas Nipperdey reports that statistics indeed indicate a degree of imbalance: "in Posen, only some 2% of Polish men married non-Polish women, and 9–10% of German men married Polish women." *Deutsche Geschichte 1866–1918*, vol. 2, *Machtstaat vor der Demokratie* (Munich: Beck, 1992), 278.
92. Mary Louise Pratt, *Imperial Eyes: Travel Writing and Transculturation* (London: Routledge, 1992), 152.
93. Valeska Bethusy-Huc, *Hans der Pole* (Berlin: A. Schall, 1907), 423.
94. Ibid., 212.
95. In her influential work on German colonial literature of Germany's precolonial era, Susanne Zantop shows how the depiction of individual, gendered relationships between colonizer and colonized allegorically served to stake larger claims about the essential nature of the colonial encounter. Zantop, *Colonial Fantasies.*
96. Bock, *Zug nach dem Osten,* 122.
97. Ibid., 289.
98. Ibid., 356.
99. Viebig, *Das schlafende Heer,* 51–52.
100. McClintock, *Imperial Leather,* 53.

101. See Bernhard Stasiewski, "*'PolnischeWirtschaft'* und Johann Georg Forster: eine wortgeschichtliche Studie," *Deutsche wissenschaftliche Zeitschrift im Wartheland* 2–3 (1941): 207–16.

102. Maria Lammich, *Das deutsche Osteuropabild in der Zeit der Reichsgründung* (Boppard am Rhein: Boldt, 1978). Lammich closely investigates the language used to describe the Poles in the popular press (in *Die Gartenlaube, Die Grenzboten,* and *Westermanns Monatshefte*).

103. Orłowski, "*Polnische Wirtschaft.*"

104. Albert Emil Brachvogel, *Der Fels von Erz* (Berlin: Janke, 1872); Höcker, *Polnische Wirthschaft.* On Zell and Genée's unpublished manuscript, "Polnische Wirtschaft," see Orłowski, "*Polnische Wirtschaft,*" 32.

105. Hasso von Zitzewitz, *Das deutsche Polenbild in der Geschichte: Entstehung—Einflüsse—Auswirkungen* (Cologne: Böhlau, 1991), 104.

106. Liepe, *Die Spinne,* 11.

107. Ibid., 19, 22.

108. Walter Olma, "Das Polenbild im deutschen Heimatroman: Clara Viebigs Erfolgsroman *Das schlafende Heer* als Beispiel," in *Studien zur Kulturgeschichte des deutschen Polenbildes 1848–1939,* ed. Hendrik Feindt (Wiesbaden: Harrassowitz, 1995), 120.

109. The implications for German housekeeping practices were profound. See Reagin, "The Imagined Hausfrau."

110. Recent historical studies offer richly detailed accounts of the ways in which Max Sering—and more generally, the *Verein für Sozialpolitik* (Social Policy Association) to which he belonged—linked inner colonization to overseas colonialism. See Zimmerman, *Alabama in Africa;* and Robert L. Nelson, "From Manitoba to the Memel: Max Sering, Inner Colonization, and the German East," *Social History* 35 (2010): 439–57.

111. Max Sering, *Die innere Kolonisation im östlichen Deutschland* (Leipzig: Duncker und Humblot, 1893), 172.

112. Alfred Brenning, *Innere Kolonisation* (Leipzig: B. G. Teubner, 1909), 54.

113. A view shared, for example, by Friedrich Ernst von Schwerin, "Zur inneren Kolonisation in Pommern. Umblick und Ausblick," *Preußische Jahrbücher* 86, no. 2 (November 1896): 319. Schwerin laments the breakup of large estates and describes incoming German colonists tending toward criminal and degenerate behavior. He therefore concludes that the "large landowners should remain the leaders of the entire rural population, also in economic life."

114. Viebig, *Das schlafende Heer,* 124–25.

115. For a differentiated treatment of the debates surrounding the settlement of Catholics in the East, see Helmut Walser Smith, "Protestants, Catholics, and Poles: Religious and Nationality Conflicts in the Empire's Ethnically Mixed Areas, 1897–1914," chap. 6 in *German Nationalism and Religious Conflict: Culture, Ideology, Politics, 1870–1914* (Princeton: Princeton University Press, 1995), 169–205.

116. Moritz Gehre, *Die neue deutsche Kolonisation in Posen und Westpreußen* (Grossenhain: A. Hentze, 1899), 36.

117. Viebig, *Das schlafende Heer,* 269.

118. Ibid., 181.

119. Ibid., 518.
120. Ibid., 403.

CHAPTER 3

1. See Sibylle Benninghoff-Lühl, "Afrika—die koloniale Enttäuschung," chap. 5.1 in *Deutsche Kolonialromane 1884–1914 in ihrem Entstehungs- und Wirkungszusammenhang* (Bremen: Veröffentlichungen aus dem Übersee-Museum, 1983), 143–48.

2. Said, *Orientalism*, 19.

3. Ibid., 3.

4. Friedrich Scherer, *Adler und Halbmond: Bismarck und der Orient 1878–1890* (Paderborn: Schöningh, 2001); Haim Goren, ed., *Germany and the Middle East: Past, Present, and Future* (Jerusalem: Hebrew University Magnes Press, 2003); Malte Fuhrmann, *Der Traum vom deutschen Orient: Zwei deutsche Kolonien im Osmanischen Reich 1851–1918* (Frankfurt am Main: Campus Verlag, 2006).

5. Todd Kontje, *German Orientalisms* (Ann Arbor: University of Michigan Press, 2004); Nicholas A. Germana, *The Orient of Europe: The Mythical Image of India and Competing Images of German National Identity* (Newcastle: Cambridge Scholars, 2009); Andrea Fuchs-Sumiyoshi, *Orientalismus in der deutschen Literatur: Untersuchungen zu Werken des 19. und 20. Jahrhunderts, von Goethes West-östlichem Divan bis Thomas Manns Joseph-Tetralogie* (Hildesheim, NY: G. Olms, 1984); Andrea Polaschegg, *Der andere Orientalismus: Regeln deutsch-morgenländischer Imagination im 19. Jahrhundert* (Berlin: W. de Gruyter, 2005); Nina Berman, *Orientalismus, Kolonialismus und Moderne: Zum Bild des Orients in der deutschsprachigen Kultur um 1900* (Stuttgart: M & P, 1999); Iman Attia, *Die "westliche Kultur" und ihr Anderes: Zur Dekonstruktion von Orientalismus und antimuslimischem Rassismus* (Bielefeld: transcript, 2009).

6. See Kontje, *German Orientalisms.*

7. Edward Said, *Culture and Imperialism* (London: Vintage, 1994), 51.

8. Axel Dunker, *Kontrapunktische Lektüren: Koloniale Strukturen in der deutschsprachigen Literatur des 19. Jahrhunderts* (Paderborn: Wilhelm Fink, 2008).

9. Axel Dunker, "'Unter lauter pechschwarze Kerle, die von Kultur und Ehre nichts wissen': Theodor Fontane: *Effi Briest*," in Dunker, *Kontrapunktische Lektüren*, 151–65; Claudius Sittig, "Gieshüblers Kohlenprovisor: Der Kolonialdiskurs und das Hirngespinst vom spukenden Chinesen in Theodor Fontanes *Effi Briest*," *Zeitschrift für deutsche Philologie* 122 (2003): 544–63; Rolf Parr, "Kongobecken, Lombok und der Chinese im Hause Briest: Das 'Wissen um die Kolonien' und das 'Wissen aus den Kolonien' bei Theodor Fontane," in *Fontane und die Fremde: Fontane und Europa*, ed. Konrad Ehlich (Würzburg: Königshausen und Neumann, 2002), 212–28; Judith Ryan, "The Chinese Ghost: Colonialism and Subaltern Speech in Fontane's *Effi Briest*," in *History and Literature: Essays in Honor of Karl S. Guthke*, ed. William S. Donahue and Scott Denham (Tübingen: Stauffenburg, 2000), 367–84; Reinhard Finke, "' . . . der Äquator läuft ihnen über den Bauch': Namen und Geschichten zu Afrika in Fontanes *Effi Briest* und anderswo," in *Romantik und Ästhetizmus*, ed. Bettina Gruber and Gerhard Plumpe (Würzburg: Königshausen und Neumann, 1999), 297–315; Peter Utz,

"Effi Briest, der Chinese und der Imperialismus: eine 'Geschichte' im geschichtlichen Kontext," in *Zeitschrift für deutsche Philologie* 103 (1984): 212–22; Ingrid Schuster, "Exotik als Chiffre: Zum Chinesen in *Effi Briest*," *Wirkendes Wort* 33 (1983): 115–25; Ulrike Rainer, "*Effi Briest* und das Motiv des Chinesen: Rolle und Darstellung in Fontanes Roman," *Zeitschrift für deutsche Philologie* 101 (1982): 545–61.

10. Hugo Aust and Hubertus Fischer, eds., *Fontane und Polen: Fontane in Polen* (Würzburg: Königshausen und Neumann, 2008); Hubertus Fischer, "Polnische Verwicklungen," in *Fontane und die Fremde, Fontane und Europa,* ed. Konrad Ehlich (Würzburg: Königshausen und Neumann, 2002), 262–75; Benjamin Breggin, "Fontane's Aesthetics of the Slavic Race," *German Life and Letters* 56 (2003): 213–22; Mirosław Ossowski, "Das Polenbild des jungen und des alten Fontane," in *Literatur und Politik in der Heine-Zeit: die 48er Revolution in Texten zwischen Vormärz und Nachmärz,* ed. Hartmut Kircher and Maria Kłańska (Cologne: Böhlau, 1998), 219–34; Werner Rieck, "Polnische Thematik im Werk Theodor Fontanes," *Fontane-Blätter* 61 (1996): 84–112; Walter Müller-Seidel, "Fontane und Polen," in Hendrik Feindt, *Studien zur Kulturgeschichte des deutschen Polenbildes 1848–1939* (Wiesbaden: Harrassowitz, 1995), 41–64; Siegfried Sudhof, "Das Bild Polens im Werk Theodor Fontanes," *Acta Universitatis Wratislaviensis* 34 (1978): 101–11; Dietrich Sommer, "Das Polenbild Fontanes als Element nationaler Selbstverständigung und -kritik," *Weimarer Beiträge* 16, no. 11 (1970): 173–90.

11. Dunker, "Unter lauter pechschwarze Kerle," 151.

12. See Ryan, "The Chinese Ghost," 383–84; less convincingly, Utz, "Effi Briest," 222.

13. The "anxiety of reverse diffusion" is a term adapted from those introduced by Steven Arata ("reverse colonization") and J. M. Blaut ("diffusionism"). See Stephen D. Arata, "The Occidental Tourist: *Dracula* and the Anxiety of Reverse Colonization," *Victorian Studies* 33, no. 4 (1990); and Blaut, *Colonizer's Model.*

14. Blaut, *Colonizer's Model,* 5.

15. Having learned fluent English, mastered English social customs, and even memorized the English train schedule, Dracula eludes the defensive borders of the English metropolis and infiltrates London. Passing as English, he is not readily identifiable as Other and is thus able to pursue his plan to reproduce himself, threatening to turn the English population into fellow vampires in the process. With his thinly disguised, voracious sexual appetite, Dracula threatens to deracinate the entire English population. See Arata, "Occidental Tourist."

16. Arata, "Occidental Tourist," 623.

17. Anon., "Die Ueberflutung Deutschlands mit Slawen," *Alldeutsche Blätter* (May 19, 1895).

18. Drummond, "'Einen kräftigen Damm'"; Wippermann, *Die Deutschen und der Osten,* 26–27, 34, 40–42, 65.

19. This plurality of "Easts" in the German tradition has been argued from both literary-discursive and cultural-historical angles. See respectively Kontje, *German Orientalisms,* and Wippermann, *Die Deutschen und der Osten.*

20. Benninghoff-Lühl, *Deutsche Kolonialromane,* 85.

21. See Kristin Kopp and Klaus Müller-Richter, eds., *Die Großstadt und das Primitive: Text, Politik, Repräsentation* (Stuttgart: M & P, 2004).

22. The *bel étage* was the representative first floor of buildings in Berlin, which had higher ceilings and larger rooms than apartments located on other stories and was thus preferred by members of the upper classes who lived in the city.

23. Theodor Fontane, *Effi Briest,* in *Theodor Fontane: Sämtliche Werke,* vol. 7, ed. Edgar Gross (Munich: Nymphenburger, 1959), 189. Except where noted, all subsequent citations refer to this edition. Except where noted, all translations are mine.

24. The first edition of Karl Emil Franzos's book was published in 1876 under the title *Halb-Asien: Land und Leute des östlichen Europa* (Stuttgart: Adolf Bonz und Comp, 1876). However, the book was extremely popular, and several volumes containing various collections of the original stories along with new ones were published throughout the late 1870s and 1880s.

25. Karl Emil Franzos, *Halb-Asien: Land und Leute des östlichen Europa* (Stuttgart: J. G. Cott'sche Buchhandlung Nachfolger, 1914), 1.

26. Anon., "Eine Culturskizze aus Ostpreußen," *Preußische Jahrbücher* 62 (1888): 75.

27. Fontane, *Effi Briest,* 189.

28. Ibid., 204.

29. See Martin Belgard, *Parzellierung und innere Kolonisation in den 6 östlichen Provinzen Preußens 1875–1906* (Leipzig: Duncker und Humblot, 1907), 287–86, where Belgard laments the increase in Polish landownership and population in the various eastern Prussian regions, including Pomerania. The region was predominantly Polish and Kaschubian, such that Instetten refers to it as "the Kaschubian hinterland." See Fontane, *Effi Briest,* 204.

30. Utz, "Effi Briest," 220.

31. Fontane, *Effi Briest,* 203–4.

32. Ibid., 204–5.

33. Ibid., 205.

34. See Edith H. Krause, "Desire and Denial: Fontane's *Effi Briest,*" *Germanic Review* 74, no. 2 (Spring 1999): 117–29.

35. Fontane, *Effi Briest,* 180.

36. Ibid., 172.

37. McClintock, *Imperial Leather.*

38. Fontane, *Effi Briest,* 305, where Sidonie von Grasenabb complains of a lack of good upbringing (*Zucht*) as she watches the forester's daughter flirt, indirectly accusing Effi of sharing in her behavior.

39. Ibid., 222, where the women of the landed aristocracy criticize Effi's dress for "not being discreet enough for a lady of social position."

40. Ibid., 256.

41. Ibid., 224.

42. Ibid., 191

43. Ibid., 177.

44. Ibid., 242.

45. *Deutsches Wörterbuch,* ed. Gerhard Wahrig (Munich: Mosaik, 1987), s.v. "apart."

46. See Müller-Seidel, "Fontane und Polen," 55–56.

47. Ibid.

48. Whiton, *Wandel des Polenbildes,* 174.

49. Theodor Fontane, *Sämtliche Werke,* vol. 6 (Munich: Nymphenburger, 1963), 261.

50. Ibid., 292.

51. Freytag, *Soll und Haben,* II:155.

52. Fontane, *Sämtliche Werke,* vol. 21, book 1 (Munich: Nymphenburger, 1963), 225.

53. Fontane, *Effi Briest,* 311. Translation taken from *Theodor Fontane: Effi Briest,* trans. Hugh Rorrison and Helen Chambers (London: Penguin, 1995), 120.

54. Fontane, *Effi Briest,* 311.

55. Fontane, *Effi Briest,* 295.

56. See Wojtczak, *Literatur der Ostmark,* 104–14.

57. Fontane, *Effi Briest,* 278.

58. Ibid., 279.

59. Nancy Kaiser, *Social Integration and Narrative Structure: Patterns of Realism in Auerbach, Freytag, Fontane, and Raabe* (New York: Peter Lang, 1987).

60. This is the argument of Utz, "Effi Briest," which I find largely unconvincing.

61. Fontane, *Effi Briest,* 319.

62. Theodor Fontane to Joseph Viktor Widmann, Nov. 19, 1895, in *Fontanes Briefe in zwei Bänden,* ed. Gotthard Erler (Berlin: Aufbau, 1968), 2:386. This is the only known comment recorded by Fontane concerning the Chinese.

63. Fontane, *Effi Briest,* 284.

64. Ibid., 203.

65. Ibid., 306.

66. Drummond, "'Einen kräftigen Damm.'"

67. Anon., "In der Brandung," *Alldeutsche Blätter* 7 (Nov. 15, 1892), Beilage, 81.

68. Rolf Parr, "Der Bismarck-Mythos—kulturelle Folie für Theodor Fontane," *Fontane Blätter* (1993), 31–47.

69. Fontane, *Effi Briest,* 271. Translation taken from Rorrison and Chambers, *Effi Briest,* 84.

70. This strategy of professional advancement via voluntary peripheralization involved stations both in the colonies and in the areas undergoing inner colonization. Indeed, *Die Ostmark* advertised this possibility: "Whoever has undergone the advanced school of national duty-fulfillment under the highly difficult conditions there [in the Eastern Marches] will certainly be regarded as a proven man in his later career." Erich Liesegang, "Aus Unserer Ostmark," *Die Ostmark* 2 (Feb. 1897): 75. See also Carl Busse's *Das Gymnasium zu Lengowo,* where the narrator remarks, "The government needed competent German officials. It drew them from all over Prussia. He who wanted to make a career came to Posen. He who stood the test of the difficult conditions here had good prospects." Busse, *Gymnasium zu Lengowo,* 55.

71. Henry H. H. Remak, "Politik und Gesellschaft als Kunst: Güldenklees Toast in Fontanes *Effi Briest,*" in *Formen realistischer Erzählkunst,* ed. Jörg Thunecke (Nottingham: Sherwood Press Agencies, 1979), 550–62.

72. Fontane, *Effi Briest,* 268.

73. Heinrich Heine, "Vitzliputzli," in *Romanzero* (Hamburg: Hoffmann und Campe, 1851), 78–103.

74. Fontane, *Effi Briest,* 287.

75. Ibid., 315.

76. Ibid., 351.

77. Utz, "Effi Briest."

78. Heinz Gollwitzer, *Die gelbe Gefahr: Geschichte eines Schlagworts Studien zum imperialistischen Denken* (Göttingen: Vandenhoeck und Ruprecht, 1962). J. Zwenger, "Ein Tag in China," *Gartenlaube* (1894), 797–800.

79. Fontane, *Effi Briest,* 373.

80. Ibid.

81. Ibid., 318. Also significant is the nature of Crampas's trip to Stettin: Crampas brings back news that the Prussian troops scheduled to be garrisoned in Kessin will be stationed elsewhere. Effi had thought of these Husaren as "quite actually the guardians of paradise and innocence" (Fontane, *Effi Briest,* 314). As such, they would have constituted a reinforcement of Bismarck's border.

CHAPTER 4

1. Some of the material in this chapter is adapted from my article "Cartographic Claims: Colonial Mappings of Poland in German Territorial Revisionism," in *Visual Culture in Twentieth-Century Germany: The Text as Spectacle,* ed. Gail Finney (Bloomington: Indiana University Press, 2006), 199–213.

2. Bernhard von Bülow, *Deutsche Politik* (Berlin: Reimar Hobbing, 1916), 287.

3. Imanuel Geiss, *Der polnische Grenzstreifen, 1914–1918: Ein Beitrag zur deutschen Kriegszielpolitik im Ersten Weltkrieg* (Lübeck: Matthiesen, 1960).

4. Annemarie H. Sammartino, *The Impossible East: Germany and the East, 1914–1922* (Ithaca: Cornell University Press, 2010), 30–43; Geiss, *Grenzstreifen;* Salomon Grumbach, *Das annexionistische Deutschland* (Lausanne: Payot, 1917), 133–40.

5. Woodruff D. Smith, *German Colonial Empire* (Chapel Hill: University of North Carolina Press, 1978), 225.

6. Smith, *Ideological Origins,* 177.

7. Geiss, *Grenzstreifen.*

8. Broszat, *Polenpolitik,* 183.

9. Carl Jentsch, "Der Feind im Osten," *Die Grenzboten* 1 (1915): 16.

10. Conrad Bornhak, "Deutsche Schutzgebiete in Europa," *Die Grenzboten* 10 (March 7, 1917): 295.

11. See Hans Siegfried Weber, *Ansiedlung von Kriegsinvaliden* (Berlin: Deutsche Verlags-Anstalt, 1915); Curt Thomalla, "Ansiedlung Kriegsverletzter," *Die Grenzboten* 22 (May 30, 1917): 265–74; H. L. Dannenberg, *Sieg ohne Landgewinn?* (Dresden: Verlag "Das größere Deutschland," 1918).

12. Jens P. Ackermann, "Ein Wissenschaftler als politischer Publizist im Ersten Weltkrieg," chap. 9 in *Die Geburt des modernen Propagandakrieges im Ersten Weltkrieg: Dietrich Schäfer, Gelehrter und Politiker* (Frankfurt am Main: Peter Lang, 2004), 155–239; Roger Chickering, "Dietrich Schäfer and Max Weber," in *Max Weber and His Contemporaries,* ed. Wolfgang J. Mommsen and Jürgen Osterhammel (London: German Historical Institute, 1987), 334.

13. Sammartino, *Impossible Border,* 30.

14. Geiss, *Grenzstreifen,* 54.

15. Dietrich Schäfer, "Länder- und Völkerkarte Europas" (Berlin: Dietrich Riemer [Ernst Vohsen], 1916). Scale: 1:4,000,000.

16. Dietrich Schäfer, *Unser Recht auf die Ostmarken* (Berlin: Deutscher Ostmarken-Verein, 1911), 3; Dietrich Schäfer, "Geschichtliche Einleitung," in *Die deutsche Ostmark,* ed. Der deutsche Ostmarkenverein (Lissa i. P.: Oskar Eulitz, 1913), 16.

17. Guntram Henrik Herb, "A Concern for Accuracy," in *Under the Map of Germany,* 34–45.

18. The contemporary "reader" of this map will not approach it with the same degree of reverence for its scientific accuracy—because the quality of its paper, coloration, and fonts already quietly suggest the object's outdatedness.

19. Louis B. Thomas claims that red even makes the space it covers look larger than it would had this space been given a different color. See his "Maps as Instruments of Propaganda," *Surveying and Mapping* 9, no. 2 (April–June 1949): 80.

20. J. B. Harley refers to the "silence on maps." J. B. Harley, "Maps, Knowledge, and Power," in *The Iconography of Landscape: Essays on the Symbolic Representation, Design, and Use of Past Environments,* ed. Denis Cosgrove and Stephen Daniels (Cambridge: Cambridge University Press, 1988), 290.

21. Dietrich Schäfer, *Karte der Länder und Völker Europas: Volkstum und Staatenbildung* (Berlin: Dietrich Riemer [Ernst Vohsen], 1916), booklet accompanying the map, 1–2.

22. Schäfer, *Karte der Länder und Völker Europas,* booklet, 4.

23. Smith, *German Colonial Empire,* 222.

24. For an account of the postwar proceedings, see Horst Gründer, *Geschichte der deutschen Kolonien,* 3rd ed. (Paderborn: Schöningh, 1995), 213–31.

25. *Materialien, betreffend die Friedensverhandlungen, Teil IV, Mantelnote der Antwort der Aliierten und Assoziierten Mächte auf die deutschen Gegenvorschläge. Autorisierte Ausgabe* (Charlottenburg: Im Auftrag des Auswärtigen Amtes, 1919), 83, quoted in Horst Gründer, ed., "*. . . da und dort ein junges Deutschland gründen": Rassismus, Kolonien und kolonialer Gedanke vom 16. bis zum 20. Jahrhundert* (Munich: Deutscher Taschenbuch Verlag, 1999), 316. See also Heinrich Schnee, *Die koloniale Schuldlüge,* 12th ed. (Munich: Knorr und Hirth, 1940), 30–31.

26. Ingo Haar, *Historiker im Nationalsozialismus: Deutsche Geschichtswissenschaft und der "Volkstumskampf im Osten"* (Göttingen: Vandenhoeck und Ruprecht, 2000), 32.

27. Herb, *Under the Map of Germany,* 15–16.

28. Ibid., 19.

29. Ibid.

30. Ibid., 13–45.

31. Peter Fischer, *Die deutsche Publizistik als Faktor der deutsch-polnischen Beziehungen 1919–1939* (Wiesbaden: Harrassowitz, 1991), 50, 62–70, 128–29.

32. Herb, *Under the Map of Germany,* 79. His translation of the *Verhandlungen des 20. Deutschen Geographentages zu Leipzig, vom 17. bis 19. Mai 1921* (Berlin: Dietrich Reimer, 1922).

33. Herb, *Under the Map of Germany,* 80.

34. Ibid., 101.

35. Carl Diercke, *Schulatlas Mittelausgabe,* 3rd ed. (Braunschweig: Westermann, 1928), 68–69. In his discussion of this map, Herb lists *Dierckes Schulatlas* as a distant second to *Putzgers historischer Schulatlas* but shows that it nonetheless reached broad circulation. Herb, *Under the Map of Germany,* 97.

36. Benedict Anderson, *Imagined Communities: Reflections on the Origin and Spread of Nationalism* (London: Verso, 1991), 175–76.

37. The 1928 film *Karte und Atlas* is located in the German Federal Archives under the call number M 1083.

38. Guntram Henrik Herb was the first to identify this feature of the Diercke Schulatlas. Herb, *Under the Map of Germany,* 97–98.

39. Karl Haushofer, "Die suggestive Karte?" *Grenzboten* 81 (1922): 17–19.

40. A. Hillen Ziegfeld, "Kartographik, Wesen und Aufgabe," *Volk und Reich* (May–June 1927): 257–60; Ziegfeld, "Die deutsche Kartographie nach dem Weltkriege," in *Volk unter Völkern,* ed. Karl Christian von Loesch (Breslau: Hirt, 1925), 429–45; Ziegfeld, "Kartengestaltung—Sport oder Waffe?" *Zeitschrift für Geopolitik* 12 (1935): 243–47.

41. Franz Braun, ed., *Geopolitischer Geschichtsatlas,* vol. I, *Das Altertum* (Dresden: Ehlermann, 1927).

42. Herb, *Under the Map of Germany,* 53–65.

43. Karl Haushofer, *Grenzen in ihrer geographischen und politischen Bedeutung* (Berlin: Kurt Vowinckel, 1927), 11.

44. Peter Fischer recounts the content of the Kulturfilm *Land unterm Kreuz,* in which the children of areas ceded to Poland are shown starving because the irrational severing of transportation networks at the new border has cut off the flow of commerce to these regions. Fischer, *Die deutsche Publizistik,* 140, footnote 94.

45. Karl Haushofer, "Das Wissen von der Grenze und die Grenzen des deutschen Volkes," in *Deutsche Rundschau* 198 (1924): 233ff., quoted in Fischer, *Die deutsche Publizistik,* 42.

46. Fischer, *Die deutsche Publizistik,* 43.

47. Herb, *Under the Map of Germany,* 56–62.

48. Ibid., 61–62.

49. Anon., "Wohin gehört Posen?" *Die Grenzboten* 46 (Nov. 25, 1918): 158.

50. Moritz Weiß, "Unzweifelhaft deutsches Land!" *Die Grenzboten* 14 (April 2, 1919): 19.

51. Ibid., 22.

52. Haar, *Historiker im Nationalsozialismus,* 31.

53. Doug MacDougal, *Frozen Earth: The Once and Future Story of Ice Ages* (Berkeley: University of California Press, 2004), 127–28.

54. Susan A. Crane, *Museums and Memory* (Palo Alto: Stanford University Press, 2000), 194.

55. Albrecht Penck, *Das deutsche Reich* (Vienna: F. Tempsky, 1887). See Gerhard Engelmann, *Ferdinand Richthofen 1833–1905; Albrecht Penck 1858–1945: Zwei markante Geographen Berlins* (Stuttgart: Steiner, 1988), 25–35.

56. Herb, *Under the Map of Germany,* 23–24.

57. Michael Burleigh, *Germany Turns Eastwards: A Study of* Ostforschung *in the Third Reich* (New York: Cambridge University Press, 1988), 20.

58. Albrecht Penck, "Deutscher Volks- und Kulturboden," in *Volk unter Völkern,* ed. Karl Christian von Loesch (Breslau: Ferdinand Hirt, 1925), 62–73.

59. Ibid., 62.

60. Penck, "Deutscher Volks- und Kulturboden," 64.

61. Hartmut Böhme, "Vom Cultus zur Kultur(wissenschaft): Zur historischen Semantik des Kulturbegriffs," in *Literaturwissenschaft—Kulturwissenschaft: Positionen, Themen, Perspektiven,* ed. Renate Glaser and Matthias Luserke (Opladen: Westdeutscher Verlag, 1996), 48–68.

62. Ibid., 68.

63. Friedrich Ratzel, *Deutschland: Einführung in die Heimatkunde* (Leipzig: Grunow, 1898), 255.

64. Ibid.

65. Penck, "Deutscher Volks- und Kulturboden," 70.

66. Ibid., 69.

67. Ibid.

68. Ibid., 65.

69. Ibid., 65–66.

70. Wilhelm Volz, "Zur Einführung," in *Der ostdeutsche Volksboden: Aufsätze zu den Fragen des Ostens,* ed. Wilhelm Volz (Breslau: Ferdinand Hirt, 1926).

71. Gründer, *Geschichte,* 218.

72. Paul Heinrich Kuntze, *Das Volksbuch unserer Kolonien* (Leipzig: Dollheimer, 1938).

73. This map is not present in the book's second edition.

74. Rudolf Kötzschke and Wolfgang Ebert, *Geschichte der ostdeutschen Kolonisation* (Leipzig: Bibliographisches Institut, 1937), 149–55.

75. Kuntze, *Volksbuch unserer Kolonien,* 12.

CHAPTER 5

1. For an example of such argumentation, see Rudolf Kötzschke, "Über den Ursprung und die geschichtliche Bedeutung der ostdeutschen Siedlung," in *Der ostdeutsche Volksboden: Aufsätze zu den Fragen des Ostens,* ed. Wilhelm Volz (Breslau: Ferdinand Hirt, 1926), 7–26.

2. See Jan Chodera, *Die deutsche Polenliteratur 1918–1939: Stoff- und Motivgeschichte* (Poznań: Wydawnictwo Naukowe Uniwersytetu im. Adama Mickiewicza, 1966), and Dorothea Friedrich, *Das Bild Polens in der Literatur der Weimarer Republik* (Frankfurt am Main: Peter Lang, 1984).

3. Hampe, *Zug nach dem Osten.*

4. Curt Kühns, *Marienburg* (Berlin: Verlag der grünen Volksbücher, 1920); Wilhelm Kotzde, *Die Burg im Osten: Das Schicksal einer Ritterschaft* (Stuttgart: Steinkopf, 1925); Hans Venatier, *Vogt Bartold: Der große Zug nach dem Osten* (Leipzig: Schwarzhäupter, 1939).

5. This architectural distinction is already evident in Gustav Freytag's *Soll und Haben.* There, the Polish estate acquired by the German aristocrats has a half-built stone manor on the property. This is the only stone structure in the vicinity, for the

neighboring Polish aristocrats lived in dilapidated wooden houses. The stone structure is found half-finished, because the previous Polish owners had been unable to build it to completion—this task is left to the new German owners.

6. In addition to multiple printings of Ernst Wichert's three-volume novel *Heinrich von Plauen* (Dresden: Reißner, 1869), representative titles would include Werner Jansen, *Geier um Marienburg* (Braunschweig: G. Westermann, 1925); Hanna Bahlke, *Der Kampf um die Marienburg* (Berlin: J. Beltz, 1931); Marie Frey, *Die Marienburg: Historischer Roman von der Grenzwacht im deutschen Osten* (Berlin: F. Zillefsen, 1922).

7. Tobias Nagl, *Die unheimliche Maschine: Rasse und Repräsentation im Weimarer Kino* (Munich: edition text & kritik, 2009), 221–30.

8. For a detailed historical account of interwar overseas-colonial films, see Nagl, *Die unheimliche Maschine.*

9. Films are located at the Bundesarchiv-Filmarchiv in Berlin under the following call numbers:

> *Auf deutschen Farmen in Deutsch-Südwestafrika* (n.d.), M 2867.
> *Die Weltgeschichte als Kolonialgeschichte* (Hans Cürlis, 1926), M 8057.
> *Deutsch-Ostafrika 1914–1918* (n.d.), M 3336.

10. Marcia Klotz, "Global Visions: From the Colonial to the National Socialist World," *European Studies Journal* 16, no. 2 (1999): 37–68. Klotz also notes that the colonial nations (most notably Spain) themselves only turn white at those historical moments when they are actively colonizing other geographic spaces. With the decline of their empires, European spaces become black, reinforcing the ideological notion that a white European identity was established through the act of generating diffusions. See also Nagl's reading of this film in *Die unheimliche Maschine,* 342–50.

11. Films located at the Bundesarchiv-Filmarchiv in Berlin under the following call numbers:

> *Pommern* (n.d.), M 385.
> *Schlesien* (n.d.), M 60990.

12. See Sabine Hake, "Mapping the Native Body: On Africa and the Colonial Film in the Third Reich," in *The Imperialist Imagination: German Colonialism and Its Legacy,* ed. Sara Friedrichsmeyer et al. (Ann Arbor: University of Michigan, 1998), 163–88. See also Marcia Klotz, "Epistemological Ambiguity and the Fascist Text: *Jew Süss, Carl Peters,* and *Ohm Krüger,*" *New German Critique* 74 (Spring–Summer 1998): 91–124.

13. Nagl finds only one revisionist colonial film in the strict sense to have been produced: Konrad Wiene's *Ich hatt' einen Kameraden* (1926). Nagl, *Die unheimliche Maschine,* 226.

14. Nagl, *Die unheimliche Maschine, 47.* See also Wolfgang Kabatek, *Imagerie des Anderen im Weimarer Kino* (Bielefeld: transcript, 2003), 58–63, where a similar argument is pursued.

15. Jerzy Maśnicki, *Niemy kraj: polskie motywy w europejskim kinie niemym (1896–1930)* (Danzig: Słowo/obraz terytoria, 2006), 165–67.

16. The figure of Etzel is loosely based upon Attila the Hun but not equivalent with this historical figure. I thus refer to "Etzel" throughout. See Francis G. Gentry et al., eds., *The Nibelungen Tradition: An Encyclopedia* (New York: Routledge, 2002), 67.

17. Anton Kaes, *Shell Shock Cinema: Weimar Culture and the Wounds of War* (Princeton: Princeton University Press, 2009), 153–66.

18. Joachim Heinzle, "Einleitung: Der deutscheste aller deutschen Stoffe," in Heinzle and Waldschmidt, *Die Nibelungen,* 9. Heinzle shows that this mode of reception was particularly important in negotiating the figure of Hagen, who is the villainous murderer of Siegfried in the first half of the epic, a role incompatible with his heroic persona in the second half.

19. The guilt of this betrayal was variously attributed. For some, it was an international scheme to lure Germany to Versailles with a promise of a negotiated peace, and then demanding the nation's complete capitulation instead; for others, the betrayal was simply enacted by those who signed this traitorous treaty on Germany's behalf. For many, it was those within the German nation itself—Communists, the pacifists, or the Jews—who could be thrown under suspicion for undermining the war effort at home.

20. Anton Kaes, "Der Mythos des Deutschen in Fritz Langs Nibelungen-Film," in *Deutsche Meister, böse Geister? Nationale Selbstfindung in der Musik,* ed. Hermann Danuser and Herfried Münkler (Schliengen: Edition Argus, 2001), 326–42. Kaes, *Shell Shock Cinema,* 145–46.

21. One notable exception can be found in Carl Otto Czeschka's book illustrations from 1909, reproduced in Franz Keim, *Die Nibelungenlied* (Frankfurt am Main: Insel, 1972), 26–27.

22. Joachim Heinzle, "Zweimal Hagen oder: Rezeption als Sinnunterstellung," in *Die Nibelungen: Ein deutscher Wahn, ein deutscher Alptraum: Studien und Dokumente zur Rezeption des Nibelungenstoffs im 19. und 20. Jahrhundert,* ed. Joachim Heinzle and Anneliese Waldschmidt (Frankfurt am Main: Suhrkamp, 1991), 21–40.

23. G. W. F. Hegel, *Vorlesungen über die Ästhetik,* in *Werke,* vol. 13, ed. Eva Moldenhauer, Karl Markus Michel, and Helmut Reinicke (Frankfurt am Main: Suhrkamp, 1986), 352–53.

24. See Klaus von See, "Das Nibelungenlied—ein Nationalepos?" in Heinzle and Waldschmidt, *Die Nibelungen,* 43–110.

25. Ibid., 57.

26. Karl Busch, *Das Nibelungenlied in deutscher Geschichte und Kunst* (Munich: Allgemeine Vereinigung Die Kunst dem Volke, 1934), 3–6, 15, 36, quoted in Klaus von See, "Das Nibelungenlied—ein Nationalepos?" 84.

27. Hans von Salzwedel, *Der schwarze Lupno* (Weimar: Verlag für Volks- und Heimatkunde, 1926).

28. Fritz Lang, "Worauf es beim Nibelungen-Film ankam," in *Die Nibelungen: Ein deutsches Heldenlied* (Ufa-Decla Film Pamphlet, 1924), 13.

29. Ibid., 14.

30. Kaes, *Shell Shock Cinema,* 146. Kaes's reading echos Klaus Kreimeier's sense that the border crossings each have military resonance: "Siegfried's entrance at King Gunther's palace at Worms, the entrance of the Burgundians at Brunhild's, the entrance of the Burgundians at Attila's: troop deployments that precede mass death." Klaus Kreimeier, "Der Schlafwandler: Fritz Lang und seine deutschen Filme," in *Film, Stadt, Kino, Berlin,* ed. Uta Berg-Ganschow, Wolfgang Jacobsen, and Rudolf Arnheim (Berlin: Argon Verlag, 1987), 104.

31. David Bordwell, *Narration in the Fiction Film* (Madison: University of Wisconsin Press, 1985), 186.

32. Davies, *God's Playground,* 394.

33. The Silesian War saw three major border skirmishes on August 16–24, 1919; August 19–25, 1920; and May 2–July 5, 1921.

34. Broszat, *Polenpolitik,* 202.

35. Tiessen, "Der Friedensvertrag," 203–20.

36. Ibid., 203.

37. Ibid., 212.

38. Davies, *God's Playground,* 401.

39. Linksrheiner [pseud.], "Die Versklavung des Rheins," *Die Grenzboten* (March 10, 1921): 241–43.

40. Meanwhile, in the Polish ceded territories, German schoolchildren were also seeing a reversed colonial politic. See Georg Cleinow, "Polnische Irrungen," *Die Grenzboten* 40 (Oct. 3, 1917): 1.

41. Linksrheiner [pseud.], "Weiße und farbige Franzosen am Rhein," *Die Grenzboten* 18 (May 5, 1920): 124–25.

42. Ibid., 124–27.

43. Tiessen, "Der Friedensvertrag," 218–19.

44. As such, this border can be compared to the wall erected by Death in Fritz Lang's 1921 film *Der müde Tod.* This wall also gained mythic dimensions, for the extent of its reach was never shown. The wall would have lost this function had it been shown in a cross section as is the gorge in the *Nibelungen.*

45. Friedrich Naumann, *Mitteleuropa* (Berlin: Georg Riemer, 1916 [ca. 1915]), 6–7 (emphasis in the original).

46. Siegfried Kracauer, *Von Caligari zu Hitler: Eine psychologische Geschichte des deutschen Films* (Frankfurt am Main: Suhrkamp, 1984), 159, 103.

47. Siegfried Kracauer, "The Mass Ornament," in *The Mass Ornament: Weimar Essays,* ed. Thomas Y. Levin (Cambridge: Harvard University Press, 1995), 76.

48. Rudolf Klein-Rogge, "Von Dr. Mabuse zu König Etzel" (from the 1924 Ufa-Decla advertising brochure). Reproduced in *Fritz Lang: Die Nibelungen,* ed. Enno Patalas and Fritz Göttler (Munich: Kulturreferat der Landeshauptstadt München, 1986), 35–36.

49. The fact that the threshold to Alberich's mystical kingdom is also guarded by an invisible/camouflaged figure hiding in a tree is significant. It points to a nature/culture dichotomy, which separates the civilized society at Worms from that of parallel communities that seem to exist in another, less-developed time.

50. Thea von Harbou, "Aus dem Manuskript des Films 'Die Nibelungen,'" in *Das Kulturfilmbuch,* ed. Edgar Beyfuss and Alex Kossowsky (Berlin: Carl P. Chryselius, 1924), 257; image 268: "Vor der Etzelburg."

51. Haushofer, *Grenzen.*

52. Friedrich Ratzel, *Die Erde und das Leben: eine vergleichende Erdkunde* (Leipzig: Bibliographisches Institut, 1901–2), 670.

53. ck [pseud.], "Kriemhilds Rache: Des Nibelungenfilmes zweiter Teil," *Vossische Zeitung* (April 30, 1924).

54. Herbert Jhering, "Der Zweite Nibelungen-Film," in *Von Reinhardt bis Brecht:*

Vier Jahrzehnte Theater und Film, vol. 2: *1924–1929,* ed. Edith Krull (Berlin: Aufbau-Verlag, 1959), 476.

55. Ibid.

56. Ibid., 477.

57. The Decla film catalog as well as the commemorative brochure accompanying the film's premier both include a special acknowledgment on their credits page: "The Huns' armor, costumes, and weapons were all designed by Heinrich Umlauff, and were produced in the workshops of his ethnographic museum in Hamburg." "Der Nibelungenfilm: Seine Schöpfer und seine Mitarbeiter," 148.

58. Lotte Eisner, *Fritz Lang* (London: Secker and Warburg, 1976), 79.

59. "Der Nibelungenfilm: Seine Schöpfer und seine Mitarbeiter," in *Das Verleih-Programm 1923/24* (catalog of Der Decla-Bioskop-Verleih, 1923–24), 149.

60. Cited in Isabel V. Hull, *Absolute Destruction: Military Culture and the Practices of War in Imperial Germany* (Ithaca: Cornell University Press, 2005), 135.

61. Harbou, "Aus dem Manuskript," 254–55, images 260, 262.

62. Ibid., 259.

63. Lutz Koepnick, "Unsettling America: German Westerns and Modernity," *Modernism/Modernity* 2, no. 3 (1995): 3.

CONCLUSION

1. Adolf Hitler, *Reden des Führers. Politik und Propaganda Adolf Hitlers, 1922–1945,* ed. Erhard Klöss (Munich: Deutscher Taschenbuch Verlag, 1967), 208.

2. Much research has been done on the Nazi plans in the East. Studies that treat this issue through the lens of colonialism include Elizabeth Harvey, *Women and the Nazi East: Agents and Witnesses of Germanization* (New Haven: Yale University Press, 2003); David Furber, "Going East: Colonialism and German Life in Nazi-Occupied Poland" (doctor's thesis, SUNY Buffalo, 2003); Wendy Lower, *Nazi Empire-Building and the Holocaust in Ukraine* (Chapel Hill: University of North Carolina Press, 2005); and Carroll P. Kakel, *The American West and the Nazi East: A Comparative and Interpretive Perspective* (New York: Palgrave Macmillan, 2011), which was published after the completion of this project.

3. Mechtild Rössler, Sabine Schleiermacher, and Cordula Tollmien, eds., *Der "Generalplan Ost": Hauptlinien der nationalsozialistischen Planungs- und Vernichtungspolitik* (Berlin: Akademie Verlag, 1993); Bruno Wasser, *Himmlers Raumplanung im Osten: der Generalplan Ost in Polen, 1940–1944* (Basel: Birkhäuser, 1993).

4. "Der 'Deutsche Osten': Mythos? Realität? Verlorenes Traumland?" in *Narrative des Nationalen. Deutsche und polnische Nationsdiskurse im 19. und 20. Jahrhundert,* ed. Izabela Surynt and Marek Zybura (Osnabrück: fibre, 2010), 385.

5. English-language brochure accompanying "Called: German Life in Central and Eastern Europe," an exhibition by the Stiftung Zentrum gegen Vertreibung (Berlin, 2009), 12.

6. Ibid., 23.

Bibliography

Achinger, Christine. *Gespaltene Moderne: Gustav Freytags* Soll und Haben: *Nation, Geschlecht und Judenbild.* Würzburg: Königshausen und Neumann, 2007.

Ackermann, Jens P. "Ein Wissenschaftler als politischer Publizist im Ersten Weltkrieg." In *Die Geburt des modernen Propagandakrieges im Ersten Weltkrieg: Dietrich Schäfer, Gelehrter und Politiker,* 155–239. Frankfurt am Main: Peter Lang, 2004.

Améry, Jean. "Schlecht klingt das Lied vom braven Mann." *Neue Rundschau* 1 (1978): 84–93.

Anderson, Benedict. *Imagined Communities: Reflections on the Origin and Spread of Nationalism.* London: Verso, 1991.

Arata, Stephen D. "The Occidental Tourist: *Dracula* and the Anxiety of Reverse Colonization." *Victorian Studies* 33, no. 4 (1990): 621–44.

Arndt, Ernst Moritz. *Ernst Moritz Arndts ausgewählte Werke in sechzehn Bänden.* Edited by Heinrich Meisner and Robert Geerds. 16 vols. Leipzig: Max Hesses Verlag, 1908.

Arnold, Robert F. *Geschichte der deutschen Polenlitteratur [sic] von den Anfängen bis 1800.* Halle: Max Niemeyer, 1900.

Attia, Iman. *Die "westliche Kultur" und ihr Anderes: Zur Dekonstruktion von Orientalismus und antimuslimischem Rassismus.* Bielefeld: transcript, 2009.

Aust, Hugo, and Hubertus Fischer, eds. *Fontane und Polen: Fontane in Polen.* Würzburg: Königshausen und Neumann, 2008.

Becker, Sabina. "Erziehung zur Bürgerlichkeit: Eine kulturgeschichtliche Lektüre von Gustav Freytags *Soll und Haben* im Kontext des Bürgerlichen Realismus." In *150 Jahre* Soll und Haben, edited by Florian Krobb, 29–46. Würzburg: Königshausen und Neumann, 2005.

Belgard, Martin. *Parzellierung und innere Kolonisation in den 6 östlichen Provinzen Preußens 1875–1906.* Leipzig: Duncker und Humblot, 1907.

Below, Ernst. *Ostmark und Krummstab.* Berlin: Janke, 1897.

Benninghoff-Lühl, Sibylle. *Deutsche Kolonialromane 1884–1914 in ihrem Entstehungs- und Wirkungszusammenhang.* Bremen: Veröffentlichungen aus dem Übersee-Museum, 1983.

Berg, Max. *Am alten Markt zu Posen: Polenroman aus der deutschen Ostmark.* Lissa i. P.: F. Ebbecke, 1907.

Berman, Nina. *Orientalismus, Kolonialismus und Moderne: Zum Bild des Orients in der deutschsprachigen Kultur 1900.* Stuttgart: M & P, 1999.

Bethusy-Huc, Valeska. *Hans der Pole.* Berlin: A. Schall, 1907.

Bhabha, Homi K. "Of Mimicry and Man: The Ambivalence of Colonial Discourse." *October* 28 (Spring 1984): 125–33.

Blackbourn, David. *The Conquest of Nature: Water, Landscape, and the Making of Modern Germany.* New York: Norton, 2007.

Blaut, J. M. *The Colonizer's Model of the World: Geographic Diffusionism and Eurocentric History.* New York: Guilford, 1993.

Bleiber, Helmut, and Jan Kosim, eds. *Dokumente zur Geschichte der deutsch-polnischen Freundschaft, 1830–1832.* Berlin: Akademie-Verlag, 1982.

Bock, Annie. *Der Zug nach dem Osten.* Berlin: Vita, 1898.

Böhme, Hartmut. "Vom Cultus zur Kultur(wissenschaft): Zur historischen Semantik des Kulturbegriffs." In *Literaturwissenschaft—Kulturwissenschaft: Positionen, Themen, Perspektiven,* edited by Renate Glaser and Matthias Luserke, 48–68. Opladen: Westdeutscher Verlag, 1996.

Bordwell, David. *Narration in the Fiction Film.* Madison: University of Wisconsin Press, 1985.

Brachvogel, Albert Emil. *Der Fels von Erz.* Berlin: Janke, 1872.

Braun, Franz, ed. *Geopolitischer Geschichtsatlas.* Vol. I, *Das Altertum.* Dresden: Ehlermann, 1927.

Breggin, Benjamin. "Fontane's Aesthetics of the Slavic Race." *German Life and Letters* 56 (2003): 213–22.

Brenning, Alfred. *Innere Kolonisation.* Leipzig: B. G. Teubner, 1909.

Brockhaus' Konversations-Lexikon. 14th ed. 16 vols. Leipzig: F. A. Brockhaus, 1894–96.

Broszat, Martin. *Zweihundert Jahre deutsche Polenpolitik.* Frankfurt am Main: Suhrkamp, 1972.

Brüggen, Ernst von der. "Auswanderung, Kolonisation und Zweikindersystem." *Preußische Jahrbücher* 49 (1882): 295.

Brüggen, Ernst von der. *Russia To-day.* Translated by M. Sandwith. London: Digby, Long, 1904.

Bülow, Bernhard von. *Deutsche Politik.* Berlin: Reimar Hobbing, 1916.

Burleigh, Michael. *Germany Turns Eastwards: A Study of* Ostforschung *in the Third Reich.* New York: Cambridge University Press, 1988.

Busse, Carl. *Das Gymnasium zu Lengowo: Ein Schulroman aus der Ostmark.* Stuttgart: Engelhorn, 1907.

Calloway, Colin G., Gerd Gemünden, and Susanne Zantop, eds. *Germans and Indians: Fantasies, Encounters, Projections.* Lincoln: University of Nebraska Press, 2002.

Carter, T. E. "Freytag's *Soll und Haben:* A Liberal Manifesto as a Best-Seller." *German Life and Letters* 21, no. 4 (July 1968): 320–29.

Chickering, Roger. "Dietrich Schäfer and Max Weber." In *Max Weber and His Contemporaries,* edited by Wolfgang J. Mommsen and Jürgen Osterhammel, 334–44. London: German Historical Institute, 1987.

Chodera, Jan. *Die deutsche Polenliteratur 1918–1939: Stoff- und Motivgeschichte.* Poznań: Wydawnictwo Naukowe Uniwersytetu im. Adama Mickiewicza, 1966.

Conrad, Sebastian. *Deutsche Kolonialgeschichte.* Munich: C. H. Beck, 2008.

Conrad, Sebastian. *Globalisierung und Nation im Deutschen Kaiserreich.* Munich: Beck, 2006.

Conze, Werner. "Nationsbildung durch Trennung: Deutsche und Polen im preußischen Osten." In *Innenpolitische Probleme des Bismarck-Reiches,* edited by Otto Pflanze, 95–119. Munich: R. Oldenbourg, 1983.

Crane, Susan A. *Museums and Memory.* Palo Alto: Stanford University Press, 2000.

Dabag, Mihran. "National-koloniale Konstruktionen in politischen Entwürfen des Deutschen Reichs um 1900." In *Kolonialismus: Kolonialdiskurs und Genozid,* edited by Mihran Dabag, Horst Gründer, and Uwe-K. Ketelsen, 19–66. Munich: Wilhelm Fink Verlag, 2004.

Dannenberg, H. L. *Sieg ohne Landgewinn?* Dresden: Verlag "Das größere Deutschland," 1918.

Davies, Norman. *God's Playground: A History of Poland.* Vol. 2, *1795 to the Present.* New York: Columbia University Press, 1982.

Dohnke, Kay. "Völkische Literatur und Heimatliteratur 1870–1918." In *Handbuch zur "Völkischen Bewegung" 1871–1918,* edited by Uwe Puschner, 651–84. Munich: Sauer, 1996.

Drummond, Elisabeth A. "'Einen kräftigen Damm gegen die polnische Hochflut zu errichten': Natur und Kultur im deutschen Ostmarkendiskurs, 1886–1914." In *Die nationale Identität der Deutschen: Philosophische Imaginationen und historische Realität deutscher Mentalität,* edited by Wolfgang Bialas, 99–114. Frankfurt am Main: Peter Lang, 2002.

Dunker, Axel. *Kontrapunktische Lektüren: Koloniale Strukturen in der deutschsprachigen Literatur des 19. Jahrhunderts.* Paderborn: Wilhelm Fink, 2008.

Eichendorff, Joseph von. *Der letzte Held von Marienburg.* Königsberg: Bornträger, 1830.

Eisner, Lotte. *Fritz Lang.* London: Secker and Warburg, 1976.

Eley, Geoff. *Reshaping the German Right: Radical Nationalism and Political Change after Bismarck.* New Haven: Yale University Press, 1980.

Engelmann, Gerhard. *Ferdinand Richthofen 1833–1905; Albrecht Penck 1858–1945: Zwei markante Geographen Berlins.* Stuttgart: Steiner, 1988.

Fabian, Johannes. *Time and the Other: How Anthropology Makes Its Object.* New York: Columbia University Press, 1983.

Feindt, Hendrik. "Dreißig, sechsundvierzig, achtundvierzig, dreiundsechzig: Polnische Aufstände in drei Romanen von Freytag, Raabe und Schweichel." In *Studien zur Kulturgeschichte des deutschen Polenbildes 1848–1939,* edited by Hendrik Feindt, 15–40. Wiesbaden: Harrassowitz, 1995.

Feld, Hans. "Hamburgs Indianer-Territorium." *Film-Kurier* 139 (June 18, 1930).

Fenske, Hans. "Imperialistische Tendenzen in Deutschland vor 1866: Auswanderung, überseeische Bestrebungen, Weltmachtträume." *Historisches Jahrbuch* 97–98 (1978): 336–83.

Fenske, Hans. "Ungeduldige Zuschauer: Die Deutschen und die europäische Expansion 1815–1880." In *Imperialistische Kontinuität und nationale Ungeduld im 19. Jahrhundert,* edited by Wolfgang Reinhard, 87–123. Frankfurt am Main: Fischer Taschenbuch Verlag, 1991.

Finke, Reinhard. "'. . . der Äquator läuft ihnen über den Bauch': Namen und Geschichten zu Afrika in Fontanes *Effi Briest* und anderswo." In *Romantik und Ästhetizmus,* edited by Bettina Gruber and Gerhard Plumpe, 297–315. Würzburg: Königshausen und Neumann, 1999.

Fischer, Hubertus. "Polnische Verwicklungen." In *Fontane und die Fremde, Fontane und Europa,* edited by Konrad Ehlich, 262–75. Würzburg: Königshausen und Neumann, 2002.

Fischer, Peter. *Die deutsche Publizistik als Faktor der deutsch-polnischen Beziehungen 1919–1939.* Wiesbaden: Harrassowitz, 1991.

Fitzpatrick, Matthew P. *Liberal Imperialism in Germany: Expansionism and Nationalism, 1848–1884.* New York: Berghahn, 2008.

Fitzpatrick, Matthew P. "Narrating Empire: *Die Gartenlaube* and Germany's Nineteenth-Century Liberal Expansionism." *German Studies Review* 30, no. 1 (2007): 97–120.

Fließ, Erich. *Die drei Erinnyen.* Berlin: R. Eckstein, 1896.

Fontane, Theodor. *Effi Briest.* Translated by Hugh Rorrison and Helen Chambers. London: Penguin, 1995.

Fontane, Theodor. *Fontanes Briefe in zwei Bänden.* Edited by Gotthard Erler. Berlin: Aufbau, 1968.

Fontane, Theodor. "Gustav Freytag: *Soll und Haben.*" *Literaturblatt des deutschen Kunstblattes* (July 26, 1855).

Fontane, Theodor. *Sämtliche Werke.* Edited by Kurt Schreinert. Munich: Nymphenburger, 1963.

Fontane, Theodor. *Werke, Schriften und Briefe.* 2nd ed. 3 vols. Edited by Walter Keitel and Helmuth Nürnberger. Munich: Hanser, 1970.

Franke, Julia. *Solidarność 1830: Niemcy i Polacy po Powstaniu Listopadowym = Polenbegeisterung: Deutsche und Polen nach dem Novemberaufstand 1830.* Warsaw: Zamek Królewski, 2005.

Franzos, Karl Emil. *Halb-Asien: Land und Leute des östlichen Europa.* Stuttgart: J. G. Cott'sche Buchhandlung Nachfolger, 1914.

Frenssen, Gustav. *Peter Moors Fahrt nach Südwest.* Berlin: G. Grote, 1906.

Freud, Sigmund. *The Uncanny.* Translated by David McLintock. London: Penguin, 2003.

Freytag, Gustav. *Soll und Haben.* 58th ed. 2 vols. Leipzig: S. Hirzel, 1902.

Friedrich, Dorothea. *Das Bild Polens in der Literatur der Weimarer Republik.* Frankfurt am Main: Peter Lang, 1984.

Friedrichsmeyer, Sara, Sara Lennox, and Susanne Zantop. "Introduction." In *The Imperialist Imagination: German Colonialism and Its Legacy,* edited by Sara Friedrichsmeyer, Sara Lennox, and Susanne Zantop, 1–29. Ann Arbor: University of Michigan Press, 1998.

Fuchs-Sumiyoshi, Andrea. *Orientalismus in der deutschen Literatur: Untersuchungen zu Werken des 19. und 20. Jahrhunderts, von Goethes West-ostlichem Divan bis Thomas Manns Joseph-Tetralogie.* Hildesheim: G. Olms, 1984.

Fuhrmann, Malte. *Der Traum vom deutschen Orient: Zwei deutsche Kolonien im Osmanischen Reich 1851–1918.* Frankfurt am Main: Campus, 2006.

Furber, David. "Going East: Colonialism and German Life in Nazi-Occupied Poland." PhD diss., SUNY Buffalo, 2003.

Galos, Adam, Felix-Heinrich Gentzen, and Witold Jakóbczyk. *Dzieje Hakaty.* Poznań: Instytut Zachodni, 1966.

Gehre, Moritz. *Die neue deutsche Kolonisation in Posen und Westpreußen.* Grossenhain: A. Hentze, 1899.

Geiss, Imanuel. *Der polnische Grenzstreifen, 1914–1918: Ein Beitrag zur deutschen Kriegszielpolitik im Ersten Weltkrieg.* Lübeck: Matthiesen, 1960.

Gentry, Francis G., Winder McConnell, Ulrich Müller, and Werner Wunderlich, eds. *The Nibelungen Tradition: An Encyclopedia.* New York: Routledge, 2002.

Germana, Nicholas A. *The Orient of Europe: The Mythical Image of India and Competing Images of German National Identity.* Newcastle: Cambridge Scholars, 2009.

Gollwitzer, Heinz. *Die gelbe Gefahr: Geschichte eines Schlagworts: Studien zum imperialistischen Denken.* Göttingen: Vandenhoeck und Ruprecht, 1962.

Goren, Haim, ed. *Germany and the Middle East: Past, Present, and Future.* Jerusalem: Hebrew University Magnes Press, 2003.

Grabowski, Elisabeth. *Der weiße Adler: Ein Kulturbild aus der Ostmark.* Kattowitz: Phönix-Verlag, 1909.

Grumbach, Salomon. *Das annexionistische Deutschland.* Lausanne: Payot, 1917.

Gründer, Horst. *Geschichte der deutschen Kolonien.* 3rd ed. Paderborn: Schöningh, 1995.

Gründer, Horst, ed. *". . . da und dort ein junges Deutschland gründen": Rassismus, Kolonien und kolonialer Gedanke vom 16. bis zum 20. Jahrhundert.* Munich: Deutscher Taschenbuch Verlag, 1999.

Haar, Ingo. *Historiker im Nationalsozialismus: Deutsche Geschichtswissenschaft und der "Volkstumskampf im Osten."* Göttingen: Vandenhoeck und Ruprecht, 2000.

Hagen, William W. *Germans, Poles, and Jews: The Nationality Conflict in the Prussian East, 1772–1914.* Chicago: University of Chicago Press, 1980.

Hahn, Eva, and Hans Henning Hahn. "Nationale Stereotypen. Plädoyer für eine historische Stereotypenforschung." In *Stereotyp, Identität und Geschichte: die Funktion von Stereotypen in gesellschaftlichen Diskursen,* edited by Hans Henning Hahn, 17–56. Frankfurt am Main: Peter Lang, 2002.

Hahn, Hans Henning, and Eva Hahn. "Der 'Deutsche Osten': Mythos? Realität? Verlorenes Traumland?" In *Narrative des Nationalen: Deutsche und polnische Nationsdiskurse im 19. und 20. Jahrhundert,* edited by Izabela Surynt and Marek Zybura, 379–96. Osnabrück: fibre, 2010.

Hake, Sabine. "Architectural Hi/stories: Fritz Lang and *The Nibelungs.*" *Wide Angle* 12, no. 3 (July 1990): 38–57.

Hake, Sabine. "Mapping the Native Body: On Africa and the Colonial Film in the Third Reich." In *The Imperialist Imagination: German Colonialism and Its Legacy,* edited by Sara Friedrichsmeyer, Sara Lennox, and Susanne Zantop, 163–88. Ann Arbor: University of Michigan Press, 1998.

Hampe, Karl. *Der Zug nach dem Osten: die kolonisatorische Großtat des deutschen Volkes im Mittelalter.* Leipzig: Teubner, 1921.

Hannaford, Ivan. *Race: The History of an Idea in the West.* Washington, DC: Woodrow Wilson Center Press, 1996.

Harbou, Thea von. "Aus dem Manuskript des Films 'Die Nibelungen.'" In *Das Kulturfilmbuch,* edited by Edgar Beyfuss and Alex Kossowsky, 246–60. Berlin: Carl P. Chryselius, 1924.

Harley, J. B. "Maps, Knowledge, and Power." In *The Iconography of Landscape: Essays on the Symbolic Representation, Design, and Use of Past Environments,* edited by Denis Cosgrove and Stephen Daniels, 277–312. Cambridge: Cambridge University Press, 1988.

Harvey, Elizabeth. *Women and the Nazi East: Agents and Witnesses of Germanization.* New Haven: Yale University Press, 2003.

Haushofer, Karl. "Die suggestive Karte?" *Grenzboten* 81 (1922): 17–19. Reprinted in *Bausteine zur Geopolitik,* edited by Karl Haushofer, Erich Obst, Hermann Lautensach, and Otto Maull, 286–306. Berlin: Vowinckel, 1928.

Haushofer, Karl. *Grenzen in ihrer geographischen und politischen Bedeutung.* Berlin: Kurt Vowinckel, 1927.

Hegel, G. W. F. *Vorlesungen über die Ästhetik.* In *Werke,* vol. 13, edited by Eva Moldenhauer, Karl Markus Michel, and Helmut Reinicke. Frankfurt am Main: Suhrkamp, 1986.

Heine, Heinrich. "Vitzliputzli." In *Romanzero,* 78–103. Hamburg: Hoffmann und Campe, 1851.

Heinzle, Joachim. "Zweimal Hagen oder: Rezeption als Sinnunterstellung." In *Die Nibelungen: Ein deutscher Wahn, ein deutscher Alptraum: Studien und Dokumente zur Rezeption des Nibelungenstoffs im 19. und 20. Jahrhundert,* edited by Joachim Heinzle and Anneliese Waldschmidt, 21–40. Frankfurt am Main: Suhrkamp, 1991.

Heinzle, Joachim, and Anneliese Waldschmidt, eds. *Die Nibelungen: Ein deutscher Wahn, ein deutscher Alptraum: Studien und Dokumente zur Rezeption des Nibelungenstoffs im 19. und 20. Jahrhundert.* Frankfurt am Main: Suhrkamp, 1991.

Herb, Guntram Henrik. *Under the Map of Germany: Nationalism and Propaganda, 1918–1945.* London: Routledge, 1997.

Herder, Johann Gottfried. *Reflections on the Philosophy of the History of Mankind.* Edited by Frank E. Manuel. Chicago: University of Chicago Press, 1968.

Höcker, Paul Oskar. *Polnische Wirthschaft.* Berlin: Bong, 1896.

Hofmann, Wolfgang. "Das Ansiedlungsgesetz von 1904 und die Preußische Polenpolitik." *Jahrbuch für die Geschichte Mittel- und Ostdeutschlands* 38 (1989): 251–85.

Hull, Isabel V. *Absolute Destruction: Military Culture and the Practices of War in Imperial Germany.* Ithaca: Cornell University Press, 2005.

JanMohamed, Abdul R. "The Economy of Manichean Allegory: The Function of Racial Difference in Colonialist Literature." In *"Race," Writing, and Difference,* edited by Henry Louis Gates Jr., 78–106. Chicago: University of Chicago Press, 1985.

Jhering, Herbert. "Der Zweite Nibelungen-Film." In *Von Reinhardt bis Brecht: Vier Jahrzehnte Theater und Film,* vol. 2, *1924–1929,* edited by Edith Krull, 475–77. Berlin: Aufbau-Verlag, 1959.

Kabatek, Wolfgang. *Imagerie des Anderen im Weimarer Kino.* Bielefeld: transcript, 2003.

Kaes, Anton. "Der Mythos des Deutschen in Fritz Langs Nibelungen-Film." In *Deutsche Meister, böse Geister? Nationale Selbstfindung in der Musik,* edited by Hermann Danuser and Herfried Münkler, 326–42. Schliengen: Edition Argus, 2001.

Kaes, Anton. *Shell Shock Cinema: Weimar Culture and the Wounds of War.* Princeton: Princeton University Press, 2009.

Kaiser, Nancy. *Social Integration and Narrative Structure: Patterns of Realism in Auerbach, Freytag, Fontane, and Raabe.* New York: Peter Lang, 1987.

Katz, Jakob. *Die Hep-Hep-Verfolgungen des Jahres 1819*. Berlin: Metropol-Verlag, 1994.

Keim, Franz. *Die Nibelungenlied*. Frankfurt am Main: Insel, 1972.

Ketelsen, Uwe-K. "Der koloniale Diskurs und die Öffnung des europäischen Ostens im deutschen Roman." In *Kolonialismus: Kolonialdiskurs und Genozid*, edited by Mihran Dabag, Horst Gründer, and Uwe-K. Ketelsen, 67–94. Munich: Wilhelm Fink, 2004.

Klein-Rogge, Rudolf. "Von Dr. Mabuse zu König Etzel." In *Fritz Lang: Die Nibelungen*, edited by Enno Patalas and Fritz Göttler, 35–36. Munich: Kulturreferat der Landeshauptstadt München, 1986.

Klotz, Marcia. "Epistemological Ambiguity and the Fascist Text: *Jew Süss, Carl Peters,* and *Ohm Krüger*." *New German Critique* 74 (Spring–Summer 1998): 91–124.

Klotz, Marcia. "Global Visions: From the Colonial to the National Socialist World." *European Studies Journal* 16, no. 2 (1999): 37–68.

Knoop, Otto. *Ostmärkische Sagen, Märchen und Erzählungen*. Lissa i. P.: Oskar Eulitz, 1909.

Koepnick, Lutz. "Unsettling America: German Westerns and Modernity." *Modernism/Modernity* 2, no. 3 (1995): 1–22.

Kontje, Todd. *German Orientalisms*. Ann Arbor: University of Michigan Press, 2004.

Kopp, Kristin, and Klaus Müller-Richter, eds. *Die Großstadt und das Primitive: Text, Politik, Repräsentation*. Stuttgart: M und P, 2004.

Kötzschke, Rudolf. "Über den Ursprung und die geschichtliche Bedeutung der ostdeutschen Siedlung." In *Der ostdeutsche Volksboden: Aufsätze zu den Fragen des Ostens*, edited by Wilhelm Volz, 7–26. Breslau: Ferdinand Hirt, 1926.

Kötzschke, Rudolf, and Wolfgang Ebert. *Geschichte der ostdeutschen Kolonisation*. Leipzig: Bibliographisches Institut, 1937.

Koziełek, Gerard. *Polenlieder: eine Anthologie*. Stuttgart: P. Reclam, 1982.

Kracauer, Siegfried. "The Mass Ornament." In *The Mass Ornament: Weimar Essays*, ed. Thomas Y. Levin, 75–86. Cambridge: Harvard University Press, 1995.

Kracauer, Siegfried. *Von Caligari zu Hitler: Eine psychologische Geschichte des deutschen Films*. Frankfurt am Main: Suhrkamp, 1984.

Krause, Edith H. "Desire and Denial: Fontane's *Effi Briest*." *Germanic Review* 74, no. 2 (Spring 1999): 117–29.

Kreimeier, Klaus. "Der Schlafwandler: Fritz Lang und seine deutschen Filme." In *Film, Stadt, Kino, Berlin*, edited by Uta Berg-Ganschow, Wolfgang Jacobsen, and Rudolf Arnheim, 89–109. Berlin: Argon, 1987.

Krobb, Florian. "Einleitung: *Soll und Haben* nach 150 Jahren." In *150 Jahre* Soll und Haben, edited by Florian Krobb, 9–28. Würzburg: Königshausen und Neumann, 2005.

Król, Eugeniusz Cezary. *Polska i Polacy w propagandzie narodowego socjalizmu w Niemczech 1919–1945*. Warsaw: Collegium Civitas Press, 2006.

Kruck, Alfred. *Geschichte des Alldeutschen Verbandes, 1890–1939*. Wiesbaden: Steiner, 1954.

Kuntze, Paul Heinrich. *Das Volksbuch unserer Kolonien*. Leipzig: Dollheimer, 1938.

Kurpiun, Robert. *Die Schwarzweißen*. Dresden: Lehmann, 1920.

Laak, Dirk van. *Über alles in der Welt: Deutscher Imperialismus im 19. Und 20. Jahrhundert*. Munich: C. H. Beck, 2005.

Lammich, Maria. *Das deutsche Osteuropabild in der Zeit der Reichsgründung.* Boppard am Rhein: Boldt, 1978.

Lamprecht, Karl. "Die Lehren der Kolonisation Ostdeutschlands für die Politik der Gegenwart." *Die Ostmark* 3, (1898): Part I: 77–80; Part II: 90–92.

Lang, Fritz. "Worauf es beim Nibelungen-Film ankam." In *Die Nibelungen: Ein deutsches Heldenlied* (Ufa-Decla Film Pamphlet, 1924), 12–16.

Langhans, Paul. *Deutscher Kolonial-Atlas.* 2nd ed. Gotha: Justus Perthes, 1897.

Lewis, Martin W., and Kären E. Wigen. *The Myth of Continents: A Critique of Metageography.* Berkeley: University of California Press, 1997.

Liepe, Albert. *Die Spinne.* Berlin: F. Zillessen, 1902.

Liesekounig, Jürgen. "'Branntweintrinkende Wilde': Beyond Civilisation and Outside History: The Depiction of the Poles in Gustav Freytag's *Soll und Haben.*" *Yearbook of European Studies* 13 (1999): 133–47.

List, Friedrich. "Die Ackerverfassung, die Zwergwirtschaft und die Auswanderung." In *Friedlich List: Aufsätze und Abhandlungen aus den Jahren 1831–1844,* edited by Edgar Salin, Artur Sommer, and Otto Stühler, 418–548. Berlin: Reimar Hobbing, 1928.

List, Friedrich. *Das nationale System der Politischen Oekonomie. Neudruck nach der Ausgabe letzter Hand, eingeleitet von Professor Dr. Heinrich Waentig.* 5th ed. Jena: G. Fischer, 1928.

Liulevicius, Vejas Gabriel. *The German Myth of the East: 1800 to the Present.* Oxford: Oxford University Press, 2009.

Liulevicius, Vejas Gabriel. *War Land on the Eastern Front: Culture, National Identity, and German Occupation in World War I.* Cambridge: Cambridge University Press, 2000.

Loomba, Ania. *Colonialism/Postcolonialism.* London: Routledge, 1998.

Lower, Wendy. *Nazi Empire-Building and the Holocaust in Ukraine.* Chapel Hill: University of North Carolina Press, 2005.

MacDougal, Doug. *Frozen Earth: The Once and Future Story of Ice Ages.* Berkeley: University of California Press, 2004.

Mai, Uwe. *"Rasse und Raum": Agrarpolitik, Sozial- und Raumplanung im NS-Staat.* Paderborn: Schöningh, 2002.

Maśnicki, Jerzy. *Niemy kraj: polskie motywy w europejskim kinie niemym (1896–1930).* Danzig: Słowo/obraz terytoria, 2006.

McClintock, Anne. *Imperial Leather: Race, Gender, and Sexuality in the Colonial Contest.* New York: Routledge, 1995.

Müller, Michael G., Bernd Schönemann, and Maria Wawrykowa, eds. *Die "Polen-Debatte" in der Frankfurter Paulskirche: Darstellung, Lernziele, Materialien.* Frankfurt am Main: Georg-Eckert-Institut für Internationale Schulbuchforschung, 1995.

Müller-Seidel, Walter. "Fontane und Polen." In *Studien zur Kulturgeschichte des deutschen Polenbildes 1848–1939,* edited by Hendrik Feindt, 41–64. Wiesbaden: Harrassowitz, 1995.

Nagl, Tobias. *Die unheimliche Maschine: Rasse und Repräsentation im Weimarer Kino.* Munich: Edition Text + Kritik, 2009.

Naumann, Friedrich. *Mitteleuropa.* Berlin: Georg Riemer, 1916.

Nelson, Robert L. "From Manitoba to the Memel: Max Sering, Inner Colonization, and the German East." *Social History* 35 (2010): 439–57.

Nelson, Robert L., ed. *Germans, Poland, and Colonial Expansion to the East: 1850 through the Present.* New York: Palgrave Macmillan, 2009.

Neubach, Helmut. *Die Ausweisungen von Polen und Juden aus Preussen 1885/86: ein Beitrag zu Bismarcks Polenpolitik und zur Geschichte des deutsch-polnischen Verhältnisses.* Wiesbaden: Harrassowitz, 1967.

"Der Nibelungenfilm: Seine Schöpfer und seine Mitarbeiter." In *Das Verleih-Programm 1923/24* (Catalog of Der Decla-Bioskop-Verleih, 1923–1924).

Nipperdey, Thomas. *Deutsche Geschichte 1866–1918.* Vol. 2, *Machtstaat vor der Demokratie.* Munich: Beck, 1992.

Noyes, John. "Imperialist Man, Civilizing Woman, and the European Male Masochist." *Acta Germanica: Jahrbuch des Südafrikanischen Germanistenverbandes* (1996): 41–65.

Noyes, John. "National Identity, Nomadism, and Narration in Gustav Frenssen's Peter Moor's Journey to Southwest Africa." In *The Imperialist Imagination: German Colonialism and Its Legacy,* edited by Sara Friedrichsmeyer, Sara Lennox, and Susanne Zantop, 87–105. Ann Arbor: University of Michigan Press, 1998.

Olma, Walter. "Das Polenbild im deutschen Heimatroman: Clara Viebigs Erfolgsroman *Das schlafende Heer* als Beispiel." In *Studien zur Kulturgeschichte des deutschen Polenbildes 1848–1939,* edited by Hendrik Feindt, 102–29. Wiesbaden: Harrassowitz, 1995.

Orłowski, Hubert. *"Polnische Wirtschaft": zum deutschen Polendiskurs der Neuzeit.* Wiesbaden: Harrassowitz, 1996.

Ossowski, Mirosław. "Das Polenbild des jungen und des alten Fontane." In *Literatur und Politik in der Heine-Zeit: die 48er Revolution in Texten zwischen Vormärz und Nachmärz,* edited by Hartmut Kircher and Maria Kłańska, 219–34. Cologne: Böhlau, 1998.

Osterhammel, Jürgen. *Kolonialismus: Geschichte, Formen, Folgen.* Munich: C. H. Beck, 1997.

Pachnicke, Arthur. *Auf Posten im Osten: Erzählung aus der Ostmark und Kleinstadt.* Berlin: Curt Wigand, 1908.

Parr, Rolf. "Der Bismarck-Mythos—kulturelle Folie für Theodor Fontane." *Fontane Blätter* (1993): 31–47.

Parr, Rolf. "Kongobecken, Lombok und der Chinese im Hause Briest: Das 'Wissen um die Kolonien' und das 'Wissen aus den Kolonien' bei Theodor Fontane." In *Fontane und die Fremde: Fontane und Europa,* edited by Konrad Ehlich, 212–28. Würzburg: Königshausen und Neumann, 2002.

Penck, Albrecht. *Das deutsche Reich.* Vienna: F. Tempsky, 1887.

Penck, Albrecht. "Deutscher Volks- und Kulturboden." In *Volk unter Völkern,* edited by Karl Christian von Loesch, 62–73. Breslau: Ferdinand Hirt, 1925.

Pietraszek, Edward. "Zwischen Geldverdienen und Aufstieg: Polnische Arbeitsmigranten in Deutschland von 1871 bis 1939." In *Vom Wandergesellen zum "Green-Card"-Spezialisten: interkulturelle Aspekte der Arbeitsmigration im östlichen Mitteleuropa,* edited by Klaus Roth, 107–34. Münster: Waxmann, 2003.

Pilf, Traugott. *Geschichten aus der Ostmark.* Lissa i. P.: Oskar Eulitz, 1908.

Piskorski, Jan M., ed. *Historiographical Approaches to Medieval Colonization of East Central Europe: A Comparative Analysis against the Background of other European Inter-Ethnic Colonization Processes in the Middle Ages.* New York: Columbia University Press, 2002.

Piskorski, Jan M. "The Medieval Colonization of Central Europe as a Problem of World History and Historiography." *German History* 22, no. 3 (2004): 323–43.

Plischke, Hans. *Von Cooper bis Karl May: Eine Geschichte des völkerkundlichen Reise- und Abenteuerromans.* Düsseldorf: Droste-Verlag, 1951.

Polaschegg, Andrea. *Der andere Orientalismus: Regeln deutsch-morgenländischer Imagination im 19. Jahrhundert.* Berlin: W. de Gruyter, 2005.

Połczyńska, Edyta. *Im polnischen Wind: Beiträge zum deutschen Zeitungswesen, Theaterleben und zur deutschen Literatur im Grossherzogtum Posen, 1815–1918.* Poznań: Wydawnictwo Naukowe Uniwersytetu im. Adama Mickiewicza, 1988.

Połczyńska, Edyta, and Maria Wojtczak. "Die Provinz Posen in der deutschen Literatur um die Jahrhundertwende." *Convivium: Germanistisches Jahrbuch* (1996): 83–106.

Pratt, Mary Louise. *Imperial Eyes: Travel Writing and Transculturation.* London: Routledge, 1992.

Rainer, Ulrike. "*Effi Briest* und das Motiv des Chinesen: Rolle und Darstellung in Fontanes Roman." *Zeitschrift für deutsche Philologie* 101 (1982): 545–61.

Ratzel, Friedrich. *Deutschland: Einführung in die Heimatkunde.* Leipzig: Grunow, 1898.

Reagin, Nancy. "Domesticity and 'Germanization' in Occupied Poland." In *Sweeping the German Nation: Domesticity and National Identity in Germany, 1870–1945,* 181–217. New York: Cambridge University Press, 2007.

Reagin, Nancy. "The Imagined Hausfrau: National Identity, Domesticity, and Colonialism in Imperial Germany." *Journal of Modern History* 73 (2001): 54–86.

Remak, Henry H. H. "Politik und Gesellschaft als Kunst: Güldenklees Toast in Fontanes *Effi Briest.*" In *Formen realistischer Erzählkunst,* edited by Jörg Thunecke, 550–62. Nottingham: Sherwood Press Agencies, 1979.

Renz, B. [Hugo Behrens]. *Die polnische Gefahr und andere Novellen.* Berlin: Hermann Hillger, 1905.

Rieck, Werner. "Das Polenthema in der deutschen Literatur zur Zeit des Konstitutionsreichstags und des Kosciuszko-Aufstandes." *Weimarer Beiträge* 6 (1980): 5–27.

Rieck, Werner. "Polnische Thematik im Werk Theodor Fontanes." *Fontane-Blätter* 61 (1996): 84–112.

Ritzenhofen, Ute. "'Amerikas Italien.' Texas in der Auswanderungs- und Reiseliteratur der 1840er Jahre." In *Reisen im Diskurs: Modelle der literarischen Fremderfahrung von den Pilgerberichten bis zur Postmoderne,* edited by Anne Fuchs and Theo Harden, 171–87. Heidelberg: Universitätsverlag C. Winter, 1995.

Rossbacher, Karlheinz. *Heimatkunstbewegung und Heimatroman: Zu einer Literatursoziologie der Jahrhundertwende.* Stuttgart: Klett, 1975.

Rössler, Mechtild. *"Wissenschaft und Lebensraum," geographische Ostforschung im Nationalsozialismus: Ein Beitrag zur Disziplingeschichte der Geographie.* Berlin: Reimer, 1990.

Rössler, Mechtild, Sabine Schleiermacher, and Cordula Tollmien, eds. *Der "Generalplan Ost": Hauptlinien der nationalsozialistischen Planungs- und Vernichtungspolitik.* Berlin: Akademie Verlag, 1993.

Rothfels, Hans. "Das erste Scheitern des Nationalstaats in Ost-Mittel-Europa 1848/49." In *Deutscher Osten und Slawischer Westen,* edited by Hans Rothfels and Werner Markert, 5–16. Tübingen: J. C. B. Mohr [Paul Siebeck], 1955.

Ryan, Judith. "The Chinese Ghost: Colonialism and Subaltern Speech in Fontane's *Effi Briest.*" In *History and Literature: Essays in Honor of Karl S. Guthke,* edited by William S. Donahue and Scott Denham, 367–84. Tübingen: Stauffenburg, 2000.

Said, Edward. *Culture and Imperialism.* London: Vintage, 1994.

Said, Edward. *Orientalism.* New York: Vintage, 1979.

Salzwedel, Hans von. *Der schwarze Lupno.* Weimar: Verlag für Volks- und Heimatkunde, 1926.

Sammartino, Annemarie H. *The Impossible East: Germany and the East, 1914–1922.* Ithaca: Cornell University Press, 2010.

Schäfer, Dietrich. "Geschichtliche Einleitung." In *Die deutsche Ostmark,* edited by Der deutsche Ostmarkenverein, 1–62. Lissa i. P.: Oskar Eulitz, 1913.

Schäfer, Dietrich. *Karte der Länder und Völker Europas: Volkstum und Staatenbildung.* Berlin: Dietrich Riemer [Ernst Vohsen], 1916. Booklet accompanying the map "Länder- und Völkerkarte Europas."

Schäfer, Dietrich. "Länder- und Völkerkarte Europas." Berlin: Dietrich Riemer [Ernst Vohsen], 1916. Scale: 1:4,000,000.

Schäfer, Dietrich. *Unser Recht auf die Ostmarken.* Berlin: Deutscher Ostmarken-Verein, 1911.

Scherer, Friedrich. *Adler und Halbmond: Bismarck und der Orient 1878–1890.* Paderborn: Schöningh, 2001.

Schnee, Heinrich, ed. *Deutsches Kolonial-Lexikon.* Leipzig: Quelle und Meyer, 1920.

Schnee, Heinrich. *Die koloniale Schuldlüge.* 12th ed. Munich: Knorr und Hirth, 1940.

Schuster, Ingrid. "Exotik als Chiffre: Zum Chinesen in *Effi Briest.*" *Wirkendes Wort* 33 (1983): 115–25.

Schwerin, Friedrich Ernst von. "Zur inneren Kolonisation in Pommern. Umblick und Ausblick." *Preußische Jahrbücher* 86, no. 2 (Nov. 1896).

Seeba, Hinrich C. "'So weit die deutsche Zunge klingt': The Role of Language in German Identity Formation." In *Searching for Common Ground: Diskurse zur deutschen Identität, 1750–1871,* edited by Nicholas Vazsonyi, 45–57. Cologne: Böhlau, 2000.

Sering, Max. *Die innere Kolonisation im östlichen Deutschland.* Leipzig: Duncker und Humblot, 1893.

Serrier, Thomas. "'Deutsche Kulturarbeit in der Ostmark.' Der Mythos vom deutschen Vorrang und die Grenzproblematik in der Provinz Posen (1871–1914)." In *Die Nationalisierung von Grenzen: Zur Konstruktion nationaler Identität in sprachlich gemischten Grenzregionen,* edited by Michael G. Müller and Rolf Petri, 13–33. Marburg: Herder-Institut, 2002.

Serrier, Thomas. *Provinz Posen, Ostmark, Wielkopolska: Eine Grenzregion zwischen Deutschen und Polen, 1848–1914.* Marburg: Herder-Institut, 2005.

Sittig, Claudius. "Gieshüblers Kohlenprovisor: Der Kolonialdiskurs und das Hirngespinst vom spukenden Chinesen in Theodor Fontanes *Effi Briest.*" *Zeitschrift für deutsche Philologie* 122 (2003): 544–63.

Smith, Helmut Walser. *German Nationalism and Religious Conflict: Culture, Ideology, Politics, 1870–1914.* Princeton: Princeton University Press, 1995.

Smith, Woodruff D. *German Colonial Empire.* Chapel Hill: University of North Carolina Press, 1978.

Smith, Woodruff D. *The Ideological Origins of Nazi Imperialism.* New York: Oxford University Press, 1986.

Sommer, Dietrich. "Das Polenbild Fontanes als Element nationaler Selbstverständigung und -kritik." *Weimarer Beiträge* 16, no. 11 (1970): 173–90.

Spurr, David. *The Rhetoric of Empire: Colonial Discourse in Journalism, Travel Writing, and Imperial Administration.* Durham: Duke University Press, 1993.

Stasiewski, Bernhard. "'*Polnische Wirtschaft'* und Johann Georg Forster. Eine wortgeschichtliche Studie." *Deutsche wissenschaftliche Zeitschrift im Wartheland* 2–3 (1941): 207–16.

Steinecke, Hartmut. "Gustav Freytag: *Soll und Haben* (1855): Weltbild und Wirkung eines deutschen Bestsellers." In *Romane und Erzählungen des Bürgerlichen Realismus,* edited by Horst Denkler, 138–52. Stuttgart: Philipp Reclam, 1980.

Steinmetz, George. *The Devil's Handwriting: Precoloniality and the German Colonial State in Qingdao, Samoa, and Southwest Africa.* Chicago: University of Chicago Press, 2007.

Stockinger, Ludwig. "Polen als 'grüne Stelle'? Ästhetische und politische Implikationen des Polenbildes bei Gustav Freytag." *Convivium: Germanistisches Jahrbuch Polen* (2001): 99–127.

Sudhof, Siegfried. "Das Bild Polens im Werk Theodor Fontanes." *Acta Universitatis Wratislaviensis* 34 (1978): 101–11.

Surynt, Izabela. *Das "ferne," "unheimliche" Land: Gustav Freytags Polen.* Dresden: Thelem, 2004.

Thomas, Louis B. "Maps as Instruments of Propaganda." *Surveying and Mapping* 9, no. 2 (April–June 1949): 75–81.

Tiessen, Ernst. "Der Friedensvertrag von Versailles und die politische Geographie." *Zeitschrift für Geopolitik* 4 (April 1924): 203–20.

Tims, Richard Wonser. *Germanizing Prussian Poland: The H-K-T Society and the Struggle for the Eastern Marches in the German Empire, 1894–1919.* New York: AMS Press, 1966.

Tönnies, Ferdinand. "Innere Kolonisation in Preußen: Insbesondere in den ehemaligen Provinzen Posen und Westpreußen." In *Ferdinand Tönnies: Gesamtausgabe,* vol. 15, *1923–1925,* edited by Dieter Haselbach, 3–24. Berlin: de Gruyter, 2000.

Treitschke, Heinrich von. *Politik. Vorlesungen gehalten an der Universität zu Berlin.* 2 vols. Leipzig: Hirzel, 1922.

Trzeciakowski, Lech. *The Kulturkampf in Prussian Poland.* New York: Columbia University Press, 1990.

Utz, Peter. "Effi Briest, der Chinese und der Imperialismus: eine 'Geschichte' im geschichtlichen Kontext." *Zeitschrift für deutsche Philologie* 103 (1984): 212–22.

Vick, Brian E. *Defining Germany: The 1848 Frankfurt Parliament and National Identity.* Cambridge: Harvard University Press, 2002.

Volz, Wilhelm. "Zur Einführung." In *Der ostdeutsche Volksboden: Aufsätze zu den Fragen des Ostens,* edited by Wilhelm Volz. Breslau: Ferdinand Hirt, 1926.

Warmbold, Joachim. *Germania in Africa: Germany's Colonial Literature.* New York: Peter Lang, 1988.

Wasser, Bruno. *Himmlers Raumplanung im Osten: der Generalplan Ost in Polen, 1940–1944*. Basel: Birkhäuser, 1993.

Weber, Hans Siegfried. *Ansiedlung von Kriegsinvaliden*. Berlin: Deutsche Verlags-Anstalt, 1915.

Wegener, Michael. "Die Heimat und die Dichtkunst." In *Trivialliteratur: Aufsätze*, edited by Gerhard Schmidt-Henkel Berlin: Literarisches Colloquium: 1964.

Wehler, Hans-Ulrich. *Krisenherde des Kaiserreichs 1871–1918: Studien zur deutschen Sozial- und Verfassungsgeschichte*. Göttingen: Vandenhoeck und Ruprecht, 1970.

Werber, Niels. *Die Geopolitik der Literatur: Eine Vermessung der medialen Weltraumordnung*. Munich: Hanser, 2007.

Whiton, Helga B. *Der Wandel des Polenbildes in der deutschen Literatur des 19. Jahrhunderts*. Bern: Peter Lang, 1981.

Wigard, Franz, ed. *Stenographischer Bericht über die Verhandlungen der deutschen constituirenden Nationalversammlung zu Frankfurt am Main*. Frankfurt am Main: J. D. Sauerländer, 1849.

Wippermann, Wolfgang. "Antislavismus." In *Handbuch zur "Völkischen Bewegung" 1871–1918*, edited by Uwe Puschner, Walter Schmitz, and Justus H. Ulbricht. Munich: Sauer, 1996.

Wippermann, Wolfgang. *Der "deutsche Drang nach Osten." Ideologie und Wirklichkeit eines politischen Schlagwortes*. Darmstadt: Wissenschaftliche Buchgesellschaft, 1981.

Wippermann, Wolfgang. *Die Deutschen und der Osten: Feindbild und Traumland*. Darmstadt: Primus, 2007.

Wippermann, Wolfgang. "'Gen Ostland wollen wir reiten!' Ordensstaat und Ostsiedlung in der historischen Belletristik Deutschlands." In *Germania Slavica*, edited by W. H. Fritze, 187–235. Berlin: Duncker und Humblot, 1980.

Wippermann, Wolfgang. "Die Ostsiedlung in der deutschen Historiographie und Publizistik: Probleme, Methoden und Grundlagen der Entwicklung bis hin zum Ersten Weltkrieg." *Germania Slavica* (1980): 41–69.

Witten, M. von [Margaret von Gottschall]. *Nach Ostland wollen wir reiten*. Lissa i. P.: Oskar Eulitz, 1909.

Wojtczak, Maria. "Hinter den Kulissen des Ostmarkenvereins: Zur Entstehungsgeschichte der 'Ostmarkenromane.'" *Studia Germanica Posnaniensia* 22 (1995): 65–76.

Wojtczak, Maria. *Literatur der Ostmark: Posener Heimatliteratur, 1890–1918*. Poznań: Wydawnictwo Naukowe Uniwersytetu im. Adama Mickiewicza, 1998.

Wolff, Larry. *Inventing Eastern Europe: The Map of Civilization on the Mind of the Enlightenment*. Palo Alto: Stanford University Press, 1994.

Young, Robert. *Colonial Desire: Hybridity in Theory, Culture, and Race*. London: Routledge, 1995.

Zantop, Susanne. *Colonial Fantasies: Conquest, Family, and Nation in Precolonial Germany, 1770–1870*. Durham: Duke University Press, 1997.

Zantop, Susanne. "Colonialism, Cannibalism, and Literary Incorporation: Heine in Mexico." In *Heinrich Heine and the Occident: Multiple Identities, Multiple Receptions*, edited by Peter Uwe Hohendahl and Sander L. Gilman, 110–38. Lincoln: University of Nebraska Press, 1991.

Ziegfeld, A. Hillen. “Die deutsche Kartographie nach dem Weltkriege.” In *Volk unter Völkern,* edited by Karl Christian von Loesch, 429–45. Breslau: Hirt, 1925.

Ziegfeld, A. Hillen. “Kartengestaltung—Sport oder Waffe?” *Zeitschrift für Geopolitik* 12 (1935): 243–47.

Ziegfeld, A. Hillen. “Kartographik, Wesen und Aufgabe.” *Volk und Reich* (May–June 1927): 257–60.

Zimmerman, Andrew. *Alabama in Africa: Booker T. Washington, the German Empire, and the Globalization of the New South.* Princeton: Princeton University Press, 2010.

Zitzewitz, Hasso von. *Das deutsche Polenbild in der Geschichte. Entstehung—Einflüsse—Auswirkungen.* Cologne: Böhlau, 1991.

Index

Page numbers in italics refer either to the main entry or to the place where the term itself is defined.